Elementary Teachers
Corresponds to the third year
for Elementary Children.

TEACHER
Year 3

Published by:

Mesoamerica Region Discipleship Ministries
http://discipleship.mesoamericaregion.org/
SdmiResources.MesoamericaRegion.org

© 2019 - All rights reserved
All rights reserved

ISBN: 978-1-63580-124-8

Category: Christian Education

Translated from Spanish to English by: Nkele Cyr, Monte Cyr

Unless otherwise stated, all the Bible references are taken from the NIV version.

Reproduction of this material is permitted only for use in the local church.

These lessons are adapted from material originally published by
WordAction Publications.

SDMI

Mesoamerica Region

TABLE OF CONTENTS

HELPS FOR THE TEACHER

I. GENERAL ASPECTS OF THE LESSON AND THE UNIT

INTRODUCTION TO EACH UNIT

In it you will find the biblical basis for the whole unit, the biblical references, the lesson purpose, the titles of the lessons and the reasons why the students need the teaching of the unit.

EACH LESSON CONTAINS:

Biblical References

Points out the biblical passage from which the lesson was taken. It can refer to one or more books or passages of the Bible. You must read the passage(s) and become familiar with them.

Lesson Objective

It clarifies where you should go with your students and what you should achieve through the teaching and learning process.

Memory Verse

It's considered more appropriate to use a single bible verse for the whole unit, with the purpose of emphasizing the central truth.

II. PREPARE YOURSELF TO TEACH!

PREPARE YOURSELF TO TEACH!

This second section presents a help for the biblical study passage, which will expand your knowledge on the subject. It also includes a biblical context and the way in which children of this age learn. For greater effectiveness, take into account the following:

- Pray and ask for God's direction.
- Read the Bible passage several times and write down in a notebook the central ideas you find.
- Consult other versions of the Bible, biblical commentaries, biblical dictionaries, etc.
- Compare your ideas with those presented in this book.
- Meditate on each of them, and reflect on how the passage applies to your own life and the lives of your students.

III. DEVELOPMENT OF THE LESSON

The different points of the lesson's development are identified here. The Bible story must be presented with methods in which your students are actively participating. Be sure that the key points are clear in the minds of the children. You can practice the presentation of the theme at home to be at ease in front of the students. Cheer up! The work is of the Lord, and you are an instrument in His hands to carry it out.

Bible story and Application for life

This is the moment for the student to reflect on his or her daily life. It's time to guide them to ask how their life is compared to what the Bible teaches. In general, these are activities with questions to answer in a personal way. Direct the child towards reflection and don't manipulate their answers, since these must be sincere and personal.

IV. ACTIVITIES

a. In this section you will find another series of reinforcement activities for the lesson, such as tasks on the activity sheets and games.
b. Memorization of the verse, games.
c. To End: moments of prayer and reflection.

Suggestions:

- Keep in mind that it's best to prepare your lesson throughout the week, giving God's Holy Spirit opportunities to teach you, give you illustrations for the lesson, etc.
- Visit your students at least once every semester.
- Pray for and communicate with your students through letters, texts, phone calls, invitations, etc. Be sure to quickly contact them/visit them if they miss a class.
- Send a note to the student and / or parents and mention special facts in the student's life, such as birthdays, special days, etc.

- Encourage your students through contests to motivate them to attend, learn, memorize verses, invite their friends, etc.
- Arrive early to be sure you have the room ready for the class.
- When preparing lessons, take into account the age, needs and problems of elementary kids.
- As the teacher, you are also a friend, counselor and Christian model worth imitating.

SUGGESTIONS FOR BIBLE MEMORIZATION

1. WHAT DOES THE VERSE SAY?

Have your students express what the verse says by using their senses.

See
- In the Bible.
- Visual Aids: on the chalk/white board, signs, posters, flashcards, etc.

Hear
- Read it out loud.
- Record it and play it back.

Speak
- Repeat it after listening to it.
- Read it together and individually.
- Sing it.

Touch
- Write the verse.
- Fill in the blank.
- Solve a crossword
- Use hand motions

2. WHAT DOES IT MEAN?

Explore the definitions.
- Let the kids express what they understand about each Bible verse.
- Explain words they don't understand.

Discuss the context.
- For more explanation, use Bible commentaries, dictionaries and other resources.
- Investigate the background of the verse.
- Who is speaking and to whom are they speaking?

Illustrate it.
- Show pictures/illustrations of the text.
- Create your own drawings.
- Use hand motions, sign language or act it out.

3. HOW DO I APPLY IT TO MY LIFE?

Discuss the following:
- The daily life application of this verse.
- In which circumstances will it be useful and what effect will it have on your life and others' lives.

Remember a Bible verse:
- When you are being tempted.
- When you are troubled.
- When you want to encourage others.

The Students, Their Behavior And The Teacher

1. Understand Your Students and Allow For Normal Behavior.

- Children are active and curious.
- They aren't miniature adults: we must always differentiate between bad behavior and immaturity.

2. Create An Atmosphere That Promotes Good Behavior.

- Let children know that you love them and appreciate them.
- Show interest in what happens to them outside of class.
- Be organized in how you handle the students.
- Provide clear and consistent guidelines; let the children know what you expect of them.
- Don't show favoritism.

3. Acknowledge Your Position As A Teacher.

- Be in charge of the class.
- Be a figure of authority that students can follow.
- Become a friend to your students.
- Explain to them what is expected of them and give them good examples.

4. Use Methods That Involve the Children and Capture Their Interest.

- Be prepared and get to the classroom before any of the children.
- Provide a variety of activities that are appropriate for your students' ages.
- Use activities that capture their interest and ability.
- Allow children to choose some of the activities.

5. Focus on Positive Behavior.

- Limit the number of rules.
- When you correct a child, discuss it with their parent, guardian, or the person responsible for them.

WHAT DO YOU DO WHEN A CHILD MISBEHAVES?

1. Find the Cause of the Problem.

- Does the child have learning or medical problems that prevent their participation in class?
- Does he try to control the class?
- Is he academically talented and therefore bored with the class?
- When you know the cause of the problem, you may be able to correct it after talking with the child's parents.

2. Take Control of the Situation.

- Ignore behavior that doesn't interrupt the class.
- Include the child in learning activities.
- Let him see that you are observing his misconduct.
- Approach the child in a loving manner.
- Tell the child, quietly, what you want him to do.
- Teach students the consequences of continued misconduct.

3. Talk to Parents or the Person Responsible for the Child.

- If you know that you will most likely have to talk to his parents or guardian, do it, don't delay.
- Start by telling the parents what you appreciate about their child.
- State the problem and ask for their ideas of how to resolve the problem..

GET TO KNOW THE ELEMENTARY STUDENT

- They are very active, and are fine-tuning their muscle coordination.
- Their ability to count, paint, paste, cut and fold are improving progressively.
- Their reasoning is based on previous experiences or interaction with concrete objects.
- They learn more by doing than by watching.
- They seek approval from adults and their peers.
- They value justice, and don't understand when the rules change.
- They have basic skills (reading, writing, organizing, classifying) developed enough to achieve objectives.
- They are learning the concepts of time, space and distance.
- Companionship is very important. At this age they care more about being accepted by their peers than by adults.
- They are learning to know the perspectives of other people and recognize that a problem can have several solutions.

Considering the characteristics of the development stage of your students, we include some tips to improve the dynamics of your class:

- Use visual aids, illustrations and varied examples to help them understand abstract ideas.
- Establish firm standards.
- Guide the discussions with questions that help them understand the concept, and use examples to illustrate it.
- Plan some activities to work in small groups.
- Ask students to give you ideas to plan projects to help members of the church and the community, and to participate in them. Emphasize the importance of missions work.
- Provide opportunities for them to discuss and think about moral issues. Present open ended stories for them to complete and make decisions.

Christian Education material for children

Mesoamerica Region Discipleship Ministries presents with satisfaction its complete collection of Christian education (Sunday School) books.

They were designed for teachers of children and for students from 4 to 11 years of age.

Children will learn the lessons of the Bible according to their age. And, by the end of their elementary school years, they will have gone through the challenging biblical stories, as well as various topics appropriate to each stage of their childhood and pre-adolescence.

This material was designed as different steps to achieve a holy life. It contains clear and possible goals.

The teacher's book will help equip those who have the beautiful task of leading children to connect with the message that will change their lives forever.

By promoting the child to the next year-according to his age-he will have studied only once each of the books. When he reaches 12 years of age - if he started with the first book - he will have studied the eight books of this valuable collection.

The books are designed to be used in Sunday school classes, happy hours, Saturday Bible schools, children's clubs, discipleship classes, and schools in general.

This series aims to:

a. Challenge the children to learn the Word of God.

b. Encourage them to grow in their Christian experience as children of God.

c. Guide them to accept Jesus as their savior and Lord.

d. Help them grow in their faith

e. Help them become part of the faith community, the church.

The following table will help you identify the corresponding book according to the age of the students:

- Preschoolers:4 and 5 years old (Year / book 1 and 2).

- Elementary:6, 7, 8 years of age (Year / book 1, 2 and 3).

- Words of Life (preadolescents):9, 10, 11 years of age (Year / book 1, 2 and 3).

Teaching Resources

Dear Teacher:

We have prepared a series of teaching resources that will improve the dynamic of your class. Each lesson has an activities section, please use the materials below to encourage your students to use their motor skills as well as help them gain a deeper understanding of the lesson. Prepare extra activities and crafts for the kids who visit your class.

RECIPES

Recipes for Play Dough or Molding Clay

Flour and Salt Dough
Ingredients:
2 or 3 Cups of Flour
¾ Cup Fine Salt
½ Cup Warm Water
Food Coloring

Instructions:
Mix the flour with the salt and add the warm water little by little as you stir. If you want it to be colorful, add drops of food coloring as it thickens. The consistency of the dough will depend on the amount of water you add. Store in a closed container in the fridge.

Cooked Dough
Ingredients:
2 Cups of Flour
1 Cup Salt
1 Tablespoon Vegetable Oil
2 Teaspoons
Food Coloring

Instructions:
Mix the dry ingredients and then add the water and the vegetable oil. Cook the mix over low heat until it thickens, stirring it constantly. Take it off the heat and let it cool. To Marke it the color you want, add drops of food coloring while you mix the dough. If kept in a closed container, it should last for over a month.

Mud Dough
Ingredients:
2 Cups of Dirt
2 Cups of Sand
½ Cup of Salt
Water

Instructions :
Mix the dirt, sand, and salt, and then add water a little at a time until you get a consistency that's good for molding.

Finger Paint

Ingredients:
1 ¼ Cup Corn Starch
½ Cup Powdered Soap
3 Cups Boiling Water
1 Tablespoon Glycerin
Food Coloring

Instructions:
Dissolve the starch in cold water. Pour it into the warm water slowly as you stir to avoid clumps. Add the soap and the glycerin. To add color, use food coloring. This recipe isn't toxic. If stored in plastic cups, it should last several days.

White Glue

Ingredients:
4 Cups Water
1 Cup Wheat Flour
½ Cup Sugar
½ Cup Vinegar

Instructions:
Boil 3 cups of water. Meanwhile in a container, mix one cup of water and the flour, sugar, and vinegar. When the water starts to boil, add the mix and stir slowly over the heat. If there are clumps, stir it more. If it's too thick, add water. If it's too thin, boil it for longer. Store in a jar with a lid.

PAPER FOR CARDS AND CRAFTS

1. Soak 6 sheets of paper or pages from a magazine torn into small pieces in hot water.
2. Put it in the blender with half a cup of oatmeal or flowers or vegetables such as carrots or celery.
3. Strain the mixture and add 4 tablespoons of glycerin and 6 tablespoons white glue.
4. Spread the paste on a plastic sheet/tray with a rolling pin or stick until thin and even.
5. Let it dry in the sun for two days.
6. You can use this paper to make cards, bookmarks, letters, etc.

THE IMPORTANCE OF STUDENTS ADVANCING IN SUNDAY SCHOOL

Dear Leader and Sunday School Teacher;

As in school, children in our church Sunday Schools should be able to be promoted to a higher level of Sunday School. As a classroom teacher, it's very important that you be prepared to promote the students at the end of the church year or, at the end of the school year - whichever is easiest. To accomplish this, talk to the Sunday School Superintendent of your church or your pastor.

You can prepare in advance a "ceremony" and give a certificate (included in this book) to each child passing to the next class. The ceremony can be performed in the sanctuary for all the congregation to participate in. Invite parents and relatives of the children. This will be a good time for them to get to know and attend the rest of the service and hear the Word of God.

It's important to have teachers of the classes that the children are graduating from, as well as entering into as special participants in the ceremony. It will be a special time for them to say good bye to their present teacher with a hug, and for the teacher of the next class to welcome them to their new class with a hug. At the ceremony, you can present a card decorated with photos of the children that have been taken during the year. It can include some memories of the child's participation while he was in class, Special prayers they said, the date in which they gave their testimony, questions that they asked, and moments of joy experienced in the class. Prepare the child in advance, so they aren't surprised in front of the entire congregation.

Talk to the Sunday School Superintendent so that at the ceremony the new Sunday School book for the following year can be given to the student(s).You can encourage the families of the church to give a book to each child (as if they were the godparents), especially the children whose parents don't attend church or are at an economic disadvantage. In every congregation there are adults whose children are already adults who would gladly participate by giving a book to a child who attends Sunday School.

It's understandable if, because of a lack of teachers, it's not possible to have classes for every age group. This however is a good reason to invite and bring more children to church, and also to prepare and train new teachers. In every congregation there are always teenagers that are eager to learn how to teach a class. Don't miss this opportunity!

We wish you the richest blessings in the challenges that the ministry of education presents to you and your congregation.

In Christ and His Ministry,

Discipleship Ministries

Sunday School Certificate

_____
(Child's Name)

Is Promoted to the Next Level Sunday School Class

Church:

Date:

"My son, pay attention to what I say…" Proverbs 4:20a

_____
Sunday School Superintendent

_____
Teacher

Year 3

Introduction-Unit I

JESUS BEGINS HIS MINISTRY

Biblical References: Luke 2:41-52; Matthew 3:1-17;4:1-11; 4:18-22; Mark 3:13-19; John 1:35-51.

Unit Memory Verse: *And Jesus grew in wisdom and stature, and in favor with God and man (Luke 2:52).*

Unit Objectives

This unit will help the elementary students to:

✗ Know the first steps of Jesus' ministry.

✗ See His growth in His knowledge of God.

✗ See His obedient attitude after His baptism.

✗ Learn the particular way that Jesus used to select His disciples

Unit Lessons

Lesson 1: Jesus learns to obey

Lesson 2: Jesus is baptized

Lesson 3: Jesus is tempted

Lesson 4: Jesus chooses his disciples

Why Elementary Students need the teaching of this unit:

It's important that elementary students know that Jesus Christ is the character of a real story. Many times, the border between the fantasy stories they see in the cartoons, and reality, is confusing. It's important that they begin to know Jesus from their childhood. Precisely, this series of lessons will allow your students to know Jesus from His early age of 12 years. Through the biblical texts, they will begin to familiarize themselves first with a young one who called people's attention to his wisdom; second, with the way he responded with Scripture to each temptation of the devil; and finally, with his special way of selecting those who would make up his inner circle. He chose neither wealthy nor influential people, but simple and even coarse men.

Jesus learns to obey

Biblical References: Luke 2:41-52

Lesson Objective: To teach the students that Jesus obeyed his Father God, and that they can do the same.

Memory Verse: *And Jesus grew in wisdom and stature, and in favor with God and man (Luke 2:52).*

PREPARE YOURSELF TO TEACH!

When we see the children of our congregation running through the corridors - loving and playing - we tend to make the mistake of so many adults: we think that our children are incapable of serious thinking and that they are spiritually immature. We must correct this way of thinking. Children have an enormous capacity to understand the spiritual nature of our world, sometimes even more clearly than we adults. That's why, as such, we can learn valuable lessons about spiritual development as we see them surrender their small lives into the mighty hands of God. Children don't know complex theology or doctrine, but they can experience reality behind high concepts.

As a teacher, help them deepen their understanding of the Bible and its Author. Their inquisitive minds and their tender hearts need to be filled with the truths of God, in the same way that the mind and heart of Jesus were as a child. These first years will determine the direction your students will follow in the future. What a great privilege and responsibility you have as their teacher.

BIBLICAL COMMENTARY

While traveling, we tell each other stories and secrets. We enjoy that time in which we are together. In the story of Luke 2:41-52, we find Jesus traveling with his family to the city of Jerusalem. There were many holiday feasts on the Jewish calendar. One of those feasts was the Passover, in which the miraculous liberation after the 400 years of Egyptian slavery was remembered. This trip in particular was very special for Jesus. A Jewish boy 13 years old would join the community as a member, in the same way that the little kids of that age do today. In this passage, Jesus would have traveled to Jerusalem in preparation for next year's events. We can imagine the emotion that he would have felt to know that in a short time, he would have the responsibilities that concern the world of adults.

When the Passover ended, Jesus' family left Jerusalem with the rest of the group and traveled a whole day. The group was big and people moved from one place to another. For that reason, it was easy for Jesus to be separated from his parents.

Joseph and Mary returned to Jerusalem in search of their son. When at last they found him, he was with the teachers of the law. Everyone was amazed at the intelligence and answers of Jesus. Joseph and Mary expressed their concern as parents when they found him. Jesus simply replied that he was doing what was best for him: to take care of his Father's business. His priorities had earthly and heavenly dimensions.

The Scripture says that Jesus obediently followed his earthly parents back to Nazareth. There he lived in submission to them, while strengthening his relationship with his heavenly Father.

Luke 5:22 reminds us that Jesus developed as a child - physically, intellectually and spiritually, and also grew "in favor with God and men." We know with certainty that at 12 years of age, he understood the importance of his relationship with God. The lessons he learned as a teenager would help him later to trust in the one who sent him to fulfill the mission of being the Savior of the world.

LESSON DEVELOPMENT

Prepare in advance the teaching materials you will use for this lesson, and try to have the classroom ready before your students arrive.

Remember to welcome visitors and collect their info to contact them during the week.

Choose one of the following activities to capture the attention of your students.

Let's take a trip

Before class, prepare a suitcase (bag or travel bag) and place it in front of the class in a visible place to illustrate the idea of traveling.

In class, ask the children to think about family trips they have recently been on. Ask them: *What did you pack to take on their trip? How long did that trip last? What did you see on the way? Where did you go?* Let the children tell about their experiences.

Let's listen to an interesting story about a trip Jesus made with his family. The trip wasn't so important, but it was the place they were going to that was important: Jerusalem. Let's see what happened and why it's important.

You got lost?

Ask: *How many of you have been lost by getting separated from your parents in a mall or a park or somewhere like that?* (It's possible that most children have had that experience.) Ask them:

- *How did you feel?*
- *How did your parents feel?*

- *Did your parents find you?*
- *Did you find your parents?*
- *What happened when they found you?*

Let the children tell their experiences. Ask: *Do you think Jesus was ever lost? Today's story tells us about something that happened to him when he was a little boy.*

BIBLE STORY

Teacher, use pictures or figures that show Jesus sitting with the teachers of the law to illustrate the biblical story to the children.

The most important thing for Jesus

Each year, Jesus' parents prepared to go to Jerusalem for a special celebration called The Passover. They prepared food, clothing, and other items that they would need during the trip. Then, they met with other family members and friends for the long walk towards that city. As they walked, they talked about what they would do and see when they arrived.

"Now that you are 12 years old, you are almost ready to be a man," Joseph said to his son Jesus. "Look carefully at the boys bigger than you, and how they prepare for the special events that are approaching."

Jesus' enthusiasm grew and grew as he approached the city. He knew that something significant was about to happen. The Passover was a very important holiday for the Jews. Sacrifices were offered, unleavened bread was eaten, it was remembered when God delivered them from death when they put the blood of the lambs on their door frames. It was remembered when God took them out of Egypt after many years of slavery. They worshiped God and he listened to the Word of God in the temple of Jerusalem.

After a few days, the party ended, and everyone returned to their homes. Joseph and Mary, while walking, talked about the time spent in the holy city and the blessings of God.

"I think Jesus had a good time," said Mary.

"He is becoming a strong boy," commented Joseph.

But the end of the day found them looking for Jesus.

"It's time to stop and rest. Where is Jesus?" Mary asked, her voice worried.

"I'll go look for him. Don't worry," answered Joseph.

Both of them started questioning the people they were traveling with: "Have you seen Jesus? Is he with your children?"

Nobody had seen him. They couldn't find him. Finally, they decided to return to Jerusalem.

"What do you think happened to him," Joseph asked.

"I hope he's okay!" exclaimed Mary with nervousness.

It took them a whole day to return to Jerusalem. There they continued looking for him.

Meanwhile, Jesus was in the temple listening to the teachers. Although he was only 12 years old, they allowed him to sit, listen and ask questions. The teachers were amazed at his knowledge and understanding.

Finally his parents found him! When they saw him with the teachers, they marveled, but they were also upset.

His mother asked him, "Why didn't you come back with us? When we didn't see you, we started to worry. We looked for you everywhere!"

Jesus was surprised. "Why were you searching for me?" he asked. "Didn't you know I had to be in my Father's house?" (Luke 2:49).

Joseph and Mary didn't understand what he was saying.

Finally, they returned to Nazareth. Although his parents didn't understand him, Jesus obeyed them. He honored God by being obedient to his earthly parents. "And Jesus grew in wisdom, in stature, and in favor with God and men" (Luke 2:52).

ACTIVITIES

Let's take a trip!

Say: *Today we're going to take a trip. What is traveling?* (Allow some to answer.) *Yes, it's going from one place to another. Our trip will take us to a place where we'll listen to our bible story.*

Let the children follow, walking around the church building, the hallways, the kitchen, and other places where other classes aren't interrupted. Tour the main sanctuary, the garden and the courtyards.

When you arrive at the place where you will tell the story, allow them to look around. Tell them: *We've finally arrived! It took us a long time. Our story today speaks of when Jesus and his family made a long journey, from Nazareth to Jerusalem. Our trip took only a few minutes, but it took them several days. Listen to what the Bible says about Jesus.* Hold your Bible open. Tell the story of Luke 2:41-52.

Then, secretly ask a child to stay in the place where you told the story as everyone else returns to the classroom with you. (Make sure there is an adult watching the child.) As the class returns to the classroom, ask: *Are you all here?* If no one answers, look around the room and count how many children there are. Pretend you are surprised because one is missing. *Who is missing? Oh _____ is missing. We must return to look for him/her.*

Go as a group to retrieve the missing child. When you return to the room with everyone, say: *He stayed where we were. He didn't return with the group. Think about how Jesus' parents felt when they realized that Jesus wasn't with them. What did Jesus say to them when they found him in the courtyard of the temple?* ("Don't you know that I need to be about my Father's business?"). *The relationship with his Father God was very important to Jesus, even though he was still a child. Jesus wanted to know God.*

The most important thing for Jesus

For this activity,, you must prepare the "magic television" model in advance. Necessary elements: scissors, glue and colored pencils. You will need for each child: 1 empty tissue box (Kleenex) in the form of a cube (or something similar) and 4 paper plates 15 cm in diameter. Follow the instructions in the Lesson 1 activity to make the "magic television".

In class, say: *Jesus wanted more than anything else to have a good relationship with God his Father. Like Jesus, you children can have a close relationship with God. How can that be achieved?* (Reading and obeying the Word of God, praying and listening to what our parents, pastors and teachers say about God, etc.)

Give them the activity sheet from the student book and ask them to write or draw something in the blank circle that they can do to be close to God. Show them the model you prepared beforehand. Give the children the boxes and the 4 cardboard plates, and help them prepare their "magic televisions."

With this activity, and as a review, ask them to tell you the bible story and the truth they learned.

Memorization

"And Jesus grew in wisdom, in stature, and in favor with God and men" (Luke 2:52).

You will need a ball or sachet full of seeds. Divide the class into two teams. They can be standing or sitting, one team facing the other. Hand the ball or bag to the first child of one of the two teams. That child will say the first word of the verse (for example: "And"). Then he must throw the ball to the first child of the opposing team, and he will say the second word ("Jesus"). The ball will continue going from child to child, in a zigzag pattern, until everyone has said a word of the text. When they finish saying it, including the reference, start over. By repeating it, the children will learn the memory verse by playing.

To end

Pray with the children asking the Lord to help them be obedient as Jesus was, and to be close to God as he was.

If necessary, arrange an altar prayer time if there are children who have been disobedient to God and/ or their parents.

Invite the little ones to return next Sunday. You can hand out cards with the names of children who wish to be prayed for. Encourage them to pray for one another.

Remind them to take the TVs home. Ask them to tell the Bible story today to their parents, siblings and friends. Tell them that, in that way, many will learn to know Jesus and know that he was obedient to his parents.

Lesson 2

Jesus Is Baptized

Biblical References: Matthew 3:1-17

Lesson Objective: Help the students know that Jesus is the Son of God, and understand that his baptism shows that he came to save us from sin.

Memory Verse: *And Jesus grew in wisdom and stature, and in favor with God and man (Luke 2:52).*

PREPARE YOURSELF TO TEACH!

Elementary students are young and don't have testimonies like their parents or other adults in the church. But it's still very important to affirm their spiritual development. Even if they're very small, they can decide to love and serve God. They observe the examples of the adults that surround them. The responsibility for their spiritual development comes from an association between the older people close to them and God. Let's try to adapt the child's perceptions about God and give him opportunities to experience God's love and grace.

These lessons about Jesus' ministry will help them better understand his life and message. As their understanding grows, so does their ability to respond to the gospel message in a positive way. Pray for the children you teach each week and ask God for His blessing to present the truths of His Word.

BIBLICAL COMMENTARY

Read Matthew 3:1-17. After Jesus moved to Nazareth with Joseph and Mary (Matthew 2:19-23), the Bible doesn't tell us much about his life. Apparently, he worked as a carpenter with Joseph, his earthly father, and probably took over the business when Joseph died. While Jesus worked in carpentry, his cousin John the Baptist preached in the desert. John's message was: "Repent, for the Kingdom of Heaven is near."

When people listened to John's preaching, they confessed their sins and were baptized in the Jordan River. The word "repentance" means to turn 180 degrees in life and go in a direction totally opposite to what the person had been doing until then. Then and today, it implies that people leave sin and take a new path towards a righteous life. But who will give us the power to march in the direction of God?

We know that we need to repent so that our sins are forgiven, but we also know that we need a real change in our hearts so as not to sin continuously. John used water baptism as a way to show that the person has chosen to stop disobeying God. The baptism with the Holy Spirit (vv. 11-12) was something Jesus would do to give people a clean heart so that they could have the power to obey God and live for him.

When the time was approaching when Jesus would begin his public ministry, he went to visit John at the Jordan River. Jesus was the Son of God; he didn't need to repent of any sin. As the Messiah, the first thing Jesus did was to announce publicly that he identified with the lost people, that he had come to save, and that he was obedient to the will of God.

When the Holy Spirit descended on Jesus "like a dove," it was God's way of telling the world that Jesus was his Son, and that he would carry out the plan of salvation for all mankind. Young children should know that when they love Jesus, they are loving someone whom God loves very much. They should know that when they repent of their sins, they are saying that they love God and want to obey Him. The Holy Spirit's the one who will help them do it.

LESSON DEVELOPMENT

Prepare in advance the teaching materials you will use for this lesson and try to have your classroom ready before your students arrive.

Remember to welcome visitors and collect their info to contact them during the week.

You can do the following activity to get the attention of the children.

What is this?

Before class, write each letter of the word "baptism" on separate cardboard squares (you can put masking tape rings behind the letter to stick it up, or punch and place a thread to hang).

In class, mix up the letters and give them to the children. Tell them: *Let's sort these letters to form a word that has a special meaning. If you have the letter that corresponds to the key that I'm going to give, bring it and hang it up.*

✖ *The first letter is the second letter of the alphabet (B)*

✖ *The second letter is the first letter of the alphabet. (A)*

✖ *The third letter is the letter before Q. (P)*

✖ *The fourth letter is the name of a cold or hot drink. (T)*

✖ *The fifth letter is a vowel with a dot. (I)*

✖ *The sixth letter is similar to a snake. (S)*

✖ *The last letter has two mountains. (M)*

Ask: *What word do we make with these letters?* (baptism). *Baptism was and is a way of showing that they had repented of their sins. It also showed that they wanted to live for God.*

When John the Baptist preached, he told people that they needed to repent and be baptized. Our Bible story today tells us about someone who did it.

BIBLE STORY

"Hi, my name is Alberto. I'm going to tell you about a strange man. His name is John and he spoke to people from the Jordan River. I asked my mom if we could go see him. Guess what? We decided to go, and we saw the most amazing things!"

"The man wore clothes made of camel hair and he had a leather belt. Someone said he ate honey and locusts. Can you imagine how horrible that's?" Then we heard him say that people needed to confess their sins and ask God for forgiveness. If they did, they then walked into the river and the man pushed them into the water. Mom told me that this is called baptism, and that's why people called him 'John the Baptist'.

"We were sitting on a rock looking and watching. Then, we heard a group of Pharisees and Sadducees approach; someone told me that these were the most important religious leaders. John saw them arrive and told them they were like vipers. That sounded like an insult! I don't think they liked what John told them. Actually, the Baptist said strange things: he talked about someone who would come, who was very powerful. He said that not even he could untie the strap on that man's shoes. He thought that the powerful lord would arrive on a white horse, and with many soldiers, or in a beautiful carriage of brilliant colors. But it wasn't like that."

"We saw a simple man come to the river. I'm sure John was thrilled to see him. Somebody whispered in my mother's ear that this man was called Jesus. I heard that he wanted to be baptized, but John didn't want to do it. We heard that John said to Jesus, 'I need to be baptized by you, why do you come to me?'"

"Jesus insisted and asked John to baptize him. Finally, John accepted. Both walked into the river and John helped Jesus descend into the water. When he came out of the water, the most fantastic thing that I have ever seen happened."

"At that moment, we saw the heavens opening and the Spirit of God descended on Jesus like a dove. The dove was spectacular, beautiful! I think I'll never see an equal to that again."

"Then we all heard a voice saying, 'This is my beloved Son, I'm very pleased with him.' Our eyes and ears couldn't believe it. We went home amazed by everything that had happened!"

ACTIVITIES

Jesus is baptized

Hand out and then follow the instructions on the lesson 2 student sheet to assemble the figures. Help the children complete the water section if they have trouble doing it. Allow them to put their figures on the table; use them to review what happened in the story.

Show the children how to push down the water from the top in order to reveal Jesus. Give their figures to them to tell the story to their family and friends.

Ask them:

- *Who baptized people?* (John the Baptist)
- *What did John say to Jesus?* (I need to be baptized by you.)
- *What happened when Jesus came out of the water?* (The Holy Spirit descended upon Jesus in the form of a dove and the voice of God was heard.)
- *How did Jesus prepare to do the work planned by God?* (He was baptized.)
- *Why do you think that was important?* (Because he showed that he loved sinners and that he had come to help them.)
- *How do we show our gratitude to Jesus for being our Savior?* (By loving God and doing what he wants us to do, receiving Jesus as our Savior.)

Pleasing God

You will need a ball. Divide the children into two groups (you can be part of one).

Ask: *What are the ways we please God and show our joy at the fact that Jesus is our Savior?* Allow them to suggest possible answers while you write them down on the board or on a poster: pray, read the Bible, go to church, obey your parents, be kind, love others, say and act truthfully, be loyal, etc.

Then, divide the class into two teams. Place chairs, or they can stand, one in front of the other. Give the ball to the first child of the first team. He will say a way

to please God (for example: pray), then he should pass the ball to the first child of the opposing team, and he will express another form (for example: reading the Bible). Thus, the ball will continue going from child to child until everyone has participated. The answers can be repeated. Say: *Doing things that please God will help you grow like Jesus. Remember: you must obey just as Jesus did!*

Memorization

You can use the previous activity with the ball for the children to learn the memory verse. When the child has the ball in his hands, he must say a word of the text, and as they ball goes from child to child, they will learn the verse by repetition. If anyone drops the ball, they have to say two words of the verse. Whoever can say the whole verse leaves the game and is given a loud applause.

Search for the lost text

Before class, write the memory verse on medium-sized cards (20 cm x 20 cm), writing one word on each card. You will need 16 cards, including the reference. Hide the cards in different places in the room before the children arrive. After praying, welcoming and repeating several times the memorized text that will be written on the board-ask the children to look for the lost words of the verse. When they have found all of the words, they are to arrange them in the correct order. You can choose three children to serve as judges and say if the passage is worded correctly.

Then, choose other children to be judges. Then, jumble up the words and have the children arrange them correctly again. The new judges will say if the text is in the correct order.

This is a very busy activity, but the children will enjoy playing and learning the text by heart.

You can repeat this type of activity during the unit and do them with any other topic that you have to address. If the number of students is large, you can divide the class into two or more groups so that everyone participates: some being judges and others who put the text in order.

Closing

Always give them the opportunity to ask about the lesson. You will be surprised to see that some show a desire to delve into the Word of God and biblical events.

Sing a chorus according to the theme of the lesson. Before dismissing them, tell them to make a circle and pray with them.

JESUS IS TEMPTED

Biblical References: Matthew 4:1-11

Lesson Objective: To teach the students that when Jesus was tempted by Satan, He decided to obey God. They can do the same thing when they are tempted to do wrong.

Memory Verse: *And Jesus grew in wisdom and stature, and in favor with God and man (Luke 2:52).*

PREPARE YOURSELF TO TEACH!

In these times when the world says that there are no absolutes, and that it's rarely said that something is really good or bad, children need to know that some decisions are wrong. The decision to disobey God is always wrong. God never changes. If he says something is wrong, it will always be wrong. However, Satan seeks to tempt human desires.

The current tendency is to prioritize the "I" and what satisfies us. God wants us to obey Him and seek Him in the first place. This lesson will help the children understand that, just as Jesus had to decide between obeying God or Satan, they will also have to make that decision. Encourage them to ask for God's help to overcome temptation, because He knows and loves them. God understands our weaknesses and can give us strength when we are tempted.

This series of lessons about Jesus' life will lead children to God. He is our example of obedience and devotion to the Creator.

BIBLICAL COMMENTARY

When Jesus was baptized, he publicly declared that he would carry out God's plan. He was committed to completing God's divine will. But in order to do that, he had to confront Satan, God's enemy. With each temptation, Satan tried to convince him to take a shortcut in the completion of the mission. And in each temptation, he faced what it meant to be the Son of God.

Jesus was tempted to put his physical needs before God's will, to change the stones into bread. Afterwards in his ministry, he would do miracles to feed thousands of people, but during the temptation, he chose not to accept the orders of the enemy.

Then, he was tempted to put God and his promises to a test, but he decided to trust in his heavenly Father.

Finally, he was tempted to enjoy his destiny before carrying out his ministry and going through the difficulties and suffering. Jesus knew that someday the Father was going to give him all the kingdoms of the word, he would be exalted, and everyone would bow before him. But before that, he would have to die on the cross. Being an obedient son, he didn't want to take a shortcut to glory.

After resisting Satan using the scriptures, Jesus knew that he was prepared for the mission that his Father had given to him: to preach and teach the Good News that God is love and wants us to believe in Him in order to be saved.

LESSON DEVELOPMENT

Welcome your students to class with affection and ensure that the classroom is clean and tidy before they arrive. Before entering today's topic, review briefly the two previous lessons and ask your students to give some examples of how faithful they were to God during this month that's about to end.

Choose one of the following activities to direct your students' attention to the Bible teaching.

Important word

Before class, write each letter of the word "temptation" on a card. Post them on the board in order, but without displaying the written letters. Then, write the definition on another card.

In class, tell your students that they will learn a new term. Ask them questions, giving everyone an opportunity to respond. Whoever answers correctly can turn over one of the letters. Prepare simple questions such as: *Should you obey your parents? Is it right to lie? Is it okay to drink something that doesn't belong to you? Should you hit your brother or sister? Is it correct to copy a classmate's homework or exam?*

When they can see several of the letters, any child can try to guess what the word is. When someone correctly guesses the word, ask them if they know what "temptation" means. Allow them to express their opinions and then, if necessary, offer the following definition: "Temptation is everything that encourages us to disobey God, making it seem right".

Tell them: *We all face temptations. Many times we have to choose between good and bad. Today our story speaks of someone who faced temptations. Let's see if he made the right decisions.*

Allow time for the children to complete the crossed words in the student book. The questions that appear at the end will help you review the lesson.

Fresh bread

Bring special bread to your class (if it's freshly baked ... much better!) to share with your students.

Place the bread on a plate, facing the children. Ask them: *If you hadn't eaten anything for a day, a week or a month, would you want to eat this bread?*

Serve each child a piece of bread and ask them how it tastes. Say: *Bread satisfies us when we are hungry. Our lesson today has to do with bread. Pay attention to the story to know what happened.*

Beat the clock

Get a kitchen timer or a stopwatch before class. Program it to make it sound at the end of a minute. Write each word of the memory verse on cards.

In class, allow children to take turns putting the cards in order before the clock sounds. When finished, let everyone read the verse out loud.

Say: *This verse tells us how Jesus grew up. He prepared for his ministry by obeying God and showing us how to please God.*

Say: *Today's Bible story shows us another way in which Jesus prepared himself to carry out God's work on earth. Let's see what happened after John baptized Jesus.*

BIBLE STORY

Give each child a sheet of paper and a pencil. Instruct them to fold the paper in half. Then, open it and fold it in half in the opposite direction. Thus the paper will be divided into four equal sections. Ask them to list them from 1 to 4. As you tell the story, pause at the end of each scene, and ask the children to draw a simple picture related to it.

A difficult test for Jesus (Matthew 4:1-11)

Scene 1: *After John baptized Jesus, the Spirit of God led him into the desert. In preparation before beginning the work that God had entrusted to him, Jesus needed to know what it was like to be tempted to disobey his heavenly Father. For 40 days and 40 nights, he didn't eat anything. Can you imagine the hunger that he would have? Then the devil said to him, "If you are the Son of God, command that these stones be turned into bread."*

Jesus was very hungry, but he told the devil, "Man doesn't live by bread alone, but by every word that comes from the mouth of God."

Scene 2: *Then, the devil took Jesus to the city of Jerusalem. He put him in the highest place in the temple and tried to tempt him again, saying, "If you are the Son of God, throw yourself down from here, because the Word of God says that the angels will take care of you if you fall. They will not let you get hurt."*

But Jesus answered him with the words of Deuteronomy 6:16: "It's written also, 'You shall not tempt the Lord your God.'"

Scene 3: *Finally, the devil took Jesus to the top of a very high mountain. From there he could see many kilometers away. And he said, "I will give you all the kingdoms of the world if you bow down and worship me."*

But Jesus answered him, "Go away from me! The Scripture says that we should only worship God. Only before him should we bow and only he should we serve."

Scene 4: *Then the devil left and the angels came to Jesus to take care of him. He had successfully passed that great test. Every time the devil tried to tempt him, he decided to obey God.*

After the story, allow some children to retell it briefly using their drawings.

ACTIVITIES

Let's join the story

Before class, get 9 sheets of paper. On each one, write one of the following numbers and phrases: 1 - 2 - 3 - Turn stones into bread - Throw yourself down from up high - Bow and and worship - Desert - Temple - Mountain.

To review the story, divide the 9 sheets among the children. While holding them, they should read the words written on them. The children with numbers 1, 2 and 3 represent the three temptations of Jesus. Instruct them to look for classmates who have information related to each temptation and that each group forms a line facing forward.

If your class is large, prepare three more sheets with Jesus' answers. If the class is small, use only six sheets, joining the number with the corresponding phrase.

Reinforce the teachings by saying: *The devil tempted Jesus three times, and each time, Jesus decided to be faithful to God. We can also decide to be obedient to God and to do his will.*

The mountain of obedience

Talk with the children about the ways we can obey God. (Possible answers: read the Bible, pray, put into practice what the Word says, do what is good, love and serve God, help others.)

Give them the student activity sheet for this lesson from the student activity book and ask: *What does this illustration show us?* (Jesus on the mountain where the devil promised to give him the kingdoms of the world if he bowed and worshiped him.) Tell them to draw or write something they can do to obey God in the space provided.

Then, tell them to cut out the mountain and line B. Show them how to build the mountain. Help children who need assistance.

Ask that some read what they wrote or show their drawing. Encourage them to show their work at home and to tell the story today.

When we face temptations

Look for illustrations or draw situations in which a boy or girl is tempted to do something wrong. Discuss with your students about each case and tell them what their response should be, following Jesus' example.

Memorization

"And Jesus grew in wisdom, in stature, and in favor with God and men" (Luke 2:52).

You will need a ball or a bag full of seeds.

Divide the class into two teams. They can sit or stand, one team in front of the other. Hand the ball or bag to the first child of one of the two teams. That child will say the first word of the verse. (For example: "And"), then he must throw the ball to the first child of the opposing team, and that child will say the second word ("Jesus"). The ball continues from child to child, from team to team, until everyone has said a word of the verse. When they reach the end of the passage and the reference, they will begin again. By repeating it, children will learn the verse by playing.

Closing

Ask the children if they have prayer requests. Pray for those requests and then for your students, asking God to help them overcome temptations as Jesus did.

Encourage them to attend the next class and tell other people today's story.

Lesson 4

Jesus Chooses His Disciples

Biblical References: Matthew 4:18-22, Mark 3:13-19, John 1:35-51.

Lesson Objective: Help the students to be followers of Jesus.

Memory Verse: *And Jesus grew in wisdom and stature, and in favor with God and man (Luke 2:52).*

PREPARE YOURSELF TO TEACH!

Elementary students believe that they can't do much for Jesus because they're so small. It's important that they know that God values them and isn't indifferent to our needs. Today, Jesus needs followers to help spread the Good News: that God loves and cares for people. There are many ways that children can be Jesus' helpers. This lesson will help the children to begin to understand what it means to be a follower of Jesus and to identify ways in which they can help in God's work in today's world.

There are examples throughout history in which children were instruments chosen by God to guide their parents to Christ. If you know of any case, tell your class. Ask your pastor to visit your class and tell a story about how children have helped make a difference. These stories will encourage your students.

BIBLICAL COMMENTARY

Jesus was prepared to do the work that his Father had sent him to do. He publicly announced this at his baptism. Jesus was an obedient Son and said "yes" to the will of God. Also, even when no one observed him during the temptations in the desert, he showed that he was an obedient Son.

Jesus knew he was ready to begin his special work for God. He knew he couldn't do things by himself. He also knew that he wouldn't remain on earth after his resurrection. That's why Jesus chose the 12 disciples as companions, to help him with the task entrusted to him by his Father God. Jesus recognized that he needed to choose and teach a group of people who would be with him each day. After his resurrection, these men and women would be prepared to take the Good News of the gospel to the whole world and tell others how much God loves them.

The first people Jesus met to help him were two brothers: Andrew and Peter. They were fishermen on the Sea of Galilee, as were the other brothers, James and John. Later, Jesus found Phillip and told him to join his team. Philip found Nathanael and told him that Jesus, the Messiah, was looking for some good helpers. So, in a short time, he had six people who would join with him in God's mission.

A few days later, others joined the group of disciples, like Matthew, the tax collector. Finally, Jesus had to choose 12 of all the people who followed him. They would be a group that Jesus would depend on to bring the Good News of God's love to the whole world. These 12 saw and heard almost all the things that Jesus did and said.

It was a wonderful privilege to be a follower of Jesus, so admirable that each disciple left what he was doing to accept the call to follow him. What we know is that the fishermen didn't leave their jobs gradually. Matthew didn't leave his work in a gradual way either. They didn't hesitate to be one of Jesus' disciples, they did it immediately, at the first opportunity, without hesitation.

21

Your students can learn that we must be ready to respond when Jesus calls us to follow him. They should also know that when they follow Jesus, they become part of the important task that began 2,000 years ago and continues today: to tell the whole world that God loved us so much that he sent his Son Jesus to die on the cross to save us from our sins. This message is called the "Good News" or the "gospel". Let's communicate to the children that God has placed under our responsibility that they must respond quickly to Jesus' call to fulfill this task throughout the world.

LESSON DEVELOPMENT

Receive your students with affection and ensure that the classroom is clean and tidy when they arrive. Before entering today's topic, review briefly the three previous lessons and ask your students to give some examples of how faithful they have been to God during this month that's about to end.

Do this activity to emphasize today's teaching:

Simon says...

Ask: *In what places are we given instructions, about what should we do?* (Allow children to explain. Possible answers: at school, at an amusement park, at a shopping center, when an object is put together, etc.) *Now let's see how well you can listen and follow instructions.*

Play "Simon says ..." with the children. Give them several instructions and on certain occasions don't say, "Simon says ..." Those who carry out the instruction without you saying "Simon says" is out of the game. For example: Simon says, touch your nose. Simon says, jump on one foot. Jump twice. (If the children jump this time, they will be out of the game.) Ask: *What must you do to win "Simon says ..."?* (Listen to the instructions and do what Simon says.) *You have to follow the instructions. It's very important to listen carefully.*

Today's story tells us about some people who listened and followed instructions. Let's listen to who they were, and what we should do to follow like them.

BIBLE STORY

After his baptism and temptation, Jesus began his ministry. One day, while walking on the beach of the Sea of Galilee, Jesus saw some fishermen. They were at the water's edge and were throwing out their nets to fish. Their names were: Simon, called Peter, and his brother Andrew. They were busy fishing the moment Jesus called them.

"Come follow me, and I will make you fishers of men," Jesus told them.

Peter and Andrew looked at each other, looked at their nets, and left them at once to follow Jesus.

While they were walking with Jesus on the beach, they saw two of their friends, James and John. The two men were sitting on the fishing boat, fixing their nets. They waved at Peter and Andrew as they passed by. Jesus looked at them and said, "Follow me and learn to catch people."

Quickly, James and John stood up, jumped out of the boat, and followed Jesus.

After a few days, the Jesus the Nazarene decided to leave the Galilee area. And he found Phillip, who was from the same city as Peter and Andrew, and he also called him to follow him.

Philip then found his friend Nathanael. "You must come and meet someone," he said. "His name is Jesus of Nazareth and he is the promised Savior, of whom Moses and the prophets wrote."

"Did you say he's from Nazareth?" Nathanael asked. "Can anything good come from there?

"Come and see," Phillip replied.

Nathanael went with Phillip. When Jesus saw them coming, he said, "Here is a true Israelite in whom there is no deception!"

Nathanael was really surprised.

"From where do you know me?" he asked.

"I saw you when you were under the fig tree, even before Philip called you," Jesus replied.

Now Nathanael was more than surprised. He knew that Jesus wasn't an ordinary person.

"Rabbi, you are the Son of God! You are the King of Israel!" he exclaimed.

Jesus looked at him. "Do you believe because I told you that I saw you under the fig tree? You will see greater things than these!"

Jesus and his followers traveled through the region. Many joined the group that listened to his teachings and saw his miracles.

One day, Jesus climbed a mountain. He invited some of his friends to go with him, and said to the 12, "You will be my assistants. You will be called apostles. I want you to stay with me and learn. I will send you to preach and give you authority to fight against the enemy."

The names of the 12 were: Simon, called Peter; Andrew; James; John; Philip; Bartholomew; Thomas; Matthew; James, son of Alphaeus; Taddaeus; Simon, the Zealot; and Judas Iscariot. These 12 came to be Jesus' special helpers. They traveled with him and helped him in his ministry here on earth. They were also called "disciples".

Jesus still needs helpers to follow him, to learn from him, to obey him, to serve him, and to be his disciples. You can be those people.

This is a good time for children to write their name and draw a portrait or paste a photo of themselves in the oval of the student's book illustration.

ACTIVITIES

Take a look at the story. Get figures or pictures that illustrate Jesus with the fishermen who started following him. You can make the figures for the children to color. Make in advance, on cardboard, a scene for a mural. Draw a background of the sea, beach and some boats; You can do it with simple and fast strokes. When telling the story, allow students to place the relevant figures on the mural. The figures of Jesus, Peter and the other apostles can have tape on the back, or you can stick a magnet to them so that they are firm when placed on the mural with the sea and beach background. Children will feel great about being "teacher's helpers" during the course of the Bible story.

It would be very interesting if you could prepare figures of additional people, including children, from today's time (you can copy them from magazines). Put on these figures the names of each student in your class. The little ones can paint the figures. Then, when making the invitation to follow Jesus, the children can go over and place the figures with their names following Jesus, next to the figures of Peter, Philip, John and the other disciples.

Drama: this story is appropriate for the children to dramatize the scenes of the fishermen, Jesus, the nets (may be a blanket or old sheet) and the 12 followers of the Master. With a simple "Come, follow me," they will grasp the idea of what Jesus did and the decision that the disciples had to make.

Teacher, remember that for children of any age, it's easier to understand ideas when they are visualized or acted out.

Memorization

As the children move towards the mural to place the figures with their names, they can repeat the memory verse times: "And Jesus grew in wisdom and stature, and in favor with God and man".

To end

When they finish placing the figures with their names, everyone can stand near the mural. There, pray for each one of them to be true disciples and followers of Jesus. End with an appropriate chorus.

 Notes:

23

Year 3

Introduction—Unit II

JESUS MAKES THE DIFFERENCE

Biblical References: Mark 1:40-44; 2:13-16; 14:66-72; John 21:1-29.

Unit Memory Verse: *Therefore, if anyone is in Christ, the new creation has come: The old has gone, the new is here!* (2 Corinthians 5:17)

Unit Objectives
This unit will help the elementary students to:
✗ Understand that those who accept Jesus will no longer be as before.

✗ Allow Christ to guide them so that they will be better people.

✗ Know that they are now followers of a God who is as powerful as he is loving.

✗ Trust that the Lord can change even the most sinful and evil person.

Unit Lessons
Lesson 5: Jesus heals the leper

Lesson 6: Jesus transforms Matthew

Lesson 7: Jesus loves the children

Lesson 8: Jesus forgives Peter

Why Elementary Students need the teaching of this unit:
For elementary students, it's not easy to understand the word "sin." Therefore, it shouldn't be assumed that they will grasp the term during class. But they are learning to discern when a person does good or bad things.

Through this unit, they will be able to see the benefits that come from being good and honest.

They will realize, too, that Jesus is a specialist in helping them to be better children, students and friends.

Lead them to understand that before they had accepted Christ in their hearts, they were under the dominion of the devil (kingdom of darkness), but now, they are children of God (kingdom of light). If they used to lie, steal or say bad words, they now know that all of this is bad and they should no longer want to repeat them.

Lead them to understand that when God gives us a new heart, we don't want to sin anymore, but to do good and honest things.

Jesus heals the leper

Biblical References: Mark 1:40-44

Lesson Objective: To help the students believe and experience the love of Jesus.

Memory Verse: *Therefore, if anyone is in Christ, the new creation has come: The old has gone, the new is here!* (2 Corinthians 5:17)

PREPARE YOURSELF TO TEACH!

One of the most effective teaching tools in all areas of learning is behavior patterns. Elementary aged children observe behaviors at home, at school and at church, and begin to incorporate them into their own actions and attitudes with ease. They can be positive or negative characteristics, depending on the circumstances.

The story of Jesus healing the leper is a dynamic lesson that will enable your students to understand compassion and care for the less fortunate. No matter how strong the child's life is in the home and how much Christian instruction he or she has, they will surely find questionable attitudes towards people in their experiences outside the home.

While they are beginning to understand the feelings and problems of other people, this new knowledge can often be "suffocated" by the need for acceptance of their peers. For your students to feel compassion and love for others, they must have role models. This will help them understand that Jesus loves them.

This lesson will show them the truth that Jesus loves people who are rejected, and that his love and care also extends to them. At the same time, the children will learn that they can take their needs and problems to Jesus.

BIBLICAL COMMENTARY

Read Mark 1:40-44. Jesus was continually in contact with people who had different physical and spiritual needs. None of them was as devastating as leprosy. Any skin disease was called leprosy.

The fact that Jesus touched a man with leprosy is of great importance. The lepers were considered ceremonially unclean, and whoever touched someone in that condition was included in the same category.

For this reason, lepers were asked to leave their family and friends and stay at a distance, away from everyone.

Jesus' compassion was much greater than any ritual. While he had respect for the law, he consistently demonstrated that the needs of the people were more important. When observing the man with leprosy, Jesus saw someone in great need and didn't worry about violating the religious protocol. When Jesus healed the leper, he did it because he loved him, not because he wanted to win favors in the eyes of public or religious leaders.

It's easy to feel compassion for good or clean people. When our friends are sick or in need, it makes sense to do something to help them. But, what if the person in need stinks, dresses in rags or is clearly different from us? Can we show compassion for that kind of person? Can we show affection for them?

In the Sermon on the Mount, Jesus spoke of how easy it is to love those who love us (Matthew 5:43-48). The difficult thing, he said, is to show love for those whom you consider enemies. It's also very difficult to really love those who seem to have no love.

Let's look at our own situation. It's not hard to love children in your class who behave well, but with children who refuse to obey, the situation is different. It's easy to hug children who are clean and well dressed, right? It's very difficult to offer the same to those who constantly smell bad or come to class with dirty clothes.

This week, you will have the task of teaching your children about God's love.

Through this interesting story, children will learn about Jesus' compassion and love. They will see that he wasn't afraid to touch someone in a deplorable condition. Jesus wasn't afraid to touch the leper, even though he could catch the disease.

However, the lesson about compassion begins before you start teaching. It begins the moment the children enter the room. According to the way you treat each of them, they will or won't experience the love and compassion of Jesus through you.

As you approach your class session this week, ask God to reflect through you Jesus' love as spoken of in today's story. Show that you are interested in the children regardless of their actions or appearance. Allow them to see a living demonstration of Jesus in their class each week.

LESSON DEVELOPMENT

Prepare in advance the teaching materials you will use for this lesson, and try to have your classroom ready before your students arrive.

Remember to welcome visitors and collect their info to contact them during the week.

Choose one of these activities to capture the children's attention by helping them learn the biblical truth of today.

Pyramid of words

Before class, prepare 16 cm x 12 cm colored cards, out of card stock or thin cardboard, in the form of bricks to build a pyramid.

Then, write on each card a word from the verse from 2 Corinthians 5:17. Place a ring of tape on the back of each card or brick.

In class, repeat the verse several times all together. Say: *The lessons in this unit will help us understand the meaning of this verse.*

Show them how to build a pyramid using the colored blocks while repeating the memory verse. Place the cards on a table with the words facing down. Each child must come, take a card / brick, read the word and place it in the correct place to form the pyramid. Allow the children to play by forming the pyramid and at the same time reciting the memory verse.

Symbol of love

You will need for each child: a square of red paper of 10 cm. x 10 cm., glue, a popsicle stick or stick from ice cream about 20 cm. long, and scissors. Before the class, fold each square in half and with a dotted line draw the shape of a heart.

During class, ask the children to cut out the heart from each square. The child will then glue the heart to the stick. When they have finished with the craft, ask them: *What does the heart represent?* (Love) *We will use the heart to illustrate today's lesson. You will raise your heart every time you hear something that indicates that Jesus showed his love to someone.*

BIBLE STORY

A leper finds help

"Unclean, unclean!" The sad and sick man shouted these words every day. He was always sitting on the street looking at the happy and healthy people who walked by. The leaders of the city had a law that required that a leper had to shout "unclean" so that nobody would come near and be infected with his illness. The infected person wasn't allowed to enter buildings or get close to other people. His clothes were torn and dirty. How difficult it must have been for him to find food! And the sores, all over his body, were painful and ugly. People pointed at him and ran the other way. The man felt very lonely.

Every day, the same thing happened. But one morning, while shouting, "unclean, unclean!" to warn people not to approach, the leper noticed a man he had never seen before.

"Is it possible?" he thought with enthusiasm. *"Is that the Jesus I've heard about, the one who they say can heal diseases? I'm dying with this terrible leprosy, and maybe this man can help me."*

Then, the man approached Jesus. On his knees, he begged saying, "If it's your will to cleanse me, you can do it."

Jesus looked at the sick man, who was kneeling before him. He loved him, and at once, he helped him. He extended his hand and touched the man saying, "I want to ... be clean."

The man got up healthy! He wasn't sick anymore! He didn't know what to think! His dream had come true! Yes, it was possible! It was no longer a dream. What people said was true. Whoever approached Jesus received healing, forgiveness, mercy and hope.

"Oh, thank you, Jesus!" the man exclaimed, while observing that his arms and legs, which had been covered with sores moments before, were now clean and soft. His skin was new. The man exclaimed with happiness, *"I'm so grateful and happy that I must hurry and tell everyone what has just happened to me!"*

But Jesus told him, "Look, don't tell anyone anything, but go, show yourself to the priest and offer a sacrifice for your purification to show that you were healed."

The joyful man answered, "Thank you, thank you, I'll do it immediately. I'm so happy!"

Then he disappeared into the crowd, telling people what Jesus had done for him.

It was a wonderful day for the man. In the morning, he had awakened sick, leprous and unclean, but that night, he went to bed clean and healthy, understanding also that Jesus loved him, despite his terrible illness.

ACTIVITIES

Jesus makes the difference

Give the children the activity sheet from the student book (lesson 5). Allow the children to look at the two scenes and read the instructions to them. Let them compare the pictures and talk about the differences between the two scenes.

Be sure that each child understands the concept of before and after Jesus healed the leper. Ask: *In what situation was the man in when he asked Jesus for help?* (He was sick with leprosy). *What did Jesus do?* (He healed him) Say: *Jesus healed him, that's why he became a new man. Our memory verse talks about a new creation. The leper experienced the blessing that Christ brought him.*

Give the children time to color the picture.

Let's sing praises

Say: *Can you imagine how the leper felt when Jesus healed him? No doubt he understood how much Jesus loved him. Jesus loves you and loves everyone, no matter what we are like or what problems we have. Let's sing praises to the Lord with joy and give thanks for his love* (Prepare in advance two happy and appropriate choruses.)

What if they were us?

For this activity, prepare cutouts from magazines and newspapers of "different" people: people sick in bed, children and adults in wheelchairs, children with eyeglasses or with guide dogs, anyone who expresses the idea of "different". Hand out a picture to each child and ask: *What do you see in that picture? How would you feel if that were you, sitting in that wheelchair or lying in that bed? Does Jesus love that person? Can Jesus heal that person if he chooses to?* Emphasize the healing power of God. Talk about how sad it must be for those people when we avoid them or make fun of them. Say: Let's ask the Lord to help us be merciful, to tell those people that Jesus is a God of love and that they are loved by him and for us.

Memorization

Therefore, if anyone is in Christ, the new creation has come: The old has gone, the new is here! (2 Corinthians 5:17)

Repeat the memory verse several times with the class. This memorization activity can be used in the four lessons of the unit (lessons 5 to 8). Before class, write the memory verse on a piece of cardboard or on a blackboard. For example: "Therefore, if _____ is in _____, the new _____ has come; The _____ has gone; the _____ is here" (2 Corinthians 5:17). Leave blank spaces for the children to complete with the corresponding words, which will be written on pieces of cardboard and hidden in different places in the room. The children should look for the words, run to the blackboard and place them in the correct places, until the memory verse is completed. (These will be noisy times, warn classroom teachers near your classroom.) You can make two sets of cardboard with the text to divide the class into two groups. The competition will be very fun for the children.

Say: *This verse is one of the happiest in the Bible. It means that Jesus loves you very much and that if you ask him, he can change your life. He helps you and can be your Savior. In the same way that he cleansed and healed the leper in our history, Jesus can cleanse you and forgive your sins.*

Provide time for children to complete the Student book activity page: "Hidden Verse".

To end

Gather the children for a time of prayer. Say: *Thank you, God for showing us your love through the story of Jesus healing the leper. Thanks for loving us. Help us to have more love for others, especially for those who aren't loved, for those who are sick and for those who are different from us. Amen.*

For the week: Ask the children to look for opportunities to help and pray for someone in an unfortunate situation. Tell them that next Sunday they will be able to tell the rest of the class how they felt helping that person.

 Notes:

Jesus transforms Matthew

Biblical References: Mark 2:13-17

Lesson Objective: To help elementary students know that people can be followers of Jesus no matter what they have done in the past. Jesus is always willing to forgive whoever asks.

Memory Verse: *Therefore, if anyone is in Christ, the new creation has come: The old has gone, the new is here!* (2 Corinthians 5:17)

PREPARE YOURSELF TO TEACH!

When is it the appropriate time to stop treating children as babies and begin to place our trust in them? The answer is: as soon as possible. But in the case of elementary-aged students, we need to remember that their ability to think in the concrete surpasses the domain of the abstract. We must be sure to speak to them in a way that's understandable to them.

This lesson is about forgiveness and salvation. It may seem like a very high concept for first and second grade children, but it's not. Love is the basis of Jesus' forgiveness, and these children understand what love is, whether they receive it regularly or not. However, it's more difficult to convey to them the idea of sin. At this age, it's easier to see faults and sins in others than to recognize them personally. This lesson will introduce the fact that we are all sinners and need to be forgiven by Jesus. This will offer an opportunity for children to pray and ask Jesus for forgiveness for their sins.

It's in this age of concrete concepts when children can come to know Jesus as their personal Savior. They trust what adults say and feel love when their parents, relatives, teachers or other people offer it to them. During the preparation of your class, pray that the children will be sensitive to the message and that they become followers of the Master.

BIBLICAL COMMENTARY

Why does Jesus eat with sinners?

What an interesting question! Those who asked it were teachers of the law. They were men with many years of study and contemplation. Their lives involved learning the law of God and their task was to impart that knowledge to others.

It was appropriate for those teachers to ask a deep theological question. If they believed that Jesus was the Son of God, as he claimed to be, they should have been eager to ask and also absorb his teachings. But if they didn't believe, they had the right to ask deep questions to expose Jesus as a fake.

For that reason, they wanted to know why Jesus ate with sinners. It was a fact that went beyond their comprehension. If Jesus was the Son of God, could he associate with such people? And if he was a fraud, why would he risk everything for such an obvious mistake?

So, "why does he eat with sinners?" was the big question, and it seemed that no one could give an appropriate answer.

Last week, we learned how Jesus showed compassion for an "unclean" leper and healed him. These "sinners" weren't physically ill, but they were as unclean as the leper. They were "good" Jews and were warned to stay away from tax collectors, adulterers, thieves and those who refused to follow the law. Good people didn't eat with sinners, because eating together meant they were friends or "equal to them".

So, why did Jesus eat with sinners?

First, this group of "sinners" included a former sinner named Levi (or Matthew). Previously, Jesus had asked Levi to follow him. Immediately, Levi left his job of collecting taxes and his disordered lifestyle to follow Jesus. His life changed. Jesus was at the party celebrating that new life!

Second, as a former sinner, Levi had many friends who were still in "that category". When he prepared a party to celebrate his new life, Levi invited the people he knew, that is, other sinners. Levi hadn't been a "good boy" long enough to know that he shouldn't continue to join them.

Third, and very important, this was the kind of people that Jesus had come to seek and save. Jesus didn't come to "heal the healthy", he came to reach those who needed help, the sinners.

When the Pharisees looked through the windows at Levi's party, they saw a vile and unpleasant scene. Someone who claimed to be the Son of God was associating with the unclean and sinful! They were shocked by Jesus' actions.

When Jesus looked around the room, he saw sick people. They weren't physically sick, but they were spiritually sick, and Jesus was the Great Doctor. That is the reason why he came to heal all those who asked him.

Ironically, the Pharisees were sick, but they didn't recognize him. Their very righteousness didn't let them see Jesus, nor experience the spiritual healing that only he could offer.

Instead of wondering why Jesus ate with sinners, we should thank him for doing so. Let's give thanks to God because Jesus spent time with sinners, because that includes us too, and he did it to give us a new life.

LESSON DEVELOPMENT

Prepare in advance the teaching materials you will use for this lesson and try to have your classroom ready before your students arrive.

Remember to welcome visitors and get their contact details to contact them during the week.

You can repeat the construction game of the pyramid that was done the previous week.

Now is a good time to remember the lesson of the last class. Ask some questions about what happened in that lesson. *Who did Jesus heal?* (A leper). *What kind of illness did that man have?* (Leprosy) *What was the man shouting about himself?* (Unclean, unclean). *Did Jesus heal the man?* (Yes), etc.

When the children arrive to the class, they can begin to practice the memory verse with the blocks or bricks. In advance, place the cards or bricks with the words upside down. Children can start by assembling the pyramid by placing the words in the right place.

Important word

Before class, prepare a card with the word "forgiveness" and print the definition on the back. Cover the card with packing tape or paper to laminate it.

In class, present the word "forgiveness." Say: *Today we have a fun game to help you understand a new word: "forgiveness". Forgiveness is a gift from God. When we are guilty of disobeying God, Jesus takes our sins on himself and takes our punishment. God's forgiveness unites us to him again.*

Follow the leader

Ask the children who knows how to play "Follow the Leader".

Place the children in a line one behind the other; you will be the leader Be sure there is enough space to move around in the room. If there isn't, go to a wider area. Have the word "forgiveness" and its definition written on a piece of paper while playing.

Tell the class that when you mention the word "forgiveness" or part of its meaning, they can follow you and do what you do. If you say something else that has nothing to do with the word "forgiveness", the class will stop immediately or they will stay where they are and won't follow.

Use words and phrases that have nothing to do with today's lesson so that children are sure you are saying the word "forgiveness" and its meaning. Some examples can be: zebra, skate board, butterfly, please, pass the potatoes, crooked eyes, etc. Play until the students are sure they heard the word "forgiveness" and its meaning. Laugh with them with the simple words and phrases.

BIBLE STORY

Matthew finds a Savior

It was a beautiful day and Jesus was walking near the lake, teaching people about the love of God.

"Jesus, tell us more!" they exclaimed.

Jesus spoke to them for a long time. A lot of people followed him wherever he went.

One day, Jesus and the people walked near a city. Levi, later called Matthew, was sitting collecting taxes. The tax collector looked at those who passed by without a smile ... he knew very well that he didn't like any of them. It was a very hectic day and there were many who traveled from one place to another.

Matthew's job was to collect the tax money from those who traveled outside the city or from those who entered it. Many disliked Levi because his work was for the Roman government.

Generally, the tax people collected a little extra money for themselves. For that reason, nobody said anything good about Levi. It was surprising when someone expressed something kind about this Jew, since money was probably his only friend.

"Come, follow me," said a voice.

Matthew fixed his eyes on the face of the one who had spoken to him. It was Jesus! The Master's hand was extended toward Matthew. Matthew lost his breath!

He immediately got up from his desk and followed Jesus. He didn't look back; Nor did he wonder if he had made a good decision. He didn't ask himself, "And what about my money and my earnings?" He also didn't ask Jesus where he wanted him to follow him. He only heard the Master's voice and did what Jesus said: He followed him!

The next day, Matthew decided to have a big party at his house. How could he not have a party if Jesus was there and had totally changed his life? It was the perfect time to introduce Jesus to his friends. Jesus and his disciples went to Matthew's house to eat with him. Many of his friends - tax collectors - came to the party. Some weren't honest and had cheated people. There were also other sinners around the table who didn't know Jesus.

Matthew thought: "If all these people come to my house to eat, they will listen to what Jesus has to say to them, and it's possible that they will become his followers too."

During the meal, Jesus sat in the midst of all the tax collectors and sinners. He smiled and talked with them while they ate. It must have been a very interesting conversation. The men heard about how they could receive God's forgiveness and follow Jesus.

Everyone had a great time at the party. They talked and listened to the wonderful message that Jesus had to give them. It was then that someone warned that a group of Pharisees was nearby ... observing them. They were the men who enforced the laws, and they didn't like Jesus. They didn't trust or believe in Jesus as the Savior. The Pharisees complained and were angry.

Jesus heard one of them ask, "Why does that Jesus eat with tax collectors and sinners? If he is who he says he is, then he must get away from them!"

Jesus didn't get angry with the Pharisees or tell them to go away. Instead, he looked at them and showed them something important. He said, "The healthy have no need of a doctor, but the sick do. I haven't come to call the righteous but sinners."

The Pharisees didn't understand what Jesus had told them. They continued being angry. But Matthew understood very well. He could love Jesus because Jesus loved him and loved all his friends. Jesus the Nazarene knew that tax collectors and sinners didn't act righteously. He knew that they didn't live correctly, but he wanted to help them learn about God and know that their sins could be forgiven. Jesus took advantage of this excellent opportunity to communicate the Father's message. All the people around that table in Levi's house needed forgiveness, restoration and a new life. That was the reason why he went to the party with all of them. His love and forgiveness is for all people! His love and forgiveness was and is much more important than the sins that all of them had committed.

Ask: What did Jesus say to Levi? (Follow me.) What did Levi do? (He left everything and followed Jesus.). Why do you think he invited his friends to the party in his house? (He wanted them to listen to Jesus.) What does it mean when Jesus said that the healthy don't need a doctor, but the sick do? (Jesus calls those who are sick with sin to follow him and stop sinning.)

Half puppets (sock)

You will need: a clean sock or stocking for each child, markers, fabric paint, glue, scissors, small pieces of yarn or wool, squares of waxed paper or cardboard, movable eyes or buttons.

Say: Matthew really needed a Savior and did the right thing by following Jesus. He understood the meaning of what Jesus had said, that the healthy don't need a doctor, but the one who is sick does.

Let the children comment, and guide their thinking to the idea that Jesus loves everyone and wants to forgive them.

Say: We're going to make an puppet to tell the story that we've heard.

While the children are working, review the story sequences with them.

Allow each child to make a simple puppet with the sock. Have the children place their hand or the cardboard inside the sock to trace and draw the mouth and other facial features. This will prevent ink

or glue from leaking through the back.

Children will need the help of an adult to draw the face. They can glue on movable eyes or buttons; Or, they can draw them with markers if you don't have them. You can add thick yarn or wool hair. When they are finished, ask the children to repeat the story using their puppets.

ACTIVITIES

Follow me!

Say: Jesus paid attention to Matthew and also to you. He wants your life to be different.

Give each child the activity page from lesson 6 of the student book. Guide the children to follow the instructions. When they complete their project, talk about how Jesus takes care of us.

Say: We have learned that when Jesus asked Matthew to follow him, Matthew obeyed. We also can follow Jesus. Likewise, we must not lie, or steal, or cheat others, like Matthew and his friends did. We have all been sinners because we've disobeyed God. We can ask Jesus for forgiveness and then we can be his followers. Levi decided to follow Jesus. You can also make that decision.

Encourage the children to tell the Bible story to someone in their home using the craft they made.

Memorization

Therefore, if anyone is in Christ, the new creation has come: The old has gone, the new is here! (2 Corinthians 5:17).

Repeat the memory verse several times with the class.

Say: This verse is one of the happiest in the Bible. It means that Jesus loves you very much and that if you ask him, he can change your life. He helps you and can be your Savior. In the same way that Jesus forgave Matthew in our story, Jesus can cleanse you and forgive you of your sins.

Closing

Take the opportunity to invite the children to accept Jesus as their personal Savior. Make this a special moment, so that the children really understand that they are sinners and that Jesus is willing to forgive them, if they ask him to do so.

Pray with them, and during the week engage in a conversation with the parents of those who accepted Jesus, and the pastor, to celebrate the "new birth" of their children.

Jesus Loves Children

Biblical References: Mark 10:13-16

Lesson Objective: That the children learn that Jesus loves all children and that He wants them to belong to him.

Memory Verse: *Therefore, if anyone is in Christ, the new creation has come: The old has gone, the new is here!* (2 Corinthians 5:17).

PREPARE YOURSELF TO TEACH!

This is an opportunity that's worth gold to you as an elementary teacher. Whether you have a class of two children or a class of 20, you can be sure that everyone comes from different backgrounds and environments. Some will have heard the stories of Jesus in their homes, they will have seen figures or paintings of the Master embracing the children, others will have seen Christian movies or videos, and a few will have already accepted Jesus as their personal Savior. But there will be children who haven't gone through any of these experiences.

There is no simpler message in the entire Bible than the one that you will teach this week. Jesus loves children. He loves them individually and collectively. He loves them in moments of joy as well as in times of sadness. He loves them when they make bad or good choices. He loves them unconditionally. They cannot escape his immense love.

Elementary students have tender hearts and can understand the concept that Jesus loves all children. Although for those who experience problems in their homes or at school, it will be more difficult to understand the idea that Jesus loves them individually in the same way that he loves other children. Through the Bible story and today's activities, you will lead the class through these concepts about Jesus' love for them as a group and individually. That's the way in which your students will have the desire to accept and give back God's love, and to understand that they belong to him.

BIBLICAL COMMENTARY

"Not now!" "I'm busy!" "Can't you see what I'm talking about?"

These are the expressions that children hear most of the time from adults. They are "interruptions" that walk. It's that they still have no sense of time or of occasions. They speak at inopportune times and say the wrong things. They also have the "ability" to embarrass their parents.

Trying to stop children from interrupting adult conversations didn't end with the impatient words of the disciples 2,000 years ago. Throughout history, children were placed behind the crowds and told to shut up and wait. In practically all cultures, children occupy last place.

In biblical times, especially mothers often asked well-known rabbis to bless their children, especially when the child was about to complete their first year of life.

These parents believed that the touch and blessing of Jesus would help their children. It's not surprising. They observed that Jesus healed the sick, gave sight to the blind and made the paralyzed walk.

Who knows what blessing those parents would seek! Maybe they wanted healing for their sick children. Maybe they were looking for something special for them to overcome the circumstances and diseases that killed the youngsters in those days. Or maybe Jesus' blessing would guarantee a good and prosperous life for her little ones in the future.

Unfortunately, Jesus didn't have time for the children. That's what the disciples thought, although the passage doesn't explain it. Maybe they thought, "Jesus has more important things to do. These children may not be 'clean' as rituals stipulate. There are many people (adults) that Jesus must attend to and help. Jesus is a very busy man ... children must wait."

But the disciples were wrong. When Jesus saw that the disciples rejected the children, he was angry. In the original language, this term emphasizes a very strong degree of anger. The Lord wasn't a politician trying to fall in love with children. This was the Son of God outraged because his disciples despised them.

Immediately, Jesus stopped the action of the disciples and called the children to the front of the crowd. Not only did he give them his blessing, but he used them as the object of an important lesson. What a turn about! A few minutes earlier, those children had been pushed to the back of the crowd. Now, Jesus used them as an example of what adults should be in order to enter the Kingdom of God.

Children in your class will often experience what it means to be treated as second-class citizens. Even if their parents are loving and patient, they will be forgotten by other adults. Our cultures aren't so different from Jesus' culture in those days, at least at this point.

In this lesson, children will learn how important they are to God. They will know that, regardless of how others treat them, Jesus loves each of them individually in a very special way.

LESSON DEVELOPMENT

Receive your students with affection and ensure that the classroom is clean and tidy when they arrive. Before starting today's topic, review briefly the past two lessons and ask your students to give some examples of how faithful they have been to God during these weeks.

Important words

Before class, prepare the words "forgiveness", "disciples" and "Savior" on large cards made with cardboard or card stock.

On the back, write the meaning of each word. Then, place them in a large envelope.

Forgiveness: it's God's gift. When we are sad that we disobeyed God, he takes away our sins and our guilt. Forgiveness makes us feel that we are right with God.

Disciples: they are people who love Jesus and obey his teachings. When Jesus was on earth, he chose 12 men to be his followers. They were called disciples.

Savior: a savior is someone who gives freedom to those who need it. Jesus is our Savior. He came to earth to show us God's love. Jesus died to give us freedom from our sins.

Ask the children to sit in a circle. Begin by passing an envelope with the important words to the child on your right, while playing music. When the music stops, the child with the envelope will take out a card and read the important word. If they read from the side where the word is, they can give clues to its meaning. And if they read the meaning, they can give clues about the word. For example: "FORGIVENESS": start with "F" and end with "S". That's why Jesus died for us. When a someone figures it out, they can clap or shout, "Very good!"

In the case of the word "disciple", you will have the opportunity to review the previous lesson and ask several questions prepared in advance.

If, when the music stops, the child doesn't know that word or its meaning, continue with the music until the envelope falls into the hands of another child. No one should laugh or make fun of those who don't know the Important Words. Play and repetition will help them learn..

BIBLE STORY

Children find a friend

One day, Jesus was teaching many people. Some had brought their children.

The Master spent a lot of time teaching while on earth. The crowds followed him. The parents who listened wanted their children to know Jesus. They wanted him to touch them and sit them on his lap. The parents wanted Jesus to pray for their children.

The people knew that the Lord was special. Perhaps they had seen him heal the sick and wanted that "special touch" on their children. But the disciples didn't like this. They frowned at the dads and moms.

"Stop, don't do that!" they told them.

It's possible that the disciples thought that Jesus was too busy to give children time and attention. Maybe they thought that the little ones weren't important.

But Jesus looked up, saw the disciples and listened to what they were saying.

Jesus wasn't happy with what his disciples had done. That's why he got very angry and said, "Let the children come to me, don't take them out of my presence!"

He wanted to see them. He was happy that they visited him. Jesus loved children and today he loves each one of you in particular, as well as all the little ones in the world.

Jesus told them, "God loves children. The Kingdom of God belongs to people who are like a child."

The Master knew that God cared about all people, not just adults. He loves all children.

Then Jesus looked at a little child and said to the adults, "'You must be like a child, otherwise you will not be able to enter the Kingdom of heaven."

Jesus wanted everyone to understand that they needed to reach out to God with trust and obedience like a child does.

The little ones came to where Jesus was. He lifted them up, hugged them, talked with them and blessed them.

"God loves you," Jesus said to each one. "You are very special to God."

He helped those people understand that God loves children as much as adults. Children are special to the Father. Jesus wants children to be his followers too.

Dramatization

You will need costumes, a person who represents Jesus, another 2 or 3 as the disciples and another group that acts as parents.

Encourage the children to participate in this small biblical dramatization. They can act out everything as you tell the story, or if they wish they can learn short sentences to tell the story.

ACTIVITIES

Jesus loves me

Give the students the activity page from the student book (lesson 7) with the pictures of Jesus with a child in his arms. Provide colored pencils or crayons to color them. Also, cut colored card stock squares a little larger (3 cm more on each side), than the pictures. Trim the edges in a decorative way. Make two marks on the top of the cards so that children can pierce them later. Give each child two pieces of thread or yard to pass through the holes in the squares. While they are working on this activity, review the lesson with them. Ask the children how they feel about knowing that Jesus loves them. Tell the children that they can give one of the pictures to a friend and tell them that Jesus loves him or her.

Memorization

Therefore, if anyone is in Christ, the new creation has come: The old has gone, the new is here! (2 Corinthians 5:17).

Repeat the memory verse several times with the class. Before the beginning of the class, write on a piece of cardboard or on the board words that are skipped from the memory verse. For example: "Therefore, if _____ is in _____," etc. Leave blank spaces for the children to complete with the corresponding words, which will be written on pieces of cardboard and hidden in different places in the room. Children should look up the words, find them, run to the blackboard and place them in the correct places, until the verse is complete. (These will be noisy times, warn class teachers near your classroom.) You can make two sets of cards with the text to divide the whole group in two. The competition will be very fun for the children.

Say: *This verse is wonderful. It means that Jesus loves you very much and that if you ask him, he can change your life. He helps you and can be your Savior. Jesus can cleanse you and forgive your sins.*

Closing

Discuss with the children the fact that Jesus loves all children, not only those who have heard many times about him, or those who come to church every week, or those who memorize bible verses. Ask them if they know other children that nobody wants at school or in the neighborhood. Be careful: don't let them say the name of the child that nobody loves.

The purpose of the question is to get the children in your class to pray for those less fortunate, either because they are different, have no money, or act rudely. Ask the children to pray silently. Then you pray for those "difficult" children (without repeating names), then pray for your class, that your students will love children who aren't loved. Say goodbye to the children with a hug and tell them that Jesus loves them and you love them too.

Don't forget to hand out today's crafts.

Lesson 8

Jesus Forgives Peter

Biblical References: Mark 14:66-72; John 21:1-19

Lesson Objective: To help the students understand that, just as Jesus forgave Peter when Peter denied Him, Jesus can also forgive their sins.

Memory Verse: *Therefore, if anyone is in Christ, the new creation has come: The old has gone, the new is here!* (2 Corinthians 5:17).

PREPARE YOURSELF TO TEACH!

The fear of failure is acquired from an early age. The world cries out that by our triumphs, or failures, we will be judged. This doesn't only happen at work, or with adults, but also happens in elementary classes, in the playground and playrooms, and in school cafeterias. Elementary students are familiar with success and failure. Sadly, they are also used to the popular belief that says: "If I don't succeed on the first attempt ... I'll give up".

Today's lesson shows students the truth that Jesus isn't focused on our mistakes, but that he is willing to

forgive us if we sin. Peter denied Jesus. That was sin. The children will discover in this lesson that Jesus forgave Peter when he came to him repentant. If we sin, Jesus will forgive us. We only need to go to him with true repentance for our sin. Peter did so, and as an apostle became a leader of the early church.

Your students should feel encouraged by this lesson when they hear about Peter's journey of faith. They should be encouraged to know that if they are wrong or they sin, Jesus will forgive them. They should feel happy knowing that God transforms them and works through them to bring salvation to other people, family and friends.

BIBLICAL COMMENTARY

Read Mark 14:66-72 and John 21:1-19

Remember a time when you failed Jesus? Do you remember when you "denied" the Lord in one way or another? I do!

For some of us, our failures haven't been as dramatic as Peter's. We haven't failed Jesus in a public market as happened to the apostle. But we know our faults very well. And Jesus does too.

It's easy to relate to Peter. Despite his swagger, Peter collapsed by the fire.

Moments earlier, he had promised to fight for Jesus. But it took him by surprise to see angry men, with clubs and swords, arresting his Master, and he panicked.

It's very easy to take a position in favor of the Lord in the middle of a Sunday service. In that situation, it's not difficult to be Jesus' allies. We're happy when we sing and pray, and we may even raise our hands. There are no problems!

The difficult thing is to live the Christian life in the real world, in the street. It becomes difficult when it's not popular to be a Christian. It's not easy to be loyal to Jesus when others mock or threaten us.

If you failed Jesus, you know how bad you felt. You betrayed the most important person in your life. You made a promise and broke it. Your firm commitment collapsed under the pressures. And you ask yourself, "How can Jesus trust me again?"

Still, he continues to trust us. He waits for us on the beach and prepares us breakfast. He doesn't do it to then give us a beating because of our bad attitudes. He does it because he loves us and wants to spend time with us.

And there comes the question of Jesus, "Do you love me?"

And we thought ... "I knew it! He still remembers what I did! He's angry or offended!"

But it's not like that. In the question there is an opportunity to say, "Yes, I still love you."

Without the question, we have no way of answering him. If he doesn't ask us, we cannot let him know, from our heart, that we still love him. The question gives us the opportunity to express what we desperately want to say. "I was wrong, but I still love you."

At first we think that it would have been better for Jesus to say: "I love you." But that phrase wasn't necessary. The fact that Jesus loved Peter and loves us is understandable.

He proved then, and continues proving today, his love in so many ways, not to mention his journey to the cross. Jesus never failed us, nor will he. His love for us should never be questioned.

Jesus loved a leper enough to touch him and heal him.

Jesus loved a sinner like Levi enough to call him to be one of his disciples.

Jesus loved the children enough to give them his time and use them as the center of an illustration of how we should be if we want to enter into His Kingdom.

Jesus loves you and me enough to touch us and find us in our sinful state. He loves us so much that he draws us to him. He loved us enough to die on the cross. He continues to love us, even when we do wrong.

And now, he prepares us breakfast and invites us to sit down to eat with him. Just a timely question: "Do you love me?"

LESSON DEVELOPMENT

Receive your students with affection and ensure that the classroom is clean and tidy when they arrive. Before starting today's topic, review briefly the three previous lessons and ask your students to give some examples of how faithful they have been to God during this month that's about to end.

Read again the activity "Pyramid of words" from lessons 5, 6 and 7 to practice the memory verse. When the children enter the class, they can have the cards/blocks on the table to make and repeat the verse. By now, all the children should know the verse by heart.

Ask all the volunteers who have learned it to come forward and tell the whole class, placing the pyramid blocks in the right place.

Important words

Since this is the last lesson of the unit, do the envelope game with the important words. Children should already know the words and their meaning: forgiveness, disciples and Savior.

BIBLE STORY

Peter finds forgiveness

The night was calm and dark. Peter had never been so sad in his life as he was at the moment. A few hours earlier, the soldiers had arrived and taken the Master. Peter knew that the men wanted to hurt Jesus.

Peter was confused and angry. While he was stopped in the courtyard of the palace where Jesus had been taken, Peter warmed his hands by the fire. He was trembling with cold!

He had been at Jesus' side in exciting situations when teaching about God's love for his people.

He had learned a lot from him and loved him. But that night, Peter was afraid.

"Jesus was arrested," he thought. "What can I do?"

Peter was startled when he heard someone approaching where he was. Although there were many people out there, he wanted no one to bother him.

"You were with Jesus of Nazareth!" said a woman.

"I don't know what you're saying, or who you mean!" said Peter.

He turned around and headed for a nearby courtyard. He wanted to be alone.

It wasn't long, when the woman approached Peter again. But this time she didn't speak to him, but to all who passed by and to the curious who had stopped.

"He is one of them!" she shouted, pointing at him with her finger.

But once again, he again denied it, "No, no!"

A group of people approached Peter. He was terrified.

Others who were there insisted, "You are truly one of them, because you are a Galilean and your way of speaking is similar."

Peter exploded with anger and began to curse and swear, "I don't know this man!"

Suddenly, a shuddering noise was heard in the air. It was the crowing of a rooster close by. It not only crowed once, but twice. Peter was frozen ... listening. He couldn't believe it! At that moment he remembered the words of Jesus, who loved him so much. "Before the cock crows twice, you will deny me three times!"

It was too much for Peter. He had never felt so badly. Jesus was right. Peter had denied him, and not only that, he had lied saying that he didn't know him. He had denied Jesus three times! The apostle fell to the ground in deep weeping.

A few days after Jesus was crucified, died and had been resurrected, Peter was with his friends, trying to fish in the Sea of Galilee.

The men were tired. They had been fishing all night but hadn't caught a single fish. Everyone felt very badly, they were discouraged and sad.

The morning sun shone and it was a splendid day. The glare didn't let them see clearly. But one of them spotted someone who was on the beach, as if spying on them. It was Jesus, but the fishermen didn't recognize him. He asked them, "Have you caught anything?"

"No, we haven't!" they replied.

"Put the net on the right side of the boat and you will find some fish," he replied.

Soon, the net was filled with beautiful fish. Nobody could believe it! The men rubbed their eyes and wondered who could be shouting at them from the beach.

One of them told Peter, "It's the Lord!"

Immediately, the disciple put on some clothes and threw himself into the water. Peter couldn't wait anymore, he was so excited that he went swimming to the shore. The others came to the shore with the boat dragging the net full of fish.

When they all reached the shore, they noticed that there was a small fire, with fish roasting and there was also bread. Then Jesus told them to bring more fish from what they had just caught. Peter ran and brought the heavy net. The fish were big, beautiful. There were 153 and the net didn't break.

Jesus invited them to eat. How wonderful! The tired and hungry men had a breakfast ready for them! But the most wonderful thing was who had prepared it for them.

After eating and being satisfied, Jesus began to speak to them. He turned to Peter and said, "Simon, do you love me more than these?"

"Yes Lord; You know I love you," he answered.

Jesus asked Peter if he loved him twice more.

"Yes," Peter said both times.

Jesus forgave Peter for what he had done.

While they were talking on the beach, Jesus told him some important things to do. He asked him to feed his sheep and take care of them.

Jesus didn't ask Peter to look after real sheep, but to take care of people, and to tell them about Jesus' love. The last thing the Master said to Peter was a short phrase, perhaps the most important phrase in the whole universe:

"Follow me!"

Peter followed Jesus until his death. But before that, he was one of the greatest preachers and leaders of the early church.

ACTIVITIES

The forgiven sinner

You will need: scissors, glue and pencils.

Give the children the activity sheet from lesson 8 of the student book. Explain the instructions. Ask: *How did Peter fail Jesus?* (He denied him.) *What did Jesus do for Peter?* (He forgive him). *How did Peter change?* (Peter became a great preacher and leader of the early church). *How did your life change when you were forgiven by Jesus?* (Allow the children to respond.)

Sweet verses

You will need: the activity page 113 (candy jar) of the student book, scissors, construction paper larger than the candy jar, and colored pencils or crayons. Throughout the year, you will find on different pages of the student book in the cut-out sections, the memory verse for each Unit, in candy or candy forms with the verses written on each one. When the child has memorized the memory verse, allow him to cut out the candy from that unit and stick it inside or around the jar. At the end of the year, they will be able to take the jar with sweets to their homes. That way they can repeat to their families the verses they learned.

Memorization

Since you've reached the end of Unit 2, you can do a competition. Divide the class into two groups. Ask that 2 or 3 children chosen by them (or by you) in the respective groups recite the text. The group that said the passage without error will receive special applause, or leave the classroom first, etc. Use your own creativity to reward children. Maybe use cookies, or a piece of fruit.

Closing

Ask the children to complete the activity sheet: A gift from God, and sign the letter addressed to God. Pray especially for those who accepted Jesus during this unit. Allow them to tell what they feel now that Jesus lives in their hearts and forgave them of their sins.

Encourage them to go home and tell about their new experience with the Lord to their family and friends.

Year 3
Introduction - Unit III
THE MIRACLES AND MINISTRY OF JESUS

Biblical References: Mark 1:21-28; 4:35-41; Luke 7:1-17; 9:1-6; 10:1-20.

Unit Memory Verse: *While he was still speaking, a bright cloud covered them, and a voice from the cloud said, "This is my Son, whom I love; with him I'm well pleased. Listen to him!"* (Matthew 17:5).

Unit Objectives

This unit will help the elementary students to:

✘ Discover Jesus' great power.

✘ Be amazed and always remember the miracles Jesus was able to do.

✘ Know that Jesus uses that power to free us from difficult situations.

Unit Lessons

Lesson 9: **Jesus, the best teacher**

Lesson 10: **Jesus, the best doctor**

Lesson 11: **Jesus, the most powerful**

Lesson 12: **Jesus, the best leader**

Why Elementary Students need the teaching of this unit:

Elementary students are going through an age where the capacity for wonder is very high and curiosity drives them to discover new things.

This means that the extraordinary events of Jesus are seen by them in a very special way.

Therefore, seeing Jesus who, although he looked like an ordinary man, calmed the waves of the sea with the authority of his voice, completely healed the centurion's son who was on the verge of death, and performed feats of his own, will impact your students. And it will be difficult for them to forget the power of God.

It's good to point out that Jesus didn't do miracles just to entertain people, but to attract them to himself and change their lives.

Jesus, the best teacher

Biblical References: Mark 1:21-28

Lesson Objective: To help the students understand that Jesus acted and taught in a wonderful way, so that they would believe and have faith in him.

Memory Verse: *While he was still speaking, a bright cloud covered them, and a voice from the cloud said, "This is my Son, whom I love; with him I'm well pleased. Listen to him!"* (Matthew 17:5).

PREPARE YOURSELF TO TEACH!

Many of today's cultures are visual cultures, rich in images. This reminds me of an Easter service that I attended. While the choir sang, the images of Jesus suffering on the cross came to my memory, adding another dimension to the music.

As children grow up with visual stimuli, it's very difficult to communicate with them when we don't use those resources. Also, the little ones in their class don't have the benefit of having been present when Jesus taught in the synagogue. It's difficult for us to understand the admiration that people felt in biblical times when listening to Jesus. It must have been incredible to witness the miracles and healings that took place during his ministry.

These lessons will give you the opportunity to help children experience some of that admiration. Use the activities to attract attention and encourage their imagination to better understand the stories. Guide them to the times when people listened to the teachings of Jesus. Help them understand why this Teacher was so different from all the others. His authority came from God, because he was the Son of God.

BIBLICAL COMMENTARY

Read Mark 1:21-28. When you were a child, did your teacher teach you with figures or objects? My teacher did. Over the years, I saw biblical stories illustrated with flannel graphs, with drawings on the blackboard, and also with puppets. I was exposed to a variety of newspaper objects to guide me during the lesson.

One of the lessons that I remember very vividly was when my father explained the gospel through a chemical experiment. He had a glass with a transparent liquid, to which he added another dark liquid, while he told us about how sin had stained our lives. The second liquid muddied the first until it was almost black. Then, when talking about Jesus shedding his blood for our sins, Dad added a red liquid to the cloudy glass. Magically, the liquid became transparent. It was wonderful!

Seeing the transformation was an important experience for me. Remember that "seeing" is part of our learning, regardless of how the information reaches us. Let me explain.

When we learn, how do we receive the information? Sometimes it comes through touch: touching an object, feeling its contours. Other times we learn by listening: when someone tells us a story. We also teach ourselves through reading (most of our biblical learning is done that way). And you may ask yourself, But how do we "see" that way? When we learn by touch, our fingers transmit the sensations to a kind of map in our brain. When we read a story, we see scenes in our minds. Later, when someone reminds us of that story, the images return immediately.

When we read, we translate the words into figures that represent those words. For example, if we say "fork," we will immediately draw in our mind the image of a metal, plastic or wooden article, with a handle and three or four teeth. We do this hundreds of times, every time we read a page, without being aware of what we are doing. Therefore, everything is "seen", either with our fingers, with our eyes, with our sense of smell or with mental images.

In Mark 1:21-28, the people "saw" the teachings of Jesus. Although Jesus used words, people could "see" that things were changing. His authority was physically present to them. The power of Satan was destroyed before their very eyes. Something new, extraordinary, was happening. The teachings of Jesus had the authority of God's power.

Another important aspect of "seeing" is understanding. Through the words of Jesus and the healing of the man possessed by the devil, the multitude "saw" (that means they understood) who Jesus was: the Son of God.

In your role as a children's teacher, how do you teach? Does you depend solely on your human strength, your natural creativity and some of the talents that God gave you; or do you feel God's authority behind the truths you teach your students?

Whether you give them objects to touch, tell them a story, or give them a Bible reading, children will learn better when they see in you the radiance of Jesus.

LESSON DEVELOPMENT

Prepare in advance the teaching materials you will use for this lesson and try to have your classroom ready before your students arrive.

Remember to welcome visitors and collect their contact info in order to contact them during the week.

Choose one of the following activities to catch the attention of your students in the subject of study.

How do we listen?

Ask: *What happens sometimes when you should listen carefully? Can you hear what the other person is saying if there is a lot of noise?* (Allow the children to respond.)

Say: *We're going to do the following experiment. I will read something to you. While I read, you can cover your ears, clap your hands, tap and talk to whoever is at your side. Have fun! But you should be silent when I raise my hand* (show the children raising your hand). *Very good, start!*

Read Matthew 17:5 while the children make noise. When you finish reading, raise your hand and ask, *Who heard what I read?* (possibly none)*Now listen carefully when I read.*

Reread the text. Ask: *Who can tell me what I just read this time?*

Explain that this is the memory verse this month.

Tell them: *This verse tells us that God wants us to take time to listen to Jesus' teachings. How can we do that?* (Coming to church, attending Sunday School, in a class during the week, reading the Bible, listening to the pastor's message, hearing our inner voice reminding us what Jesus wants from us and what he wants us to do, etc). *Our story is about the time when some people came to listen to Jesus.*

Important words

Write on 10 cm x 10 cm cards the words: "Son of God" and "miracle". On the other side, the meaning.

Son of God: it's a special name for Jesus. When we know Jesus, we know who God is and what he is like.

Miracle: it's an incredible event that shows the power of God. It cannot be explained in any other way.

Place the cards in a bag, and after having reviewed the meaning of the words several times, ask some volunteers to take out a card and say the meaning of that word. Remember that the game will help the children learn. Repeat this activity for each lesson of the unit. If you wish, add other words to each lesson.

BIBLE STORY

Surprise in the synagogue!

Read Mark 1:21-28 in advance.

"Here we are!" said Jesus.

He and his disciples were in the city of Capernaum. It was the Sabbath and they had arrived at the synagogue, as they did every week. When the service began, Jesus was ready to teach about God.

The people in the synagogue had a habit of listening to the teachers. Each week, the teachers of the law explained the Scriptures to them. But when Jesus spoke, everyone immediately paid close attention.

"Jesus teaches differently than the other teachers of the law!" mentioned a man to his friend.

"I know, you can tell he knows what he's talking about," said another.

"I agree," said someone else. *"He makes you feel that he really knows God."*

Suddenly, there was a loud noise in the synagogue. Everyone jumped!

(If you have a picture of Jesus in the synagogue with a group of people, this is the time to show it.)

"What was that?"

"Look at that man, he is controlled by an evil spirit!"

Jesus went to where the man was who was screaming without stopping.

The evil spirit that controlled the man said very angrily, "Ah! What do you want with us, Jesus of Nazareth? Have you come to destroy us? We know who you are: the Holy One of God."

"Be quiet and leave him!" said the Lord.

The unclean spirit, shaking him with violence and shrieking, came out of the tormented man, who immediately felt good. The evil spirit was gone. It didn't control him anymore. Everyone in the synagogue was amazed.

"What is that?" they were asking each other.

"It's a new teaching!" some said.

"And with such authority! He gives the order to the evil spirits and they obey him!" commented others.

Jesus and his friends left the synagogue. But the people didn't forget him. People told their friends what had happened that day. The news spread throughout the country.

Review of the biblical story

For this review activity, give everyone the activity sheet from the student book: **Who said it?** Guide the children to cut, paste and assemble the review wheel. You can give them a few minutes to form teams of two and play while you ask the questions about the story that appear on the wheel. Children should remember who said what is mentioned in the three biblical verses.

ACTIVITIES

Bookmarks for your Bible

Before class, write the memory verse (Matt. 17:5) on 2 cm x 15 cm paper strips. In addition, cut 4 cm x 17 cm strips from cardboard or construction paper. In class, give each child the strips with the memory verse and the cards. Instruct the children to paste the text on the construction paper. Hand out small figures or stickers for them to decorate their bookmarks. They can place their names on the back.

Say: *Jesus was an excellent teacher. His teachings and miracles proved that he was the Son of God. Place your bookmarks in your Bibles in today's story. When you get home, you can read it with your family and friends.*

Memorization

Who is the winner?

For this unit, write the memory verse on pieces of cardboard in the form of clouds or another form of your liking. Place in each of them a word from the text of Matthew 17:5.

Mix them up on a table, with the words down. After repeating the memory verse several times, encourage the children to put the passage in order.

For this memorization activity you can divide the children into two or three small groups. If so, you must prepare two or three sets of memory verses. Make it into a competition. The team that learns the text and puts it in the correct order first can receive a small prize, such as a pencil, stickers or stamps. This activity can be repeated every Sunday while teaching this unit.

To end

Ask the children to be very quiet. Prepare a series of 3 or 4 questions about the lesson and the Bible story. At the end of the review, ask a child to pray that they can remember the lesson during the week. Pray to dismiss them. Ask them to tell the Bible story to their parents, siblings and friends. They can use the wheel "Who said it?" for that.

Lesson 10

Jesus, the best doctor

Biblical References: Luke 7:1-17

Lesson Objective: That the children understand that Jesus, being the Son of God, healed diseases and raised the dead; and that same Jesus can help them today when they have needs.

Memory Verse: *While he was still speaking, a bright cloud covered them, and a voice from the cloud said, "This is my Son, whom I love; with him I'm well pleased. Listen to him!"* (Matthew 17:5).

PREPARE YOURSELF TO TEACH!

For most children, the idea that someone can be healed exists only in the stories of the Bible. Unless the children have experienced the healing of a relative, they may not be able to associate that form of God's power with their daily life.

This lesson provides an excellent opportunity for someone you know, or yourself, to testify about their healing. A testimony, combined with biblical history, will help make the power of Jesus real in the lives of children. In addition, it will create a bridge between the biblical stories and the truth of the Word of God as a reality in today's world.

Ask God to help you minister to the children in your class. As you talk about the power of Jesus, know that some of them have serious needs. Some will have disabilities that God has not healed. Others have sick parents or friends.

Use this lesson to teach about the importance of prayer in each circumstance. Remind your students that God always listens to us when we pray. Also, that God cares about their colds and scrapes in the same way he cares about other serious situations. Encourage the class to pray and ask God when they have illnesses and sufferings in their families. Tell them that it's not always God's will for us to be healed, but it's his will that we pray and learn to accept him with the confidence that he knows what is best for us.

BIBLICAL COMMENTARY

Each story has its "climax". In a joke, the "climax" arrives unexpectedly, and that's why it's funny. In a story, the climax may happen in more than one place. But still, it works the same way. The purpose is to finish the story in a powerful way. The "climax" is what will make us remember that particular story.

The story of Luke 7 has those "high points": "God has visited his people" (v. 16). That phrase is enough to encourage us, despite the suffering caused by this world sick with sin. And there is even more in this passage! We have two great demonstrations of how God helped his people through Jesus.

The first story is about a man who was self-sufficient in almost all areas of his life. As a military leader, he had a number of soldiers who did what he asked of them. But he recognized that there was an area beyond his command and power: he was unable to heal his death-sick servant. He did what he could: he sent some of his high-ranking Jewish friends to ask Jesus for help.

The second story shows us another person who didn't have resources. She was a widow and mourned the death of her only son. Not only had she lost the support of her husband, which was necessary to have prestige in society, but she was also in the process of burying the only resource that would supply her with food ... her son.

Jesus reacted to these two people. He was "amazed" (v. 9) by the centurion's faith. The centurion, in saying that Jesus didn't need to come to his house to heal the servant, showed more faith than Jesus had found in most of the Jews of his time.

In contrast, the heart of Jesus "felt sorry" (v. 13) for the widow when he came across her son's funeral. Jesus reacted to the widow's pain in the same way that he had acted at the request of the centurion.

He not only reacted, but also responded to both situations. Jesus healed the centurion's servant "by remote control." He came close to the house, but not to the house. Upon returning, the messengers to the house found the servant in good condition. In contrast, Jesus responded to the widow by acting. He touched the coffin and brought the boy back to life, thus restoring the poor woman's source of support. Then, Luke shows us the reaction of the people: "And all were afraid ..." (v. 16).

This brings us to the "climax": "God came to help people" (v. 16).

LESSON DEVELOPMENT

Prepare in advance the teaching materials you will use for this lesson and try to have your classroom ready before your students arrive.

Remember to welcome visitors and collect their info to contact them during the week.

"M" is for "Miracles", review and important word

You will need: cardboard or construction paper, scissors, paints, colored pencils, markers, figures, stickers or stamps, colored paper, etc. to decorate the letters "M".

Before class, cut out large letters "M", about 6 cm. wide, for each child.

In the class, while the children decorate their letters "M", say, *the "M" is the letter with which the word "MIRACLE" begins. What is a miracle?* (A powerful act that shows the power of God, we cannot explain that act in any other way). *What miracle did we talk about last week?* (Jesus cast out an evil spirit from a man.)

Allow time for the children to show their classmates their decorated "M" letters. Once the work is finished, place the letters "M" on display in a mural on one of the walls of the classroom. You can place them around the word "MIRACLE" and a picture of Jesus.

BIBLE STORY

"Your servant is very ill, I don't think he will improve," the Roman soldier told his commander.

"I know," the commander replied. *"I'm worried. He is a good servant. We have done everything possible to cure him, but his health keeps getting worse."*

The days passed and the servant was still very sick. Finally, the commander realized that if he didn't seek immediate help, his servant would die. What could he do?

Suddenly, he had an idea. *"Maybe that Jewish teacher, Jesus, could help my servant. I've heard wonderful stories about him! And now he has come to our town,"* he thought.

Quickly, the centurion sent a message to his Jewish friends. They were important leaders.

"Please, go to where Jesus is and ask him to heal my servant," he asked them.

The Jewish leaders were happy to do what the commander asked of them. Generally, Jews didn't help Roman soldiers. But this soldier was different from the others, so they rushed to look for Jesus.

"Jesus," they begged, *"please come to the commander's house and heal his servant. This Roman is a good man. He loves the Jews, and he even built a synagogue for us."*

Quickly, Jesus went with men. But when they were near the commander's house, someone came out to meet him.

"Sir, don't worry," he said. *"The commander told me to tell you that he isn't good enough for you to come to his house. He knows that if you say a word, his servant will be healed."*

When Jesus heard that, he marveled at the commander ... He turned and looked at the people who were with him and said, *"I tell you that not even in all of Israel have I found so much faith."* And then, addressing the centurion's friends, he said to them, *"Return to the commander's house."*

(Pause and say, Surprise! What do you think happened? Let the children guess what the first surprise in the story is.)

The commander's friends returned to the house. There they discovered the wonderful truth. The Roman commander's servant was completely healthy!

Some time later, Jesus went to the city of Nain. The disciples and a large crowd went with him. Just he was entering the city, he saw a funeral. A young man had died and they were taking him to be buried. His mother went with them.

Jesus felt sorry for the poor woman. Her husband had

long since died. She only had that one son, who took care of her. And now he was dead. What could this woman do?

"Don't cry," Jesus said to the widow. Then he went to the coffin, touched it and said, "Young man, I tell you, get up!"

(Again, pause and say, Surprise! What happened? Let the children guess what the second surprise is, then continue.)

Suddenly, the boy sat up and started talking. He was alive!

Jesus looked at the young man's mother; she was looking at him with total admiration.

"Here is your son," Jesus said.

The people were amazed and began to praise God.

"A great prophet has risen among us!" they said. "God has visited his people!"

ACTIVITIES

Testimony of health

Before the beginning of the class, invite someone to tell your students about how God healed him or her. The guest should give a testimony appropriate to the age of the children about physical health, and not talk about personal issues. It's important that it be someone who can speak at the level of the children. Allow the pastor to approve this person.

During the class, allow the visitor to testify about their healing experience. Encourage the children to ask questions.

Say, Jesus, the Son of God, has great power. He used his power to help people. Sometimes today, he heals people like he did in biblical times. Other times, Jesus offers another kind of help. No matter what we face, we can trust that Jesus will help us because he is the Son of God. There isn't anything that God cannot do!

Prepare a soda and cookies to share with the visitor and the class.

Doctor's instruments ...

Pass out the activity sheet from the student book (lesson 10). Tell them to follow the instructions on the sheet. They can cut out, color and paste on construction paper the instruments that some doctors use. Then, ask them to write each one's name: 1. thermometer, 2. syringe, 3. band aid, 4. medicine, 5. stethoscope, 6. tongue compressor, 7. instrument for looking into the ears, 8. instrument for taking blood pressure, 9. cast.

Band-Aids for everyone

Take a box of Band-Aids to the class. Write on each band-aid: "Jesus heals." Give the band-aids to the children and tell them to use them as a reminder that Jesus is the Son of God, that He can work miracles and that He shows us His power in every miracle.

Ask them to sit in a circle so that each one tells their need. Have a moment of prayer for those needs.

Memorization

Continue using the same biblical memory verse. Write each word in the form of clouds or other forms. Divide the class into two groups and give each team a set of the words for the Bible verse. The team that completes the verse first will be the winner. Encourage the losing group to continue practicing to learn the verse.

To end

Ask the children to pray for their family and friends who are sick.

Make a list on the board with the names of the sick people. Say, Because Jesus is the Son of God, we know that he has the power to help us and to heal diseases. Pray for your sick friends and family. Let's ask the Lord to heal them, but we also pray that, if it's not God's will to heal them, both they and we will learn to be happy with God's will for our lives. He can help the sick to cope with the moments of pain. He gives us strength in the midst of pain."

Jesus, the most powerful

Biblical References: Mark 4:35-41

Lesson Objective: To help the students understand that Jesus, as the Son of God, has power over the forces of nature, over diseases and over everything else. Let them know that he is with us especially when we are afraid.

Memory Verse: *While he was still speaking, a bright cloud covered them, and a voice from the cloud said, "This is my Son, whom I love; with him I'm well pleased. Listen to him!"* (Matthew 17:5).

PREPARE YOURSELF TO TEACH!

There are many things in the world that make children afraid, like storms, night noises or being away from mom and dad. There are very peculiar fears that affect every child in particular. Keep in mind that they can face very big fears in their everyday life.

Elementary-aged children have very little control over their lives. They are directed by their parents, teachers and other adults. This, in itself, can cause them fear. Although they probably will never be in a boat during a storm, their fears are equally real. It's important that as an adult who represents Jesus for their lives, you recognize that they have such feelings.

In today's lesson, children will learn that there are still strong men who are afraid of storms. It's good for children to know that adults are also afraid sometimes. Children understand the fear that comes from strong storms, thunder and lightning. This is a story with which they can identify.

The foundation of the story is that we can trust God when we are afraid.

Use this lesson to give your students an important tool: trust in God. Tell them that Jesus is with them wherever they are and that he will help and protect them when fear overwhelms them.

BIBLICAL COMMENTARY

Read Mark 4:35-41.

"What's going on?" he asked twice, trying to hide the tremor in his voice.

He and his wife had spent the last two hours in the emergency room. Another convulsion of pain hit the woman's body.

"I don't know," she said weakly.

He didn't know either. All he knew was that he was very afraid.

A doctor and a nurse entered the room.

"Please, can you help her?" the husband asked, not hiding his panic.

"Sure," said the doctor, "we'll give her something for the pain right now. Then we'll take her to the surgery room to repair the bleeding area. She will be alright."

How different it is to have knowledge about something! The man didn't know what was happening to his wife; that's why he was terrified. The doctor knew what was happening and that he would be able to solve it; therefore he wasn't afraid.

Many times, security comes from knowledge.

If we know the answers to the questions, we won't be afraid when we take an exam. If we hear a noise in our house during the night, we won't worry if we know who's making it. And we can be sure when we know that a power superior to ours is there to take care of us.

The center of Mark's story about "the storm" that struck Jesus and his disciples has to do with knowing; knowing who Jesus is and who has the power to act.

Jesus was in the same boat as his disciples, literally and symbolically. Jesus slept in the stern of the ship that was taking them to the other side of the sea. This is the story as it happened. Although Jesus was also "in the same boat," like all of us experiencing life as a human being, still he wasn't scared when the disturbed disciples woke him up and accused him of not caring about them. Jesus simply got up, "rebuked the wind and said to the sea, "Be silent, be still!" (V. 39)

Jesus knew, that's why he was calm.

Did the disciples know? They had asked each other, "Who is this?" (V. 41).

They had been with Jesus for a long time, but this demonstration of his power amazed them. He also filled them with fear. They wondered if they really knew who Jesus was. In fact, they knew him a little, but they still had a lot to learn. That question at the end of the chapter makes us ask ourselves, "Who is this?"

Do we know Jesus? Do we know him as the one who has all the answers to the most complex problems? Do we know him as our protector when we go through the darkest nights? Do we know that his power is greater than any other power in the universe?

If we don't know Jesus in that way, we will be continually anxious, because life is full of storms. On the other hand, if we truly know him, we will have peace in the middle of the storms.

May we hear Jesus whisper to our storms, "Be silent, be still!"

LESSON DEVELOPMENT

Welcome your students with affection and ensure that the classroom is clean and tidy before they arrive. Before starting today's topic, briefly review the two previous lessons and ask your students to give some examples of how faithful they have been to God during this past week.

Choose one of these following activities to get the children's attention for the lesson.

Storm noises

Place the children in a circle. Ask them to make noise imitating various types of storms (rain, thunder, wind). For the rain, have children hit the palms of their hands quickly on their legs. For thunder, ask them to hit the ground with the soles of their feet, as if they were running. For the wind, ask them to blow hard and make noise saying: Wooo! Wooo!

Play for a while. Direct the frequency and loudness of the noises of the storm. Start very smoothly, then stronger, faster, etc.

Ask them, *How do you feel when it begins to rain really hard and you hear thunder and see lightning?* (Let the children respond.)

Say: *In today's Bible story, Jesus was with his disciples when a very strong storm hit them. Let's see what happened.*

Be silent! Be still!

This is a fun game. Ask the children to stand in a row at the side or at the end of the room. Tell them, *When I cover my eyes, you can move to where I am. When I say, "Be silent! Be still!", you must stop immediately. I will open my eyes and if I see anyone moving, they will have to return to the starting place.*

Play this game as time allows.

Say: Be silent! Be still! Let's see what happened when Jesus said those words.

BIBLICAL STORY

Winds and waves are silent!

It was late. Jesus had taught many people throughout the day, therefore he was very tired. Before dark, he decided to take a break. He told his disciples, "let's go to the other side." They all climbed into the boat, untied it and started sailing. Jesus leaned back in the boat and fell asleep on a pillow.

While they were sailing, a big storm arose. The wind began to blow with fury. It rocked the boat from one side to the other. Then, it started to rain so hard that they almost couldn't see anything. A powerful storm surrounded them.

The disciples trembled with fear. They were so scared that they didn't know what to do. Everyone feared that the boat would sink.

"What will we do now? We will drown!" they shouted.

As they looked around, they noticed that Jesus wasn't helping them get water out of the boat. He was still asleep
in the back of the boat. The disciples were shocked. How could he do that? How could Jesus sleep in the middle of that terrible storm?

"Teacher!" exclaimed one of his disciples, "don't you worry that we will die?"

Rubbing his eyes, Jesus got up and looked around. He saw that the wind was shaking the boat from one side to the other. The rain hit his face as he watched the dark sky. Then he turned, looked at the sea and ordered the wind to stop blowing.

"Be silent! Be still!" was Jesus' order.

The wind stopped. The rain stopped. The storm subsided. Everything was quiet. The drenched disciples looked surprised.

The Master looked them in the eyes and asked them, "Why are you afraid? Don't you have faith?"

The disciples were amazed.

"Who is this?" one of them asked. "Even the wind and the sea obey him!"

ACTIVITIES

Choose some of the following activities to connect biblical truth with daily life.

When we are afraid

Give each child the activity sheet from the student book and a variety of colors.

Ask them, *What things make children or adults afraid? What makes you afraid?*

Be prepared to tell children something that you fear now or that you were afraid of when you were little.

Ask the children to draw on the activity sheet something that makes them feel afraid. As they do so, ask them, *What can you do when you are afraid?* (Pray, remember that God is with them.) *How can Jesus help you when you are afraid?* (By giving them peace of mind, helping them to think about what to do, changing the situation.) Once the drawings are finished, they can be placed on a mural for a few weeks. Write on the mural as the title: "Jesus, the most powerful."

Guide the children to color the figure in the student book (lesson 11). Follow the instructions on the same page. As a review, ask the questions that appear on the sheet. Encourage them by saying, *all people, both children and adults, often feel fears in different ways. Don't be ashamed, remember that you aren't the only ones to be afraid.*

Memorization

Write the memory verse on the board. After repeating it as a class several times, erase one word at a time, starting with the first, until the children have memorized the verse completely. Ask several of them to write two or three words of the verse on the board. You can divide the board into several spaces and give the opportunity for several to come and write parts of the text. Help those who are wrong, or ask whoever already knows the text to help those who don't know.

To end

Teach the children to pray when they are afraid for some reason. Encourage them to always remember that Jesus is the most powerful, that he is always with us, that his presence shines in the darkest corners, and that he is the solution to fear.

Put them in a circle. In this way, a child can pray for the fears of his partner on the right, and so on until it is finished with you, and you will pray for the whole class.

Lesson 12

Jesus, the best leader

Biblical References: Luke 9:1-16; 10:1-20

Lesson Objective: That the students understand that Jesus asked his followers to help him in his work and that he enabled them to carry it out. Help the children to be willing to do what the Lord asks of them and trust that he will help them accomplish that task.

Memory Verse: *While he was still speaking, a bright cloud covered them, and a voice from the cloud said, "This is my Son, whom I love; with him I'm well pleased. Listen to him!"* (Matthew 17:5).

PREPARE YOURSELF TO TEACH!

Generally, children this age don't have the opportunity to participate in the work of the church. In many cases, our actions reinforce the idea that they are "the church of tomorrow," instead of making them part of the church today.

This lesson will allow you to show children how Jesus wants to involve everyone in his work. This also includes the little ones. Take time to think about what activities your students can help you with during class. Don't invite them to participate only in this lesson, but rather continue to provide opportunities to serve in all classes. Help them understand that they can tell their friends about Jesus and that it's also helping God.

The only reason children often don't understand that concept is that we don't give them opportunities to serve. Let this be the week of change. Provide for this through service opportunities. Allow them to experience the joy that these occasions bring them and encourage them to make service their lifestyle.

BIBLICAL COMMENTARY

Read Luke 9:1-6; 10:1-20. The apostle Paul told us that God has put workers in the church. First apostles, then prophets, and thirdly teachers (1 Corinthians 12:27-28).

Have you ever noticed that the teachers are up on the scale, along with the other two? And have you ever had the curiosity to know why these positions were established?

Apostles: the Greek word from which this word comes means "sent." So, apostles are literally "the ones sent."

Prophets: the prophets of the Bible basically performed two tasks: hearing and transmitting God's message to the people. Frequently, the word they received from God came before certain events occurred, so the message dealt with what would happen in the future. In other times, the prophets spoke the Word of God to the people. In either case, the prophets had to speak the truth to warn of the consequences of continued sin and to help the people stay on God's path.

Teachers: the teachers assigned by God were life shapers. They were called to help people apply the truth of God to their lives. Among the first great Christian teachers was the Apostle Paul. His instructive letters still teach and form us as followers of Christ.

When Jesus sent the 12 disciples (Luke 9:1-6), he transformed his students (disciples) into apostles. He sent them to announce the Good News they had learned from him. When Jesus commissioned the 70 (Luke 10:1-20), he also transformed several of his followers into apostles. He sent them to work hard in a field spiritually prepared for the message; That field didn't have workers. The 12 and the 70 had extremely active and effective ministries. However, Jesus told them that the most important thing, beyond any success, was that they could have the knowledge that they themselves belonged to God.

As he prepared to ascend to heaven, Jesus marked out the territory that his disciples would cover with the message: "In Jerusalem, in all Judea, in Samaria, and to the ends of the earth" (Acts 1:8). He commissioned them to expand their ministry beyond the center of their world, Jerusalem, to the most remote places on the planet.

They obeyed his mandate. The apostles scattered and spread the Word. The prophets spoke the truth. And the teachers formed lives. Throughout the centuries, faithful people have done what God called them to do. They told the story of the gospel, so that it persevered from the time of Jesus to our day. And now we pass it on to our students, the next generation of God's disciples.

It is a long historical chain. It has been and continues to be a beautiful story that changes lives. Those who were sent to tell it had busy lives, often full of dangers. But thanks to the fact that in each generation there have been so many faithful people to spread the message, you and I can rejoice that our "names are written in heaven" (Luke 10:20b). Our students also deserve the same privilege. It's God's desire that they know him personally; so our duty is to go and tell them.

LESSON DEVELOPMENT

Receive your students with affection and ensure that the classroom is clean and tidy when they arrive. Before starting today's topic, review briefly the three previous lessons and ask your students to give some examples of how faithful they have been to God during this month that's about to end.

We can help

Before class: This week ask your students to help you prepare the class. Choose tasks they can do (distribute activity sheets, prepare the classroom, welcome their classmates, etc.). Write each task on a card. For more difficult tasks, write the same task on several cards. Place the cards with the written part face down on the table.

In class: Invite children to look at the cards and choose a task to perform voluntarily. Encourage them while doing their jobs. If necessary, help them. Congratulate them for their effort. (It would be good to do this activity in each class.)

Say: *You were very good helpers today. Jesus is happy when we help. In today's Bible story, we are going to see how Jesus chose his helpers.*

BIBLE STORY

"Go, preach and heal!"

Read Luke 9:1-6; 10:1-20

Many people knew about Jesus. People saw him when he came to their town. Many heard about the incredible miracles he performed.

Jesus knew that many could know God if his disciples went and spoke to people. Then one day, Jesus called his disciples.

"I have an important job for you," he told them. "I'm giving you permission and power to carry out this task. Go to the cities where I send you. Preach about the Kingdom of God, heal the sick, and cast out demons. Take nothing with you," he added. "Don't take food, money or clothes. When you arrive in a town, people will offer you their houses to stay with them. Stay with them until you leave the city."

Jesus knew that not all people would receive the disciples.

"If they don't receive you, then shake the dust from your feet and leave," he told them.

The 12 obedient disciples went from city to city preaching and healing people.

Then, the Master sent more people to do his work. He called 70, who were his followers, and he also sent them to preach and heal.

"Go, I send you as lambs in the midst of wolves," said Jesus to the 70" (Luke 10:3). "Don't carry anything. Just go, preach and heal. I will be with you."

His followers went. They preached to the people about God. Every place where they went, many sick people were healed.

"This is wonderful," the disciples said. "Jesus has chosen us to do his work."

The disciples returned to Jesus. They were excited and grateful that he included them in his work.

"Here is something more to be happy about" said the Lord. "Rejoice that your names are written in heaven."

After the bible story, say: *We can also help Jesus do his work. We can go and talk to others about the love of God. Where are places that you can go and talk about Jesus to others? What can you tell others about Jesus? What are some ways that you can share God's love with a person who is sick or hurt?*

We are Jesus' helpers. We can trust that he will help us tell others about his love and power.

ACTIVITIES

Helpers in the church

Before class, ask your pastor if your students can help in the main service. If they can, organize with the pastor that the children greet the people, distribute bulletins, or participate by collecting the offering.

In the class, say: *Today we are going to help in the service.*

Explain what they will do. Comment on the responsibilities each one will have. Say: *Jesus has chosen us to do his work. Today we are going to help Jesus by doing his work by:* (describe the tasks children will perform during the service).

Mural: Preparing to travel

You will need: markers, pencils or color paints, picture or drawing of a suitcase, scissors and glue. On thin cardboard or construction paper, write: "What do we need for the trip?" Then, in the center, paste or draw a suitcase or travel bag. Ask the children what things are necessary to take on a three-day trip. Give them a blank sheet of paper or construction paper to draw and color all the items they think are necessary for the trip. At the end, ask them to tape or glue their drawings around the suitcase.

Ask: *Is each item really necessary for the trip? If we had made this trip in Jesus' time, would he have told us to leave those things or could we take them?*

Give the children the activity sheet from the student book (lesson 12) and guide them to complete what is missing. Have the children paste or draw a picture of Jesus on the sheet. Then, helped by the holes on the sides, have them insert a piece of yarn, passing it from one hole to the other.

Let's follow the leader

Tell the children that you will be the leader and that they should follow you and do everything you do. This is a good activity to do in a yard. Form a row with the children behind you. Start marching to the sound of any song on the subject. Make gestures that children can make, such as stopping and bending their legs, jumping, raising both hands, lifting one hand, whistling, scratching their head, etc. The purpose of the activity is for children to understand what it's like to follow the leader and obey him/her.

At the end of the activity, ask some questions to review the bible story.

Say: *Just as you followed the me, your teacher-leader and did what I told you to do, so the Lord chooses leaders, that is, prophets, apostles and teachers. That's why the disciples followed him and obeyed, doing what Jesus told them to do. They were to preach the Good News of salvation.*

Memorization

Write the memory verse on the board. Teach the children the passage, word by word, and have them repeat it several times until they learn it. Then, start deleting a word and have them repeat the whole verse. Then erase another and so on until they say it by heart. Every time you delete a word, encourage them by making comments like: I'm not sure you can say it, it's very difficult, etc. (to challenge them). Celebrate when they say it well. In the end, when there isn't anything written on the board, have them repeat it one more time with all their strength.

To end

Say: What a beautiful story we learned today! How good it is to know that Jesus wants us to help him! But we have to put all our effort into doing his work as well as possible. Who is willing to do what Jesus asks?

Closing prayer: *Thank you, Lord, because we can work together in your work. Help us to trust that you will enable us to do it. We want to be excellent helpers! In your name, amen.*

 Notes:

Year 3

Introduction – Unit IV

PLAN OF SALVATION

Biblical References: Luke 22:47-53, 63-71 ; Luke 23; 24:1-12, 36-53 ; Mark 16:15-16, 19-20.

Unit Memory Verse: *God has raised this Jesus to life, and we are all witnesses of it (Acts 2:32).*

Unit Objectives
This unit will help the elementary students to:

✘ Know that Christ paid for our sins by dying on the cross for us.
✘ Be impacted by Jesus who rose from the dead.
✘ Accept with faith and gratitude that Jesus is our Savior.

Unit Lessons
    Lesson 13: Jesus died for us.
    Lesson 14: Jesus was resurrected!
    Lesson 15: Jesus is our savior.

Why Elementary Students need the teaching of this unit:

A person who dies on a cross is a figure almost incomprehensible to a child of this age because it's not a custom of the current world. Therefore he cannot understand it, or even imagine it (unless he has been told the story of Jesus since he was little).

It will be essential, then, to show pictures of Jesus' death on the cross, and explain that he was subjected to that specific type of death for two reasons: one, so that what was announced in the Old Testament would be fulfilled, and two, to pay with his death for the sins of everyone.

It's important that students don't see this only as a history lesson, but understand that Jesus' death, which occurred more than 2,000 years ago, has an effect on their lives today. And although at this age they don't have the maturity to understand the responsibility of all human beings in Jesus' death, it's necessary that they feel that because of the wickedness of all people, including children, Christ had to suffer such a sacrifice.

Give them a positive note by teaching them that death served to give them life forever, eternal life.

Jesus died for us

Biblical References: Luke 22:47-53, 63-71; Luke 23

Lesson Objective: That the children will know why Jesus came into the world and died on the cross: to die for their sins. They need to ask him for forgiveness for their sins.

Memory Verse: *God has raised this Jesus to life, and we are all witnesses of it* (Acts 2:32).

PREPARE YOURSELF TO TEACH!

Elementary-aged children aren't so small that they don't know that Jesus died on the cross for their sins. This class will be appropriate to invite the children to receive him as their Savior. However, we must do it in the most appropriate way.

Dr. Catherine Stonehouse of Asbury Theological Seminary points out that the first step that must be taken is to soak the child in the truth of God's love for him/her. According to Stonehouse, when the child understands (not only knows) that God loves them unconditionally, it's easier to go to Him to receive his forgiveness.

This lesson will give you the opportunity to help your students understand more clearly the love God has for them. He loves them in such a way that he gave Jesus, his only Son, to suffer and die on the cross. Jesus loved and welcomed the thief who repented. In the same way he loved those who plotted his death. Unfortunately today, many children don't feel unconditionally loved by anyone. Ask God to help you communicate His unconditional love to each child in your class. Pray that God will allow you to show the children that they need to respond to the one who loves them more than anyone else: Jesus.

BIBLICAL COMMENTARY

Read Luke 22:47-53; 63-71, and Luke 23.

In Mark 15:12, Pilate exclaims, "What, then, do you want me to do about what you call the King of the Jews?" Pilate hadn't realized how critical the question he was asking them was. But the eternal destiny of all humanity depended on what those people "did" with Jesus.

In today's passage we see some people "acting" in different ways in response to Pilate:

✘ The response of betrayal. This was the response of Judas and Peter, which was particularly atrocious. Betrayal is the opposite of what one would expect in a relationship. In biblical times, a kiss on the neck or on the cheek was a common way of greeting men. Judas used that sign - which represented friendship and esteem - to abandon Jesus, giving him to his enemies. Peter's denial completely changed his promise to be with Jesus until death. We also betray Jesus if we live hypocritically or abandon our commitment to him when the path becomes difficult.

✘ The response of mockery. It reflects the way in which Herod, the soldiers (except the centurion), the governors, the people and a dying thief responded to Jesus. For them, he was simply the object of a good joke. They didn't see anything particular in him or in what he represented, to be revered. Do you know people for whom nothing is sacred? When confronted by Jesus, by the people of God, or by Christian institutions, they make fun of them, sometimes reaching the point of blasphemy.

✘ The response of indifference. This was also Herod's response. He was expected to conduct a serious investigation into an alleged crime. But all he wanted was to see Jesus perform magic tricks. When Jesus refused, Herod lost interest. This is how people often respond when they discover that they cannot manipulate Jesus for their particular purposes.

✘ The response of hate. This is the most violent response, and was represented in the first place, by the religious leaders. These men worshiped power, receiving honors and having material goods. When Jesus publicly opposed them in all their arguments, there was only one thing left for them to do: eliminate him. Even today Jesus is hated by those who want to become gods, who cruelly torment, persecute and kill His followers.

✘ The response of a leader: "it doesn't matter to me." Pilate almost seemed like the good guy in the story. He recognized that Jesus didn't deserve death and made numerous efforts to avoid his execution. He sent Jesus to Herod, hoping that in this situation he would reach an agreement. Then, he proposed him for the annual program of "set a prisoner free." When that failed, he suggested that they beat Jesus to intimidate him, and then release him. But when none of those tactics worked, Pilate shrugged, washed his hands (Matthew 27:24) and walked away from Jesus. We see Pilate's response in those who are indifferent to the gospel or openly reject it.

✘ The response of acceptance. This group is small, but important. It includes the woman who cried for him, the repentant thief, the frightened centurion, and Joseph of Arimathea. Although the details given by Luke aren't very precise, we can see in these people an attempt to approach Jesus, with different levels of love and faith.

There are many ways to respond to the Lord, and each person is responsible for their choice. The question then still remains today: "What, then, do you want me to do with him who is the King of the Jews?"

LESSON DEVELOPMENT

Prepare in advance the teaching materials you will use for this lesson and try to have your classroom ready before your students arrive.

Remember to welcome visitors and collect their info to contact them during the week.

Choose some of the following activities to help children focus their attention on the topic and prepare them to learn biblical truth.

S-E-A-R-C-H biblical words

Before class, write on a blackboard S-E-A-R-C-H. Below, write the words the children suggest that start with that letter that are related to the topic of today's lesson. To do this, make a list of key phrases or clues, which will help children find the correct word.

For example:

✘ S - Disobedience to God (SIN)

✘ E - For whose sins did Jesus die? (EVERYONE'S)

✘ A - Who can be saved? (ALL)

✘ R - When someone is raised from the dead (RESURRECTED)

✘ C - Jesus was _____ on the cross (CRUCIFIED)

✘ H - Because Jesus died for our sins, if we ask him to forgive us, we will someday go there. (HEAVEN)

Tell the children: *I'm going to give you clues about some words that are in the Bible, and the letter the answer starts with. If you think you know what the word is, raise your hand and give your answer when I call on you. Then I will read another clue, and so on.*

They can play until the children find all the words.

Ask them: *How many new words did you learn in this game? Had you heard those words before? What do they mean? Our Bible story today is about those words.*

Sin - It's wrong!

Before class, write the title of the activity on a poster or construction paper and attach it to the wall at eye level with the children.

In class, show the children the word "SIN" (which will be written in large capital letters) and ask them to explain what it means.

Say: *At Easter, there is always talk that Jesus died on the cross, and that's why people can receive forgiveness of their sins. Let's think about why Jesus died.*

Give them blank pages and let each one write words or phrases naming different sins. Tell them they can decorate them with dark colors so they look ugly and dark, but so that others can read them. Children can draw pictures in relation to what they wrote, and then cut their papers in different ways. Finally, let each one stick his sheet on the mural that you put on the wall, under the title.

Ask: *What things does sin produce in the world and in people?*

Let the children talk, and repeat the main thing each one said. Add: *Jesus never did any of these bad things, but he suffered and died for those sins. We will learn more about this in our Bible story today.*

BIBLE STORY

The saddest and happiest day in history

Read Luke 22:47-53, 67-71; Luke 23

"What's that noise?" murmured some of the disciples as they struggled to stand up.

In the distance they could hear the metallic sound of swords and heavy boots. At that moment, the light of flaming torches illuminated the darkness of the garden where they were. Dozens of men, armed with clubs and swords, appeared out of nowhere. Leading the group was Judas, one of Jesus' disciples. Quickly, Judas approached Jesus and gave him the usual, friendly and respectful greeting: a kiss on the cheek.

Sadly, Jesus looked at his disciple. "Judas, are you betraying the Son of Man with a kiss?" he asked.

The disciples were now wide awake, ready to defend Jesus. Suddenly, Peter took his sword and cut off the ear of the high priest's servant.

"Enough!" said Jesus. And touching the man's ear, he healed it.

Then Jesus, turning to the crowd, said, "Am I leading a rebellion that you have come with swords and clubs. Every day I was with you in the temple courts, and you didn't lay a hand on me."

"Let's go!" yelled the temple guards, who violently took Jesus away.

Filled with panic and pain, the disciples fled for their lives, leaving Jesus behind with those who were arresting him.

That night, the temple guards beat Jesus with a whip full of small pointed pieces of metal. Then they blindfolded him. And laughing, they said, "Hey, prophet! Every time we hit you, tell us who it was."

And they insulted him by saying many other disrespectful things.

Later, they took Jesus before Pilate. And there they began to accuse him of all kinds of crimes.

"We have found that he is causing problems in our country," they said, "and that he forbids paying tribute to Caesar, saying that he himself is the Christ, the King."

Pilate asked Jesus, "Are you the King of the Jews?"

"You say it," the Master replied.

Pilate asked him other questions. Then, turning to the furious crowd, he said, "This man has not done anything wrong."

"Jesus causes everyone to get upset," the leaders said. "He has begun to do this in his hometown. And now he is doing it here."

That gave Pilate an idea. "I don't want to take care of this," he thought. "I will send Jesus to Herod. He rules in the birthplace of Jesus. Let him decide what to do with Jesus."

Then Jesus was taken to King Herod. Herod had wanted to talk with Jesus for quite some time, because he had heard many things about him. "Do some miracles," he told Jesus.

But Jesus stood there, quiet, without saying a word.

Soon, Herod became tired. And together with his soldiers, he made fun of Jesus for a while. Then, dressing him in splendid clothes, he sent him back to Pilate.

Pilate began to get upset with the religious leaders. And he told them, "Nothing this man has done is worthy of death, so I'll let him go after punishing him." Each year, Pilot released a criminal, and he hoped to use that as the basis for releasing Jesus.

"Don't do that!" exclaimed the angry crowd. "Release Barabbas to us!" (Barabbas was a bad man who was in prison for causing riots against the rulers and for murder.)

Pilate spoke to them again, wanting to release Jesus; but they shouted again saying, "Crucify him! Crucify him!"

"OK" said Pilate finally. "Here, you can have Jesus. I will have him beaten, and then you can do whatever you want with him. I'm going to set Barabbas free as you requested."

The soldiers took Jesus from there and put a heavy wooden cross on his back. Then they took him down the long road that led to the place where the criminals were crucified. But Jesus was so weak after being beaten so badly that he couldn't carry his cross.

"Hey you!" the soldiers called to a man who was standing nearby. "Carry that cross to Golgotha."

Finally they came to Golgotha, to the crucifixion mountain. The soldiers nailed Jesus' hands and feet to the cross and hung a sign over him that said: "THIS IS THE KING OF THE JEWS". Then they put the bottom of the cross in a hole in the ground and stood the cross up. Jesus' pain was terrible.

There were also two robbers being crucified at the same time, one on each side of Jesus. Jesus looked at the crowd, the religious leaders, the soldiers, and the people, and prayed saying, "Father, forgive them because they don't know what they are doing."

One of the robbers made fun of Jesus saying, "Save yourself and us."

The other robber responded saying, "Don't you fear God, since you are going to die? We are suffering because we are receiving what our bad deeds deserve; but this man did nothing bad." And then he said to Jesus, "Remember me when you come into your Kingdom."

With love, Jesus replied, "Truly I tell you that today you will be with me in paradise."

The hours passed slowly. At about 3 o'clock in the afternoon, Jesus cried out with a loud voice, saying, "Father, into your hands I entrust my spirit."

And having said this, he died.

One of the Roman soldiers, looking up, said with great surprise, "This man was truly righteous."

Among the crowd that day was a follower of Jesus called Joseph of Arimathea. He went to Pilot. "Please let me take Jesus' body," he asked. "I want to bury him."

"Take him," Pilate answered.

Then, Joseph lowered Jesus' body from the cross and took it to a grave in a garden. Filled with pain, he went home to prepare good smelling spices and perfumes to put on the body. His friend was dead! It was the saddest day in history!

After concluding the story, tell the children: The title of our Bible story is: "The saddest and happiest day in history." Why do we say that it was the saddest day? (Because evil people crucified Jesus, the Son of God.) Why do you think we can also call it the happiest day? (Because now we know that Jesus suffered and died for our sins, and rose again three days later. We can be forgiven and someday live in heaven with him forever.)

ACTIVITIES

Choose one or more of the following activities to help the children understand the plan of salvation.

Jesus is OUR Savior

Ask the children:

What were the sins committed by the people in the bible story that we just heard?

Did Jesus die for those sins?

Could he have forgiven them if they had asked him?

What kind of sins do people commit today?

Did Jesus die for those sins? Does he forgive us if we ask him?

Tell them: *Everyone has sinned. Surely we haven't murdered anyone, nor have we deceived anyone to arrest and kill an innocent person. But we have all disobeyed God. That's the reason why Jesus came to earth. He came to show us his love and to die for our sins. Anyone in the world can be forgiven for all the bad things they have done because Jesus died for their sins. I'm going to tell you how we can be forgiven and become friends with God.*

Ask the children to complete the activity sheet from the student book (lesson 13) and to write down the ABC steps a person must take to accept forgiveness for their sins: 1) **Admit** that he/she is a sinner: repentance. 2) **Believe** in faith that Jesus died for their sins and that God loves them. 3) **Claim** Jesus as their savior, and tell others that Jesus forgave their sins, that is, they already gave their lives to Jesus.

Tell them: *Perhaps some of you are sorry for having disobeyed God and want to ask Jesus today to be your Savior.*

Ask the children to bow their heads. Sing a song that talks about repentance, forgiveness of sins or surrender to Christ.

Then, say: *If you want to receive Jesus as your Savior, raise your hand.*

If anyone raises their hand, ask one of your assistants to take care of the other children. And you, along with other helpers, speak and pray with those who responded. Allow God to guide you in this task.

The cross

Help the children make their cross necklace using the directions from the activity sheet. Encourage them to use the pendant so they always remember that Jesus died for them.

Memorization

Before class, write the memory verse in large print on a piece of construction paper (*God has raised this Jesus to life, and we are all witnesses of it* (Acts 2:32).) Then, cut out each word so that they are all separated, like pieces of a puzzle to put together.

In class, read the memory verse and repeat it together several times. Then, put the words that you cut into a bag. Mix them well. Allow each child to take out a word.

Ask: *Who has the piece with the word "Jesus"? Say the verse with me.*

Let the child say it alone if he can, or with you if he can't. Then ask him to put it on the table.

Then ask: *Who has the piece with the word "witnesses"? Say the verse with me.*

Let him also say it out loud by himself if he can and put his piece on the table. Each child should place their piece on the table in the correct place until the complete verse is assembled. That way everyone will have repeated the memory verse.

To end

Make a circle with the children. Tell them to put on the necklaces with the cross. Ask some volunteers to pray, thanking God for his love shown in sending Jesus to die on the cross of Calvary and for saving them.

Encourage them to tell the Bible story to their family and explain the title: "The saddest and happiest day in history." Sing an appropriate chorus.

Jesus was resurrected!

Biblical References: Luke 24:1-12

Lesson Objective: To help students know and believe that Jesus died and was buried, but God resurrected him. Teach them that the Easter story is to celebrate that he lives.

Memory Verse: *God has raised this Jesus to life, and we are all witnesses of it* (Acts 2:32).

PREPARE YOURSELF TO TEACH!

How real and exciting can we make the resurrection for children who have their minds fixed on rabbits and chocolate eggs? The truth is that we don't have a good answer. The little ones don't show us immediately when a spiritual truth comes to them. And many times teachers don't understand the signals they send us.

As teachers, we aren't responsible for convincing children of the biblical truths; that's the task of the Holy Spirit. Our goal is to present the truth faithfully and in the best possible way, and then trust that the Spirit will help them apply it.

As you prepare the lesson, consider what the resurrection means to you. Does it bring you joy, security and hope? Does it help you know that you can find victory over your sins? Does your faith in God increase when you face daily struggles?

You "teach" your students by reflecting with your life what you say with your words. In the same way that you talk about the resurrection, you will communicate the reality of this fact to them. Therefore, whether or not you receive any indication from the children, teach this lesson with confidence. Through the resurrection, you will know that God, in His time, will make this truth real for them.

BIBLICAL COMMENTARY

Read Luke 24:1-12.

The conviction of Jesus' resurrection saturates the message of the New Testament. First, the resurrection, and later the authority and power of the Holy Spirit, enabled the apostles to carry the message of the Good News. Second, the fact of the resurrection was a central topic of the message of the apostles, as found in the book of Acts.

One of the strangest parts in the story of the resurrection is that Jesus' closest friends seemed to not remember or disbelieve the many predictions of his crucifixion and resurrection (Luke 9:21-27, 44-45, 18:31-34).

In contrast, their enemies remembered them very well. That's the reason why the religious leaders made sure that Jesus' tomb was sealed and protected by guards until the third day.

The day of rest (sabbath) was Saturday, so the "first day" of the week was Sunday. Several women went to the tomb to complete the funerary ritual, putting spices in the folds of the sheet that wrapped the body of Jesus.

As in most of the times in which people met with celestial beings, the women were deeply frightened. Luke doesn't describe the two men as angels, but they were. Their clothes were "resplendent" - in the same way the clothes of Jesus are described in the story of the transfiguration (Luke 9:29).

The fact that women were the first witnesses of the resurrection of Jesus is important. A theory against the truth of the resurrection indicates that the disciples invented that story. However, in biblical times, women weren't allowed to be official witnesses. If the disciples had plotted the resurrection story, they certainly wouldn't have involved women as eyewitnesses.

A second evidence against the "plotted theory" is that the disciples reluctantly believed that Jesus had risen. When the women gave their report, they rejected it as something that didn't make sense. Although Peter at least showed curiosity, and together with John (John 20:3-4) they went to take a look. In particular, he noticed the position of the sheet, which wasn't as if some grave robber had removed it before taking the body of Jesus. But still, Peter didn't believe; he only wondered what had happened.

Luke doesn't give all the details of the resurrection that are included in the other Gospels. But he emphasizes the certainty of the resurrection. "He isn't here, he is risen!"

The truth of the resurrection is the center of Christianity. The Applied Bible commentary says why Christ rose from the dead:

✘   Christians know that the Kingdom of heaven burst into the underworld. The world is heading towards redemption and not toward final disaster.

✘   Death was conquered and we all have the hope of resurrection and eternal life with Christ.

✘   Our testimony to the world has authority.

✘   The greatest tragedy - the crucifixion of Christ - had meaning. That means we can find meaning in the tragedies of life and have hope for the future.

✘   We are sure that Christ lives and governs his kingdom. He isn't a legend; He is alive and he is real.

✘   The power of God that raised Christ from death is available to help us live victoriously without sinning in this unholy world.

LESSON DEVELOPMENT

Prepare in advance the teaching materials you will use for this lesson and have your classroom ready before your students arrive.

Remember to welcome visitors and collect their info to call or visit during the week.

"Jesus came back to life!"

Say: *Cut out and assemble the figures from the activity sheet. When you are finished, join the dots to discover the hidden message. Take the figures home and show them to your friends and family. Tell them the story of Jesus' resurrection. They will see how exciting it is! Remember to thank God, because we have Jesus who rose from the dead. Jesus is neither on the cross nor in the grave! Everyone who listens to you will know about Jesus, and maybe even follow him. You are his disciple and you can tell his story.*

BIBLE STORY

"He isn't here, he is risen!"

Read Luke 24:1-12.

"I can't believe it!" Mary Magdalena said to her friends. "It's like a nightmare."

"I know," said another. "Why did they kill Jesus in such a horrible way?"

It was Sunday morning. Mary Magdalene, Mary the mother of James and other women who loved Jesus walked towards the grave. They wanted to finalize all the special details that people performed for a loved one who had died. The women carried jars with spices and rich perfumes. They would place the perfumes in the folds of the sheet that covered Jesus' body.

While the women walked, they talked.

"How will we enter Jesus' tomb?" asked one of them.

"That's a good question!" replied another.

"They are right!" said a third. "The leaders of the temple placed a huge rock at the entrance to the tomb and sealed it. And now they have soldiers guarding it. Maybe those same soldiers will help us remove the stone."

"Look!" cried one of the women. "The stone has been removed. The tomb is open!"

Quickly, the women entered the tomb. Jesus' body wasn't there!

"Where is Jesus' body?" they asked each other. "What happened? Who could have taken it?"

At that moment, the women saw two men standing next to them. But these weren't ordinary men. Their clothes shone like lightning. They were angels.

The women fell on their knees, very frightened.

"Why do they search for the living among the dead?" asked the angels. "He isn't here, he has risen. Don't you remember what Jesus said before he died? He told you that he would be crucified by his enemies, but that on the third day he would be resurrected."

As the angel spoke, the women began to remember Jesus' words. With enthusiasm, they ran to where Jesus' disciples were.

"The stone has been removed, the tomb of Jesus is empty!" they said excitedly. "Two angels told us that Jesus lives, just as he had told us before!

"That makes no sense!" the disciples said.

They had seen Jesus die painfully on the cross. They had seen Joseph of Arimathea place Jesus' body in the tomb. They didn't remember the words of the Master about his resurrection. Therefore, they didn't believe the women.

Peter wanted to make sure for himself. He ran to the grave. He bent down, looked at the open tomb, and saw the sheet that had been used to wrap Jesus' body. There was something strange there. Peter left that place and returned to where the disciples were. "What happened?" he asked himself. "Could it be possible that Jesus is alive?"

At the end of the story, ask the children: *What miracle did God do on Easter morning?* (He made Jesus live again.)

Who believed the Good News that Jesus was alive? (At first no one believed, later the women believed.)

Why do you think the story of the resurrection is the most important thing for Christianity?

Listen carefully to the children's responses. It's possible that some understand some of this. Say: *Today's story is the best story in the entire Bible. Christianity is the only religion in which its leader, Jesus, rose from the dead and today lives in heaven. And since*

Jesus was resurrected, we Christians know that the power of God is superior to anything else. Christians know that when we die, we will live again and we will be with God and Jesus in heaven. This is the Good News of the resurrection!

ACTIVITIES

We remember the empty tomb (drama)

Choose several children to represent different characters in the story of the resurrection. Actors: the 3 women, Peter, three or four soldiers, two angels, several disciples.

Prepare in advance a short dialogue between all the characters to dramatize the resurrection day. You can add more characters as the Gospels indicate. Use your creativity to devise the tomb with the stone removed.

Convince Peter

Say: *Let's pretend that we meet Peter when he comes back from the empty tomb. Peter is very confused by what he saw. What would we say to Peter, with our own words, to help him know and believe in the wonderful news that Jesus lives? How can we convince him?*

Choose a child to play the role of Peter and the rest of the class, with enthusiasm, give him the Good News and try to convince him that it's true. Peter will complain and say that what they tell him isn't true. In the end, a child may appear who plays Jesus, all dressed in white, who greets Peter and all those who are gathered.

Memorization

Write the memory verse on the board with the words mixed up. For example: "God, we are witnesses, Jesus ...". Then let the children go one by one to write on the board the verse with the words in the right order.

To end

Make sure children understand the true meaning of the resurrection. Give thanks to the Lord for it, because death was defeated.

Teach them this dialogue as an Easter or Resurrection greeting:

Teacher: The Lord has risen!

Students: He has risen indeed!

Then, have each student say goodbye to each other with the same greeting.

 Notes:

Jesus is our Savior

Biblical References: Mark 16:15-16, 19-20; Luke 24:36-53

Lesson Objective: That the students know that Jesus' disciples saw him return to heaven after God raised him from the dead.

Memory Verse: *God has raised this Jesus to life, and we are all witnesses of it* (Acts 2:32).

PREPARE YOURSELF TO TEACH!

Why do we spend so much time emphasizing the resurrection of Jesus to elementary-aged children? Because first and second graders are growing up in a world that emphasizes acceptance of each religious belief as valid. This concept is stated in several ways: "I believe that different religions are good ways to reach God," or "Christianity is good for Christians, but other religions are good too," or "Who am I to say that my religion is the only correct one?"

Given this spiritual climate, it's never too early to teach children the vital truths about the crucifixion, resurrection and ascension of Jesus.

First, children need to know that only Christians have a resurrected and living Lord.

Second, they need to understand that even though Jesus isn't with us bodily, he is with us through the Holy Spirit. He always continues to work in our lives.

And finally, we want children to start caring about people - some of those people are really sincere- who don't believe in Jesus. They will be eternally lost unless someone helps them know Christ and receive him as their Savior.

Whether or not they're ready to testify of Christ to their unbelieving friends, learning and deepening the fundamental concepts of faith while they're small will help them shape their lives in a Christian way.

BIBLICAL COMMENTARY

The biblical passages that we'll consider are about "endings" because they talk about the last days of Jesus on earth before his ascension. They also speak of "beginnings" - the new age of the kingdom of God on earth - and the evangelization of the world.

Read Luke 24:36-43. The events of this passage occurred the night of resurrection Sunday. And although there was a varied number and type of reports on this, the disciples doubted considerably that Jesus was alive. Those doubts were perhaps dissipated as they listened to the report of the men of Emmaus (Luke 24:13-35); however, they hadn't yet disappeared completely.

While the disciples were discussing the Emmaus report, Jesus suddenly appeared to them. John tells us that they were in a place with the doors locked (20:19). Therefore, it was obvious that Jesus had entered in a different way than normal. In his resurrected body, Jesus was free from earthly limitations.

He offered various tests to prove that he wasn't a ghost. He allowed them to touch his body, which was solid, it was human flesh, and let them examine his wounds. He also ate something, which a ghost couldn't do. Finally, the disciples were convinced.

Read Luke 24:44-49 and Mark 16:15-16. The events that Luke mentions occurred after the resurrection. We know from Acts 1:3 that Jesus remained on earth 40 days more. During that time, he appeared to his disciples and to other people on various occasions. As the passage indicates, Jesus instructed his disciples in the Old Testament teachings about the Messiah, helping them understand that he was the fulfillment of those prophecies. Most notable was Jesus' emphasis on the truth of the crucifixion and the resurrection. These historical facts are the heart of the apostles' preaching in the book of Acts.

Both Luke and Mark spoke of the message that Jesus wanted his disciples to preach, but they emphasized different ideas. Luke spoke about repentance and the forgiveness of sins through Jesus Christ. Mark emphasized the need to believe in Jesus. As the disciples knew, believing in Jesus wasn't easy; but it was and is absolutely essential for salvation.

Read Luke 24:50-53 and Mark 16:19-20. The last moments of the Master on this earth were spent in the vicinity of his greatest sufferings and triumphs. The triumphal entry, the blessing of the children, the resurrection of Lazarus, Gethsemane and his crucifixion, death and resurrection, all happened in Jerusalem and its vicinity.

While Jesus was preparing to leave the earth, he affirmed his promise of the Holy Spirit and blessed his disciples. Then, while they watched, Jesus ascended to heaven. For him and his disciples, that was the "end" of a world changing historical time. In the same way, this was the beginning of another historical time.

Jesus would continue to minister in and through people through the Holy Spirit. Authorized and sent by Jesus, the disciples would take to the whole known world the message of the crucifixion, resurrection and ascension of Jesus, who loves the world and provides complete salvation for all who believe in him and accept him as their Savior.

LESSON DEVELOPMENT

Smile as you welcome your students. Make sure the classroom is clean and tidy when they arrive. Maybe place a bouquet of flowers on the table. Before going into today's topic, review briefly the past two lessons and ask your students to tell you how faithful they have been to God this past week. You can also tell of your own experiences with the Lord.

Do you remember the last class?

Before class, prepare on two cards several sentences with the events that occurred in connection with the empty tomb, based on Luke 24:1-12. For example:

1. The disciples were filled with joy because Jesus had risen.
2. The disciples were sad because Jesus had died.
3. The disciples were sad because they had stolen the body of Jesus.
4. The women believed in the Good News, but the disciples did not.
5. No one believed that Jesus had risen.
6. How many women went to the tomb?
7. Was there a large stone covering the entrance of the tomb?
8. How many men were there in shining clothes?
9. Did the women go to the grave at 3 o'clock in the afternoon?
10. Who ran into the tomb to look?

Divide the class into two small groups and give five questions to each. Have a competition between the two groups to see who remembers better the story of the last class. The group that answers the most questions can receive a prize.

Important words

Write on cards the important words of this lesson. On one side write the word "ascension" and on the opposite side write down its meaning: the Lord Jesus was received up into heaven and sat at the right hand (right side) of God (Luke 16:19).

"Witness": a person who witnesses an event. The disciples witnessed the ascension of Jesus to heaven. They would continue to tell all the people what they saw and learned from the Master. That's why we can now worship the Lord, because others told us the beautiful story of the ascension.

Hide the cards in the classroom before the class starts. Ask the children to find them. When they have found them, they should read them (perhaps with your help) and say what each word means. Then they can choose another child to whom they will pass the card, and so on until everyone has read the words and their meaning.

BIBLE STORY

Where is Jesus?

Read Mark 16:15-16; 19-20 and Luke 24:36-53.

In a locked room in the city of Jerusalem, Jesus' disciples and their friends were sitting and talking. Everyone was scared, sad, confused and at the same time, excited. Two of Jesus' followers from Emmaus had just run into that room.

"Jesus lives!" they exclaimed excitedly. "He walked with us all the way to Emmaus, but we didn't know who he was. Then we invited him to eat dinner with us. We asked him to pray, and when he started to pray, we finally recognized him. Jesus lives!"

"That can't be true," the disciples argued. "Jesus died. We saw that he died. People don't come back to life after being dead for three days!"

"But it's true," the two men insisted.

While they were talking, Jesus appeared in the room. "Peace to you," he said.

"It's a spirit!" someone said. Everyone trembled with fear.

"Why are you troubled, and why do doubts come to your minds?" Jesus asked. "Look at my hands and my feet. I'm myself; touch me and see."

Now, the disciples had to believe the Good News. He wasn't a ghost. It was Jesus, and he really was alive!

During the next 40 days, Jesus appeared to the disciples on several occasions. He told them about all the things that had happened. He showed them the Old Testament scriptures that spoke of his crucifixion and resurrection, and he began to tell his friends about the important task he wanted them to do.

"You have seen everything that happened to me," said Jesus. "Now I want you to go all over the world and preach the Good News to all people. Tell people that if they leave their sins, they will be forgiven. He who believes in me will be saved. But those who refuse to believe in me, will not be."

"Must we begin to believe now?" the apostles asked themselves.

Jesus answered their questions quickly. "I will send you the Holy Spirit, as I promised you. But for now stay in Jerusalem until you have received power from God."

Those 40 days went by quickly. How the disciples wished to be with Jesus one more time! Then one day, he led them all to a special place on the Mount of Olives. And raising his hands, he asked for the blessing of the Father.

While he was talking, he began to ascend (go up) into heaven. And in a few moments, he disappeared. The disciples never saw him again on this earth.

Were they sad? Maybe a little, in the same way that happens to us when someone we love leaves. But the disciples were also full of joy. Jesus lives! Soon he would send the Holy Spirit to be with them all the time. And what was more important: the disciples had a job to do. They were to tell everyone that Jesus was alive and that He would forgive all their sins if they asked Him.

ACTIVITIES

"Jesus lives!"

Have the children cut out and assemble the figures from lesson 15 of the activity sheet from the student book. When they have finished assembling, tell them: Tell each other and me the story of the ascension. Try to do it at home and with your friends at school. Remember to thank God because Jesus went to heaven and is sitting next to his Father."

I want to tell others about Jesus!

Teach the children to practice natural ways to be witnesses and tell family and friends about Jesus, the Savior.

In class, dramatize these possible scenarios.

What would you say? How would you tell them?

1. A friend asks you why you can't go to an amusement park with him or her on Sunday.
2. A friend notices that you have a Bible or New Testament that you like to read, and asks you why you read it.
3. Your grandmother or grandfather isn't a Christian. He or she sees your drawings and art with Bible verses and wants to know their meaning.
4. A friend from school tells you that he doesn't believe in God.
5. Someone gave you a CD of Christian music and your friends ask you what kind of music it is.

Memorization

Write the memory verse from back to front on the board.

Ask some volunteers to come up and write it again, but this time in the correct order.

To end

Invite the children to pray. Ask them: *Do you know of someone who doesn't know Jesus?*

Allow them to name familiar people, friends, or family members. Then, divide the children into pairs. Each child will pray for the family member or friend of the other who doesn't know Jesus. Encourage the children to tell others that Jesus was resurrected and now lives with the Father.

Finish with a prayer for the names expressed by the children and asking the Lord to make them courageous to be witnesses of Jesus, as were the disciples.

 Notes:

Year 3

Introduction – Unit V

The 10 Most Important Rules

Biblical References: Exodus 19:1–20:21; 24:12-18; 32:1–33:6; 34:1-14; 1 Samuel 17:12-20; 22:1-4; 1 Samuel 24; Matthew 5:21-22,43-45; 2 Kings 5:13-27; 1 Kings 21:1-29.

Unit Memory Verse: *Obey the Lord your God and follow his commands and decrees that I give you today* (Deuteronomy 27:10).

Unit Objectives

This unit will help the elementary students to:

- ✘ Know the rules that God left us so that we can live wisely.
- ✘ Take care of their thoughts.
- ✘ Respect and love their parents.
- ✘ Know that lying brings bad consequences.
- ✘ Understand that God must always be in first place in our lives.

Unit Lessons

Lesson 16: Rules for living wisely

Lesson 17: God must be in first place.

Lesson 18: Honoring our parents

Lesson 19: Take care of your thoughts

Lesson 20: Stealing and lying bring bad consequences

Lesson 21: Greed is dangerous

Why Elementary Students need the teaching of this unit:

Elementary students must grasp, even from an early age, that the Bible is a book to live by. It's not just a story that speaks of a God who lived thousands of years ago and only left a large and difficult book to understand.

Also, it's important to help them notice that the commandments and the rules that God left for people aren't prohibitions by someone who wants to limit their freedom and even their joy. These rules are to help us avoid suffering and for our lives to pass in peace and harmony.

It will be good to show them, with the participation of the students themselves, the price that those who violate God's boundaries must pay.

Rules for living wisely

Biblical References: Exodus 19:1-20:21

Lesson Objective: To teach the children the importance of obeying the Ten Commandments that God gave to Moses so that His people would learn to live wisely.

Memory Verse: *Obey the Lord your God and follow his commands and decrees that I give you today* (Deuteronomy 27:10).

PREPARE YOURSELF TO TEACH!

Children need to know the importance of the Ten Commandments. They must understand why God gave them to the Israelites, but the main thing is to realize the vital importance that these commandments have for their lives.

The children in your class are growing up in a world very different from the world in which you grew up. For example, they hear that each person chooses what seems right for their life. They are told that it's essential to have tolerance - which means approval and acceptance - of all religions and creeds.

The Ten Commandments convey to children a different message, because they are told that God set rules to live righteously, that He expects to have the first place in their lives, and that they should treat others with respect, as He does himself.

When the children begin the study of these six lessons, which refer to the ten main rules that God established, they begin to understand that respect for God and for our fellow human beings doesn't come from a personal decision, but is born from a love relationship with the Creator. God doesn't want them to comply with His rules out of fear or as an end in themselves. On the contrary, children, like all of us, should obey the Ten Commandments because they love the Lord and want to live the way He teaches them to live.

BIBLICAL COMMENTARY

When I was a child, I thought that my parents had established certain rules so that I wouldn't do certain things, so I obeyed them; I didn't want them to get mad at me. As I grew older, I came to understand that my parents didn't impose such rules in order to control me, but to guide me and protect me. I understood that those rules reflected his love for me. Over tim, I realized that they shaped the person I am and the relationship I have with them. Now as an adult, my mother is one of my best friends, and I know I can trust my father.

When God gave the Ten Commandments at Mount Sinai, He was showing the love of a father who wants to lead his children. The Israelites had lived in slavery for hundreds of years. Therefore they had made almost no decisions on their own, but they had obeyed the laws and customs of their masters, the Egyptians. They weren't yet ready to be the people with whom God would make his covenant, and therefore they needed to learn what it meant to live in relation to a holy God and be set apart for him.

The Ten Commandments were the product of love, part of a promise that God had made to his people. What promise was that? That he would be their God and they would be his obedient people. As long as the Israelites lived in a right relationship with him, obeying his rules, he would give them His love, guidance and protection, and make them into a great nation.

As Christians, we also are a people set apart and called to live a holy life, completely dedicated to God. The Ten Commandments served as a guide for the Israelites as they traveled through the desert, and then as they became a nation that had its own land. Those same commandments are what guide us Christians to live righteously in today's world. The first four tell us how to live in a correct relationship with God. The last six tell us the way to relate to those around us. In a world in which it's generally considered that abiding by the rules depends on the personal decision of each person, we have the security and freedom that gives us in knowing what God expects from us.

LESSON DEVELOPMENT

Prepare in advance the teaching materials you will use for this lesson and try to have your classroom ready before your students arrive.

Remember to welcome visitors and collect their info to contact them during the week.

Choose one of the following activities to catch the attention of your students in the subject of study.

In advance, prepare a large-sized poster or mural with the Ten Commandments. You will use it throughout Unit V. You can write each commandment in a different color to make it more striking.

Ten crazy rules

Say: *Let's see if you can guess a number that I have in mind and what it has to do with today's lesson.*

Give them the following clues, one by one, allowing the children to give their answers.

1. It's a number that's in the Bible, in the Old Testament.
2. It's a number between 1 and 12.
3. It contains the number "1".
4. It's before "12" and after "8".

When the children have guessed the number 10, congratulate them and then tell them: *In today's lesson,*

58

this number has to do with rules. So now let's have fun inventing some crazy rules. We'll call them: "The ten craziest rules in the world."

You could suggest some examples, such as: "Never eat chocolate" or any other funny rule, as well as some serious ones. As children invent the guidelines, you will place them on the bulletin board or whiteboard. Students can also illustrate them.

After finishing this step, ask them: *Now that we have had a little fun, what do you think the number 10 will have to do with our Bible lesson today?*

This is the time to show the poster with the Ten Commandments, and read what each one says. Then ask: *Do you think that our crazy rules will work for something? Surely not, but a long time ago, God gave his people 10 very good rules, called the Ten Commandments. Over the next six weeks, we will study why these Ten Commandments that God gave us are so important.*

What are the rules for?

Ask the children to join you in sitting or standing in a circle, and pass a small smooth stone from one person to another. When you say, "The Ten Commandments", the child who has the stone in their hand will stop passing it, and you will say: *Tell us about a rule at your house.* Let the child explain a rule they have in their home. Then, ask: *Why do you think your dad (or mom, or your parents, as the case may be) made that rule?* Let the little one respond. Then continue with the game, allowing each child to take a turn of holding the stone and talking about a rule established in their own home.

After the last child has shared, you will stop passing the stone when it reaches your hands and say: *Your parents have established rules for you to obey. With them, you will live more securely and learn about life. God has 10 special rules that He expects us to obey, because they help us know how He wants His people to live. Today's bible story is about these 10 important rules. Who knows what they are called?* (The Ten Commandments).

BIBLE STORY

The Israelites saw the mountain in front of them, it was huge! They had traveled three full months to get to it.

"Camp here," said Moses. "We're staying for a while."

God had led the Israelites to that mountain. He loved them and had helped them escape from Egypt, where they had been slaves. He divided the Red Sea to help them escape from Pharaoh's army. He gave them food and water while they crossed the desert. Now, he was preparing to show his love to His people in a new way.

While the people camped at the foot of the mountain, Moses spoke with God on the mountain. God told him, "Remind my people about how I brought them out of Egypt, and then tell them, 'if you obey me in everything, you will be my special people. I will show you how to live. All the other peoples will see that you follow me and love

me. You will be my special treasure.'"

Moses returned to the camp and told them what God had told him.

The people responded, "We will do everything Jehovah has told us."

Moses went back to the mountain and said to God, "The people have promised to obey."

God said, "Tell them to prepare themselves. Today and tomorrow, they are to bathe and wash their clothes. On the third day, I will come and talk to you. The people will hear me, and then they will know that they can trust you as their leader because I chose you. But make sure they stay away from the mountain because it's holy. They can't touch it."

Moses and the people obeyed God and prepared themselves. On the third day, there was thunder and lightning on the mountain. There was a thick cloud, smoke, fire and loud noises. God was there, and the people were afraid!

Everyone in the camp shuddered. Moses took the people out of the camp to meet with God and they stopped at the bottom of the mountain. Moses climbed the mountain to meet with God.

While the people waited, God spoke to Moses. He gave Moses 10 very important rules for them to fulfill. We call these rules The Ten Commandments, through which God would show his people how they should live.

The first four commandments showed the people how to honor and respect God.

"You must not have others gods in front of me." God's people couldn't love or worship anyone but him, the only true God. They were to put God first.

"You must not make and worship any image." God told his people never to make pictures or sculptures (idols) to worship.

"You must not misuse the name of the Lord your God." God's people were to use his name only in a way that showed love and respect for him.

"Remember the Sabbath day and keep it holy." This is the special day of the Lord, and the people had to put God first, using that day to worship and rest.

The following six commandments taught them how to treat other people.

"Honor your father and your mother." God wanted his people to respect and obey their parents.

"You must not kill other people."

"You must not commit adultery." God's people must keep their marriage promises. Therefore, a woman who was married shouldn't have a romantic relationship with another man. In the same way, no married man should have a romantic relationship with another woman who wasn't his wife. The spouses had to be faithful to each other.

"You must not steal."

"You must not tell lies about others."

"You must not covet." God didn't want his people to want the things that belonged to other people.

But the people were still afraid! God seemed to be so strong and powerful!

Moses told the people, "Don't be afraid." He knew that God gave the people these rules because he loved them and wanted them in turn to love him back. The Ten Commandments would help the Israelites live as God's special people. These are 10 good ways to love and obey the Creator.

ACTIVITIES

Choose one of the following activities to catch the attention of your class in the subject of study.

Ten Commandments Mobile

Before class, prepare your own mobile from the activity sheet from the student book so that you can guide the children to build theirs. This is a craft that takes several pieces. In the class, distribute the activity sheets to the children and explain how they are to assemble their mobiles. While they work under your direction, you can review why God gave the Israelites the Ten Commandments. Ask the children, *Why do you think it's important to obey the rules that God gave in his commandments?*

Suggest that the children take their mobiles home and use them to remind themselves that in order to live properly, they must obey God's commandments. Encourage them to learn the Ten Commandments from memory.

Stone tablets

Have enough dough for each student (see the recipe at the beginning of the book). Give each child a handful of dough, a sheet of waxed paper and a toothpick. Explain that God wrote the Ten Commandments on two pieces of stone called "tablets." Have the children make two tablets with the dough and write the number 10 on each one using the toothpicks. You can show them a picture to show what the tablets were like. Use a permanent marker to write each child's name on the waxed paper. Put the tablets on the waxed paper with the name of each child, and place them in a safe place to dry. Tell the children that next week when their tablets are dry, they can take them home. In the remainder of the time, ask them questions about the Ten Commandments, such as:

- *What did God expect the Israelites to do when He gave them the Ten Commandments?* (Learn them and obey them.)

- *Why is it so important that we obey God's commandments?* (Because they help us live as God wants, and shows our love for him.)

- *How can we keep the commandments this week?*

Important words

In this lesson you can introduce the important words related to Unit V, which will support the activities you want to do with the children during the 6 lessons. Before this activity, write on the board the important words with their meaning. Explain to the children what these words mean and give them examples. They are: obey, honor and respect.

Prepare squares of 8 cm x 8 cm posterboard before the class. Write on one side one of the words "Obey", "Honor" and "Respect", and on the other side, the corresponding meaning. Place these cards in an envelope or inside a bag. Ask the children to sit in a circle. Then they are to pass the bag from one to the other around the circle. You must be facing away from them, clapping your hands. When you stop clapping, they are to stop passing the bag, and you immediately turn and look to see which child has the bag. That child must take out a card, read the word and explain what it means. If the child doesn't know the meaning, one of the other children can help them, or you can help with suggestions, giving a commandment that has to do with that word. The game is repeated so that, if possible, most children will participate and learn the important words with their meaning.

Memorization

Write the memory verse on the board: *"Obey the Lord your God and follow his commands and decrees that I give you today"* (Deuteronomy 27:10). Then, practice it several times with your students so they can learn it by heart. When the study time is over, erase the verse and write it with the words in the incorrect order. Then, ask some volunteers who already know the verse to go to the board and write the words in the correct order.

Encourage the children to study the Ten Commandments. You can study and memorize two for each class during this unit. You can write them on paper or cards. Write two commandments on each card, for each child. You can give them every day of class. In that way, they will learn and have the Ten Commandments by the end of the unit.

To end

Have the class sing a song that speaks of obedience to God's law.

Then ask them: *What does it mean to obey God?* (Do what he wants us to do.) *How can you obey God this week at home, in your neighborhood or at school?*

If you wish, you can invite them to sing the song again, and then say something like this: *We don't have to try to obey God's commandments by our own strength. We can pray asking God to help us obey them and He will.*

Pray that God will help the children to choose to obey Him during the next week.

Finally, make sure that the children take home the creations they made.

God must be in first place

Biblical References: Exodus 20:1-6; 24:12-18; 32:1–33:6; 34:1-14

Lesson Objective: To help the children identify if there are some things that matter more to them than God, and find ways to put Him first.

Memory Verse: *Obey the Lord your God and follow his commands and decrees that I give you today* (Deuteronomy 27:10).

PREPARE YOURSELF TO TEACH!

Nowadays, elementary-aged children have more and more activities and interpersonal relationships outside the home and family than in the past. In addition, they find it easier to distinguish what is right from what is wrong, as well as to differentiate reality from fantasy. As they develop these capacities further, the temptation to give more importance to other things or people than to God becomes stronger. While they are young, your students need to know this important truth: God must have the first place in their lives and, although at this age they can't fully understand it, they can listen to it and begin, little by little, to assimilate its meaning.

This lesson could pose some difficult questions for children. For example: "Do I have to love God more than Mom or Dad?" Or "Is it wrong that I want to have a video game?"

Perhaps the best way to respond to a child of this age is with clear and sure statements, such as: "When we love God more than anything else, we have more love for people," or "It's okay to want to have a video game, as long as you can be happy even if you don't have it."

In this lesson you will be able to give your students examples of what it means to put God first. The best illustration you can use is your own life. By seeing how you love and serve God, they will learn what it means to love God above all.

BIBLICAL COMMENTARY

We try to solve the problem of organization by reading books on time management or by attending workshops where we are taught to set priorities in life. We spend significant amounts of money just to find the right tool to help us organize our busy life. We are careful to enter dates and events in our agenda, in visible places, or in piles of notes stuck with magnets on the refrigerator door.

However, let's forget for a moment all those notes and tricks that we use to organize ourselves, and let's see what Exodus 20 tells us. Many years ago, God created a plan to help us manage our priorities. This plan is constituted by the Ten Commandments.

The first two commandments teach us that to correctly establish priorities, we must begin by giving God the first place in our life. Although it may sound simplistic, this is a truth capable of completely transforming our life. God separated us for himself, we are a chosen people; we are his and he is our God. This fundamental principle requires a life entirely committed to the Lord and what he wants for us. If we can understand that, it will be easier for us to put the other things in their place.

The second principle that we can apply to keep God first is to prevent anything else from having the importance of God. That means anything that can have the priority that belongs only to Him. That could be a job, a high-level position, a big house, a sports car, or maybe a certain prestige or economic position that we have or want to reach. There are many aspects of life that we can allow to rival God … to take his place of importance. This easily happens when we divide our life into areas and assign one to God at the same level as those we assign to other interests. We have received a commandment: put God first and give ourselves completely to him.

The second commandment has to do with our "image" of God. In biblical times, idols were made in which the concept of the attributes of God were expressed. For example, the figure of a bull represented His strength or ability to procreate. But no matter how hard we try, human beings can't adequately represent God by means of a visual or mental image. Just as it's wrong to worship something other than God, it's also wrong to create a visible figure to represent Him. We must trust in the revelation that God gives us through the Scriptures, his action in history, the person of Jesus Christ and the Holy Spirit.

"God first!" It's easy to say, but hard to live. However, when we voluntarily give him first place, the other priorities will fall in the right place.

LESSON DEVELOPMENT

Prepare in advance the teaching materials you will use for this lesson and have your classroom ready before your students arrive.

Remember to welcome visitors and collect their info to contact them during the week.

Who wants to be the first?

Before class, write the following on construction or other paper, and post the signs in three corners of the room. They should say:

✗ I would love to be first.

✗ It would be the same for me to be or not to be first.

✗ I wouldn't want to be first.

In class, say: *Today we will talk about what someone can feel when they are first to do something. I will read some sentences. After each sentence, each person will go to the corner where the sign describes how they feel about what I read.*

Read the three posters with the children. Then read some sentences, such as the following:

What would you think if you were the first one to ...? (Each time the children choose something, ask them why they chose to go to that particular corner with which they identified themselves.)

✗ *Choose a treat from a tray.*

✗ *Read the Bible out loud.*

✗ *Choose the TV show that will be seen at home.*

✗ *Bathe before going to bed.*

✗ *Go to bed at night.*

✗ *Open a Christmas gift.*

The importance of this activity is that the children understand what it means to be first.

BIBLE STORY

God or a golden calf?

"We will do all the things Jehovah has said. We will obey him."

This was the promise that the people made to God after He spoke to them through Moses.

God told Moses, "Go to the mountain and meet me there. I will give you the stone tablets with my laws written on them." God was giving them the Ten Commandments because he loved them, and he knew that if they obeyed his laws, they would be good and they would have joy, and they would honor him with their behavior.

Moses spoke to the leaders of the people, "In my absence, my brother Aaron and his assistant will be in charge of everything. If you have a problem, take it to them."

Moses climbed to the top of the mountain to meet God, and remained there forty days and forty nights. The Creator gave him the stone tablets, on which were written the Ten Commandments. And he also gave him other important instructions.

In the camp, at first everything seemed fine. But after a while, people started to worry. When they looked towards the mountain, all they saw was smoke and fire.

Finally, the people approached Aaron and said, "Please, make us gods that will be with us and guide us. Moses took us out of Egypt, but now we don't know what happened to him."

Aaron got tired of so much whining and so many complaints. His task was to teach the people to worship the only true God, and only him. But now he didn't have the courage to obey.

"Bring me your golden earrings," he said to the Israelites. Then, he melted the gold and gave it the shape of a beautiful calf. Then he said, "Israel, here is your god who took you out of Egypt."

The Israelites liked the gleaming golden calf. Looking at it, they felt as if God himself was there with them, and not far away on the top of a mountain.

Aaron also built an altar for the golden calf. And then he told them, "Tomorrow we will have a great celebration and we will worship God."

The next day, the town burned offerings in honor of the golden calf. They worshiped it as if it was God, and they began to celebrate. They ate, they drank, they danced and they sang. They forgot to obey the Lord and began to disobey.

God knew what they were doing. And by the way, He was very angry! He loved them very much, but they were ruining all the good plans he had for them.

Then God spoke to Moses and said, "These people are stubborn and disobey me. I'm going to destroy them completely."

"No, my God, please don't do that!" Moses begged. "You took these people out of Egypt, and if you destroy them now, the Egyptians will say that you are a wicked god. Please forgive the people."

God answered him, "Okay, I will not completely destroy them."

Moses hurried down from the mountain. He could already hear the hustle and bustle in the camp. He approached and then he saw the golden calf that the people worshiped.

Bam! Moses threw down the stone tablets. Crash! The tables broke into a thousand pieces Then he took the golden calf and threw it in the fire.

Then he asked Aaron, "What did these people do to you that you brought such great sin upon them?"

Aaron tried to explain, but his excuses were very silly, so he blamed the people. Then Moses moved away from Aaron.

"Whoever is on Jehovah's side, join me over here now!" Moses cried. And some of the people came to stand close to him.

The next day, Moses said to the people, "You have committed a great sin, but I will now go up the mountain to where Jehovah is. Maybe I'll be able to convince Him to forgive your evil."

People regretted what they had done; they all cried and took off their nice clothes and jewelry to show how badly they felt.

God forgave the people, although he also had to punish them for their sin. Then he told Moses to return to the mountain, and God himself wrote the Ten Commandments in two other tablets. And then he did something wonderful: he came close enough to Moses so that he could see God, even just a little bit.

"I'm Jehovah," he said to Moses. "I'm a merciful and holy God, slow to anger and great in mercy and truth ... who forgives sin."

Then, God made him a promise: "I will do wonders that haven't been done in all the earth, nor in any nation. But you and the people must obey me. You must not bow to any other god. Only before me!"

ACTIVITIES

"God First" (with music)

Bring something to listen to music. Prepare a few pieces of construction paper or posterboard with a number written on the top, starting with 1. Make one for each child. Ask each child to think of a keyword that refers to any situation in which a person can put God before their own interests, for example: school, home, place of entertainment, neighbors, church, etc. and write it in the empty space on their poster.

Take a few minutes and ask the students to give some of the examples that they thought of (no more than two or three) of decisions they can make in such situations to put God first. Then, have them go to different places in the room with their poster in their hand.

Tell them: *I'm going to play music. When you hear the music, walk around the room, and when the music stops, stop where you are and hold your poster above your head. I will turn around and say a number. Whoever has that number on his sign will explain to everyone a way to put God first in the situation that his sign says.*

Repeat the game several times so that everyone has the opportunity to answer.

Put God first!

Guide the students in the activity sheet craft of the student book (lesson 17). Ask the children to cut out, color, and cover the door pendant, the Bible bookmark, and the mini poster with plastic paper. While working on the craft, take the time to review the Bible story with questions like:

1. Who were the characters in the story?
2. How did the people of Israel disobey God?
3. What did God ask the people to do?
4. Why does God want to be in the first place in our lives?

Add more questions that you can prepare yourself.

Memorization

Puzzle verses

Prepare two sets of cards with one word on each card: one set with the memory verse and one set with commandments 1 and 2. Have the children form two teams and distribute a set of cards to each group. Helping each other, they will assemble the bible verse or commandments by placing each card in its corresponding place. The group that finishes first wins.

Then they can turn the cards upside down on the table, and repeat the memory verse as a group, and the commandments as a group. Then, the groups can exchange cards so that all the children learn the verse and the two commandments.

Tell them to practice Commandments 3 and 4 for the next class. They will continue with the same activity of memorizing and assembling the puzzle texts next week.

To end

Tell the children to take their crafts home to help them remember all week that they should put God first in every part of their lives. You can add something like: *When we give God first place, we are honoring him, and we receive his blessing for both us and those around us. Remember to read the Bible this week. You can place your new bookmark on the reading page of today, and re-read the story of the golden calf at home.*

Pray with the children, asking God to help them obey Him during the week, giving Him first place in all their activities and in every place.

Honoring our Parents

Biblical References: Exodus 20:12; 1 Samuel 17:12-20, 22:1-4

Lesson Objective: To help the children, inspired by David's example of obedience to his parents, to be willing to honor their parents, treating them as God commanded.

Memory Verse: *Obey the Lord your God and follow his commands and decrees that I give you today* (Deuteronomy 27:10).

PREPARE YOURSELF TO TEACH!

Their relationship with their parents is the first opportunity a child has to learn to obey authority, and this relationship helps them formulate their own understanding of God and how to relate to Him.

Elementary-aged children move around in different areas outside their home and family: school, sports, church and social activities, etc. In all those situations, they come into contact with people who, for better or for worse, influence their attitudes and behaviors. It's common for children to hear comments from their peers that ridicule their fathers and mothers alike. That's why this lesson is of vital importance. It will help children understand that God expects them to respect and honor their parents. Also, this is the way He wants us to treat him as our Heavenly Father.

This lesson will help the children discover the aspects that the word "honor" involves (their parents, in this case), such as: valuing, respecting, listening, being interested in, and obeying.

You as a teacher can show the children the meaning of honor and respect by setting an example from your own life. Tell them about the training you received from your parents, and explain how you honor them. Thus your students will learn not only from your words but also through your model.

Sadly, there are children whose parents don't seem to deserve to be honored. Be alert, therefore, to the possibility that some of your students have been victims of abuse by their parents, or that somehow they feel bad towards their parents. Pray for those children, and if you suspect they are suffering abuse, talk to your pastor.

BIBLICAL COMMENTARY

Read Exodus 20:12. Everyone deals with their relationship with their neighbor. It should be noted that the first of these six commandments, "honor your father and your mother," refers to the first relationship we have in life: the relationship with our parents.

The Hebrew word for "honor" is kabed, and it means "to be heavy," "to add weight," and this entails the idea of treating our parents with due seriousness. In this command, God took into account the needs of the children of growing Israelite community, and also those of the parents.

Children need instruction and teaching, but they don't always perceive the wisdom that comes from the directives and acts of their parents. By telling them to honor their parents, God was telling them how to behave, regardless of their feelings. If they honored them, they would become a responsible "new generation" capable of living wisely and ruling their land.

In addition, the Israelites were forming a community based on their faith in a unique God. In order for this nation to have stability and continuity, parents would need to convey the stories that described the nature of God, his deeds, as well as the traditions that came from living as God's people. For this to happen, it was necessary for the children to listen to and obey their parents.

Finally, this commandment protected parents from the conflicts that could arise with their stubborn and disobedient children, and also kept them from being mistreated or abandoned when they reached an advanced age and could no longer work and care for themselves.

Read 1 Samuel 17: 12-20. This passage presents one of the most well-known and beloved stories of the Bible: that of David and Goliath. But it also gives us the opportunity to get to know a characteristic of David that we often overlook: the way he honored his parents.

In those days, soldiers had two main sources of income: the things they got when they defeated their enemies, and the support of their own families. Since the Israelite and Philistine armies had been inactive for 40 days, they hadn't gotten anything from defeating an enemy. Concerned about his sons, Jesse sent David to take supplies to them and quickly return with news, as he had done on other occasions.

Notice that David complied with his father's request quickly, since he went out "in the morning" (v. 20). He also showed responsibility for the property of his father, when he left "the sheep in the care of a guard" (v 20). And finally, he fulfilled his father's wish, as "Jesse had commanded him" (v. 20).

Read 1 Samuel 22:1-4. At this time, David was fleeing from Saul and was exiled in enemy territory. However, the honor that he showed as a young man in his relationship with his parents accompanied him into his adult life when he continued to show respect, attention and affection for them.

David's hiding place in the caves near Adulam may have been near Bethlehem. Maybe his family joined him to give him support or for fear of the danger that Saul represented. But apparently, David didn't believe that those caves were a safe hiding place for his parents, and since they were older, they weren't able to be part of a group of warriors on the move, so David went in search of a safe haven for them in Moab, outside Saul's territory.

Respect for our parents is fundamental. By respecting them, we honor God who created them, and we show to an unbelieving world how the people of God live. Learning to trust, respect and obey our parents is of paramount importance in our relationship with God.

LESSON DEVELOPMENT

Prepare in advance the teaching materials you will use for this lesson and try to have your classroom ready before your students arrive.

Remember to welcome visitors and collect their info to contact them during the week.

Choose one of the following activities to catch the attention of your students on the subject of study.

The Commandments race

Before class, make 2 sets of 10 cards of construction paper or posterboard, and write on each of them one of the 10 Commandments. Then, mix up each set of cards and place them face down.

During the class, divide the students into two groups. Then at the same time, each team will try to put their set of the Ten Commandments into the correct order. The first group that does it correctly will read them to the rest of the class.

Honor your parents

Before class, tape a large piece of posterboard to the wall with a piece of tape or hang it on the wall. Write the following italicized parts of the following sentences in large letters, leaving spaces where the bold words should go. On separate cards, write the words that are highlighted in black (use large letters that are shaped so that the children can color or fill them with seeds or paint, if desired). Cut out the words so that the little ones can work on them.

When you start the game, the children will have the opportunity to paste the appropriate word that goes with that phrase. For example: **Listen** ... *to what your parents tell you.*

- ✘ **Listen** ... to *what your parents tell you.*
- ✘ **Learn** ... *from your parents.*
- ✘ **Help** ... *your parents with joy.*
- ✘ **Be nice** ... *to your parents.*
- ✘ **Pray** ... *for your parents.*

- ✘ **Tell** ... *your parents that you love them.*
- ✘ **Hug** ... *your parents every day.*
- ✘ **Talk** ... *with your parents every day.*
- ✘ **Smile** ... *at your parents every morning.*
- ✘ **Wash** ... *the dishes a few times a week.*
- ✘ **Help** ... *take out the trash.*

In class, direct the students' attention to the fifth commandment, explaining that today's lesson refers to the commandment "honor your father and mother."

Then ask them: *What do you think it means to "honor" our parents?*

Show them the poster on the wall, indicating that the sentences teach us some ways to honor our parents, but they all lack the first word. When they finish coloring or decorating their words, the children can then, with your help, find the sentence that is completed by the word they have in their hands. To finish, read the complete sentences.

BIBLE STORY

"I wonder how my sons are doing in the army," said Jesse, David's father. *"Are they safe? Do they have something to eat? I wonder what is happening in the war."*

Jesse's three oldest sons, David's brothers, were soldiers in King Saul's army, and they were fighting the Philistine army. The Philistines were strong and bad enemies, and things weren't going well for Saul's army. The enemy had a soldier that was a giant named Goliath, whom no one dared to challenge; so for 40 days, the two armies remained stayed where they were and didn't fight.

Remember that in those days there was no radio, T.V., or internet for people to find out what was happening in the war. The only way to know if the soldiers were okay was to go to where the army was and see them. In addition, the army leaders didn't always have enough food to give to the soldiers, so their families had to bring them food.

David, who was Jesse's youngest son, was a shepherd for his father's flock of sheep near Bethlehem. Jesse sent for him to come to him.

When David arrived, his father told him, "Go and take your brothers this roasted grain and these ten loaves of bread. Take them to the camp right away. Also, take these ten cheeses to the commander of their unit. See if your brothers are well and bring back word from them."

"Yes, father," David answered. "I'll go early in the morning."

The next day, David obeyed everything his father had told him to do. He looked for someone to take his place to watch the flock while he was gone. Then he took the food and went to Saul's army camp.

When David found his brothers, he gave them the

food and asked them how things were going.

Well, we all know what happened after that ... there was a very exciting battle in which David killed Goliath, the giant Philistine. Afterwards, he returned home with Good News for his father.

Many years passed by and David grew up. During all that time, he obeyed God and his parents. God was pleased with him, but King Saul was jealous of him. King Saul wanted to kill David because he knew that one day David would take his place and be the king of Israel. That's why David had to escape to save his life!

Finally, David found a cave that was a very good place to hide. His father, his mother and his brothers knew where he was, and they went there to be with him.

David was glad to see his family, but he cared about his parents. "My father and mother are old," he thought. "I don't think it's a good idea for them to hide with me in this dangerous place. King Saul could find them and hurt them. But they can't go with me when I have to leave the cave to fight the enemy ... What will I do to keep them safe?"

Then, God helped David devise a plan. David went to see the king of Moab, a country that Ruth, his great-great-grandmother, had come from a long time ago. The king of Moab didn't like Saul, so maybe he could help him.

David bowed to the king of Moab and said, "Please help me."

"What do you want me to do?" the king asked him.

"Please, let my mother and father stay in your land until God shows me what he will do with me. They will be more secure here than with me as I try to escape from King Saul."

"They can stay," the king agreed.

David then left his parents in Moab and returned to his hiding place. Someday, he would be king of Israel and he could bring them back home. But for now, as long as he had to run, hide and fight, he was glad that they were safe.

ACTIVITIES

You write the story

God commands us to honor our parents.

One or two weeks before the class, ask the children, or the children's parents, for pictures of their parents.

Then in class, say something like: *David honored and obeyed his parents. In what other ways can children honor their parents?* Let them express their ideas.

Direct the children's attention to the activity "You write the story" on the activity sheet from the Student book. Explain how to do it. When they finish their stories, ask for volunteers to read theirs out loud. Ask them also for their answers to the question at the end.

Ask the children to color and make their own picture frames to place the picture of their parents. If there are children who don't have pictures, they can draw them.

David's snack

Place some dry foods in the center of the table (mini bread or cookies, pieces of cake, pieces of fruit, etc.) along with napkins. Each child will take a piece of food and put it inside the napkin, so he will have prepared his "snack to go." Then take the children to a special place, a free space in the church or outside, and sit down together to enjoy the snack. Meanwhile you can review the story of David that you read before. Ask them to say how they believe a person (child or adult) can honor their parents. They can give examples of how they honor their parents now, or ways that they would like to put into practice.

Close the activity with a prayer of thanks for the snack they had, asking God to help them honor their parents.

Memorization

Necessary material: a sufficiently large cube of any material on which a word can be written on each side. You can make it from cardboard. Also, you will need glue, scissors, tape, markers.

Divide the memory verse in four pieces and choose a key word from each section:

1. *Obey the Lord your God* (key word: "obey").

2. *and follow* ("follow").

3. *His commands and decrees* ("commands").

4. *that I give you today* ("you").

5. blank

6. blank

Write the key words on four sides of the cube. These will serve as clues for the children to remember part of the verse. Don't write anything on the two remaining sides. Have the children form a circle around the table or on the floor. A volunteer will roll the cube in the manner of a dice. Depending on how it falls, the same child will read the keyword and with it form the phrase. When a blank side of the cube is rolled, you and the class can agree on some action: say the whole verse, or choose a phrase from memory, etc.

To end

Gather the children together to pray. Direct them in a prayer, and then tell them: *It's not always easy to honor and obey our parents, but God can always help us. If you find it hard to do so, tell God and ask Him for help. If you have decided to honor your parents more, ask the Lord to help you fulfill your promise. It's beautiful to honor our parents! God says we will be blessed.*

Take care of your thoughts

Biblical References: Exodus 20:13; 1 Samuel 24; Matthew 5:21-22, 43-45

Lesson Objective: That the children begin to understand that thoughts that come from feelings of hatred lead to acting in a very wrong way. That they understand how important it is to forgive those who have or are hurting them.

Memory Verse: *Obey the Lord your God and follow his commands and decrees that I give you today* (Deuteronomy 27:10).

PREPARE YOURSELF TO TEACH!

Could a child of 6 or 7 years kill someone? We can give thanks that there are few if any who have committed such a crime. However, no one ignores the violent acts that some children commit. Therefore, although the topic covered in this lesson isn't common for children of this age, it's still important.

At a time when the world says there isn't anything absolutely good or bad, children between 6 and 8 years of age need a clear direction as to what they should do with strong emotions such as anger or hatred. The constant violence to which elementary school children are exposed through the media can make their conscience insensitive. This lesson will help your students understand that God commands us to respect the lives of our fellow human beings, and that this mandate not only forbids us to kill a person, it also commands us to avoid feelings of hatred or revenge; and that we also actively seek the good of our enemies.

Although this isn't an easy thing to teach children, as our world becomes increasingly violent, this instruction becomes more important. The biblical story and the activities included in the lesson will give students practical suggestions for fulfilling the commandments of both the Old and the New Testaments. Pray for the children to choose the path of love that God tells us to take towards those who did something wrong to us.

BIBLICAL COMMENTARY

Read Exodus 20:13. "I would like to kill that man ... that woman ... that child!" Very often we hear a phrase like this that, although it's said in jest, comes from a feeling of frustration, but doesn't imply a real intention to do so. Perhaps we should reconsider this apparently "light" expression of hatred, taking into account that God doesn't take murder lightly. When he began to address interpersonal relationships in the Ten Commandments, the warning not to kill anyone came immediately after the command to obey one's parents.

In this passage, "to kill" means homicide, that is, the deliberate and vengeful destruction of a human life. God forbids killing because he is the creator of life and considers it precious.

Read Matthew 5:21-22 and 43-44. While it's good to refuse to commit an act of violence against other people, that isn't enough. Jesus shed new light on the sixth commandment because looking beyond the outer act, he could see the emotions that drive people to commit murder.

There is no passage in the Old Testament in which God tells us to "hate your enemy," but quite the opposite (Exodus 23:4-5 and Proverbs 25:21-22). Over the years, the "popular theology" among the Jews led to this misinterpretation of the law. On the contrary, Jesus said that anger against a fellow man is as sinful and destructive as homicide. The word that we translate as anger doesn't refer to a burst of anger that appears and disappears with the same ease, but it designates a devouring feeling that accumulates over time. Instead of harboring that feeling, the people of God must resist the hatred and violence that other people may cause, and replace it with a reaction that's born of love and is composed of three elements: prayer, acts of kindness, and gentle words (see Luke 6:28).

Read 1 Samuel 24. In this beautiful story, David not only fulfilled the mandate of the Old Testament, but also anticipated the teachings of Jesus. David was in grave danger. The caves in which he hid could become traps with no possibility of escape. By one of those strange turns of life, Saul himself fell into the trap, entering precisely in the cave where David was hiding. Despite the advice of his men, David didn't think of killing Saul. He even regretted having cut off the edge of his cloak, behavior that was considered an act of rebellion and disrespect towards a leader. Despite Saul's behavior, David respected his position as a king chosen by God. In addition, the young man trusted in Jehovah internally and knew that He had chosen him to be Saul's successor. But he didn't want to manipulate the circumstances to accelerate the development of the events God had planned. Instead, David "retaliated" against Saul in the manner described in Matthew and Luke.

✗ He used kind words: "my lord" and "my father" (v. 8 and 11)

✗ He acted benevolently by refusing to kill Saul at that time or any other future occasion, and promised mercy to Saul's family. In those days, the kings who assumed leadership were in the habit of ordering the death of all the family and relatives of the previous king, in order to eliminate potential rivals.

✗ Everything David said to Saul had the appearance of a prayer. And when Saul died, (2 Samuel

1) David expressed his sorrow for him with sincere lamentation.

By deciding to think and behave properly, David avoided becoming what Saul was - a tormented and vengeful man - to be instead, someone of whom God could say: "a man according to my own heart" (Acts 13:22). What a beautiful reflection of Jesus' words in Matthew 5:48! "Be perfect therefore, as your heavenly Father is perfect."

Forgiveness begins with a decision. When a person does something wrong to you, do you decide to forgive them? Do you decide to love them with God's love instead of hating them?

LESSON DEVELOPMENT

Welcome your students with affection and ensure that the classroom is clean and tidy when they arrive. Before entering today's topic, review briefly the past lessons of this unit and ask your students to give some examples of how faithful they have been to God during this last week.

What are you thinking about?

Have the children sit in a circle. While you walk around them, gently touch each one's shoulder. After a moment, stop and ask someone: *What are you thinking?* The child will answer the question and then take the teacher's place. He will walk around the outside of the circle, gently touching another children's shoulders and then stopping and asking the same question. Continue the game until each child has responded and walked.

After the game, tell them: *It was fun to know what everyone was thinking, wasn't it? But now I have a question to ask.*

Write the question on the board: *Is what we think as important as what we do? (Let them answer.)*

BIBLE STORY

David decides to love

King Saul put on his armor and prepared his sword. He had just arrived back after chasing the Philistines, but he wasn't going to rest. Now he couldn't! He had just received an important message. "David is in the desert," the message said.

And Saul thought: "This is my opportunity. I can finally kill him."

Saul was the first king of Israel. God had chosen him to be king, and at first he was a good king, but then he began to disobey God and do everything his own way. For that reason, God had to choose another king, one who would obey him.

God decided that the next king of Israel would be David, because he loved and obeyed God's commandments, and the people also loved David. That made King Saul very angry, and that's why he began to

have bad thoughts about the young man.

Again and again, Saul thought, "I hate David. He's trying to take my throne away."

That wasn't true, but the more he thought about David with hate, the more convinced he was that David was his enemy, until he thought, "I'm going to kill him."

Then he started looking for a way to kill David. Things got so bad that Jesse's son had to flee to hide in caves in the desert. He was joined by other men who trusted him, because they knew that he obeyed God. But his life was in grave danger.

Saul read the message again. Now he knew where David was, so he called his army of three thousand soldiers and went with them to look for him.

David was hiding in a cave, and he heard a noise. There was another person in the cave! He and his men looked ... There was King Saul!

Then, David's friends told him, "This is your chance to kill Saul. He is bad, he disobeys God, and he is also trying to kill you. He deserves to die! We believe that God brought him here so you can kill him."

(Read the next sentences slowly and with drama.) David quietly approached Saul like a ninja, and very carefully took the knife out of its case. In silence, he stretched out his arm towards the king ... and cut off one edge of the robe. Then, slowly and carefully, he snuck back to where his men were. Saul didn't hear or feel anything.

But David immediately felt bad. What he had done was a great lack of respect towards a king. Then he said, "I shouldn't have done that. Nor should I kill Saul. That would be very bad. God chose him to be the king of Israel. I will not hurt him.

After a few minutes, Saul left the cave. He was ready to keep looking for David. David waited until Saul was a bit far away, and then he also walked out of the cave.

"Saul!" David shouted.

The king looked back, surprised. He couldn't believe that David was so close!

David bowed down before him, and said, "Why do you listen to those who tell you that I want to hurt you?"

Then he showed him the piece of cloth, and shouted, "Look! I could have taken your life. My men begged me to do it, but I did not. I will never try to hurt you. You are the king chosen by God. Why are you still trying to kill me?"

Saul saw the cloth. It was from his robe. He couldn't believe it! Then he thought, "David could have taken my life, and I wanted to kill him."

King Saul was sad about his anger and his evil thoughts towards David, and his intention to kill him.

Finally he said, "You are a better man than me. Someday you will be king, and when you are, promise me you will not kill my family. Let them live."

"I promise," David replied.

Then, Saul went home, and David returned to his hiding place in the caves. He couldn't trust Saul, who could change his mind and try to kill him again. But he trusted that God would help him, and when God saw fit, he would allow him to be king. But until that day came, David would fulfill the commandment of God, and not kill Saul.

ACTIVITIES

Choose one of the following activities to catch the attention of the children on the subject of study.

Thinking and Doing Wheel

Help the children assemble the review wheel of the bible stories according to the instructions explained on the student activity sheet (lesson 19). Have the little ones turn the wheel towards Saul. Talk about what he did and compare it with what David thought and what he did next. Ask them: *What were the thoughts and actions that pleased God, those of Saul or those of David?* (Those of David.)

Have the children turn the wheel over, this time showing the side corresponding to Jesus and the children of today. Ask a volunteer to read what Jesus says, and ask them: *Why does Jesus tell us to love our enemies and pray for them?* (Because his advice helps us act with love and forgiveness.)

Have the children identify in each figure the correct actions. Then ask them:

- *Do you think it's easy to obey Jesus' teachings?*
- *What can we do if it's hard for us to love our enemies and pray for them?* (Ask God to help us obey.)

Conclude by saying: *If anyone is still angry and having bad thoughts, he may sin. Therefore, God wants us to have good thoughts and forgiveness, and he will help us. If we think in the right way, we will also do the right thing.*

Take distance

Form a circle with the students. Review the commandment of today's lesson, the way David fulfilled it and what Jesus said to do to our enemies. Explain: *Sometimes when we are in trouble, a friend or teacher will give us advice such as: "think twice", or "sleep on it." What they're really telling us is that before acting, we need to step back away from the problem and stop to think and pray about what we are going to do.*

When Saul was trying to kill David, David "stepped back"; He trusted God, and then he did the right thing. God wants us to do the same when someone treats us badly. Now I will read several situations to you, and I will choose one of you. Whoever I point to will step back and say, "I will obey God and do the right thing," and then tell us what he would do in that situation.

You can read these situations or others that you consider appropriate:

- *Your best friend made fun of you because you like to sleep with your stuffed animal.*
- *The classmate sitting next to you scratched your notebook.*
- *A braggart in the fifth grade stopped you at the school gate and took away all the coins you brought for snacks.*

At the end, explain: *Jesus says that we should love our enemies and pray for those who mistreat us, and that God wants his people to choose love instead of evil. This week, remember that God cares about what we think and what we do.*

Memorization

Divide the whole verse (Deuteronomy 27:10) into several phrases of a word or more, for example: "Obey the Lord", "your God", "and follow his commands". Prepare a set of cards of equal size and on each of them write some of the words that make up the verse. Place the cards face down on the table and ask a volunteer to mix them up well. In turn, each child will draw a card and, with the word or phrase that's written on it, should form a more complete short sentence, without saying the whole verse (Example: the card says: "Obey the Lord," and the child completes: "Obey the Lord your God and follow his commands"). Then, place the card face up on the table. As each child picks up a card and completes the sentence, it will be placed in its corresponding place until the complete verse on the table is assembled. The game will end when the verse is complete and can be read together. (Note: if the number of children exceeds the number of cards, 2 games or more can be played.)

To end

Ask the children to keep very quiet, and ask them: *Who can tell me how Jesus wants us to treat our enemies?* (With love, forgiveness and prayer.)

On the blackboard draw a face with an angry expression and a smiling face, and assign them the numbers 1 and 2 respectively. Then, tell the children that today's prayer will be done in two steps, explaining: First, look at the angry face and think of someone who did something unpleasant to you. Now pray silently for that person. When you finish, look at the smiley face and think about how happy you will be when you see that person again after forgiving and showing love to them. There will be no more anger, and your friendship will continue!

Finally, ask for a volunteer to pray for God to help them love and forgive those who have treated them badly.

Stealing and lying bring bad consequences

Biblical References: Exodus 20:15-16; 2 Kings 5:13-27

Lesson Objective: To help the students understand that stealing and lying are bad, that they're sins, but that God can forgive them if they repent.

Memory Verse: *Obey the Lord your God and follow his commands and decrees that I give you today* (Deuteronomy 27:10).

PREPARE YOURSELF TO TEACH!

This week's lesson explains God's commands to not steal and not lie.

This lesson will provide your students with a new way of thinking about theft. Stealing is much more than taking something that doesn't belong to you. Stealing hurts both the thief and the victim of the robbery.

In a great way, elementary-aged children want the acceptance and approval of those who have authority over them. They may lie to avoid problems or to displease their parents and teachers. They need to hear from the people who guide them that stealing and lying not only disappoints them, but disobedience to these rules causes separation from God. They need to know that Jesus doesn't accept excuses for any sin, even for sins that we can consider small or insignificant. This is a good opportunity to present the children with the truth that God will help us to obey his rules and give us his strength to not sin.

BIBLICAL COMMENTARY

It's amazing how the people around us try to break or break the rules. We all know those attitudes very well. They're reflected in behaviors such as parking in the assigned place for physically disabled people with the justification that they will only be there for a few minutes. Many times we justify our behavior but condemn that same behavior in others.

These attitudes aren't something new. In 2 Kings, chapter 5, history tells us that the prophet Elisha healed the military commander Naaman of his leprosy, a disease that terrified in biblical times, just as AIDS is for us today.

After Elisha refused to accept Naaman's payment, his servant Gehazi went after the military leader and told him that indeed Elisha would accept the gift anyway. To cover his dishonesty, Gehazi lied when confronted by Elisha about the incident. The result of the sin was that Gehazi and his whole family became lepers.

It's a blessing that our rebellions don't bring us the same sufferings that Gehazi had. If it did, we would see less deceptions, less theft and less lies in our world. We must remember that when we violate God's laws, we will suffer serious consequences as a result. Breaking the commandments of not stealing and not lying can end in legal action and even with prison, and can even bring shame and disgrace on those we love.

Our actions - good or bad - project great shadows.

Although we will not conspire to rob a bank or commit perjury in front of a jury, the temptation to break these commandments is very real in our society. Sometimes we feel tempted to tell a little lie so as not to get into trouble, or save extra money when they give us too much in change. When we don't want to spend a weekend with a relative or acquaintance, it would seem that saying a "white lie" is something of no importance.

But as followers of Jesus, we can never excuse our actions assuming there are small exceptions. God calls us to live on a higher level. The world can ignore the Ten Commandments and choose lifestyles that don't please God; but as Christians, we have been called to live differently. When he gave the Ten Commandments to his people, he was saying: "the rest of the world can live according to their own rules, but, you, my chosen people, must live in this way." When we say that we live in communion with God, our choices are grounded in his Word, including the Ten Commandments.

As you prepare to teach your children this week, keep in mind that you will make a positive or negative impact. If we fail in our goal of obeying God, the consequences will not be as severe as being punished with leprosy as happened to Gehazi. But Jesus made it clear in Luke 17:12 that he doesn't take it lightly if we cause others to sin. As he says in v. 3: "So watch yourselves!"

Keep in mind that others are looking at you and especially children need to see consistent obedience to the Word of God in those who guide and teach them.

LESSON DEVELOPMENT

Before going into today's topic, briefly review the last four lessons. Ask simple and direct questions about the characters studied and the most important events.

The puppet and the thief

Before class, get or make a puppet to use in this activity. You can make it yourself with a stocking or sock. Put the sock on your hand and draw or put on eyes (they can be buttons), make a smile (lips of fabric of another color glued on). You can make eyebrows and hair with yarn. Add a triangle-shaped nose. You can also do it with a medium-sized paper bag. Give it a name.

Say a dialogue like the following about Jaime having his money stolen:

Teacher: "Hello everyone. This is my friend Jaime. Jaime, can you tell us what happened to you this week?"

Jaime: "Something terrible happened to me! I can't believe it! Mom gave me money for my work at home. I set aside an amount for my offerings and put the rest in my wallet. I wanted to buy a special toy for which I have been saving for two months!"

Teacher: "That doesn't seem so terrible! But what happened?"

Jaime: "I took my wallet to school because when school was over, I was going to go and buy a toy. During recess, I left my wallet on my desk. When I came back after recess and opened it, some of my money was gone. Can you believe it? The money I had saved and saved ... had disappeared. I couldn't buy my toy anymore. I didn't have any money. I almost started crying there at school!"

Teacher: "That's terrible, Jaime! Someone stole the money from your wallet. And you worked for two months to save it. That really hurts."

Jaime: "That hurt a lot, and the worst thing is that I don't know if I can trust anyone anymore. I don't think I can believe in my classmates. What if it's one of my friends who took my money? It could be anyone!"

Teacher: "That's true. But there is one thing you can do. You can pray that God will help you forgive that person and that you can trust your friends once again. God will help you."

Jaime: "Can you pray with me?"

Teacher: "Yes, Jaime, of course!"

Say: *Stealing and lying hurt God and others. How did the theft hurt Jaime?* (He lost his money and also his trust in friends - he couldn't buy his toy, for which he had saved for so much time.)

Direct the children's attention to the Ten Commandments poster. Ask a child to read Commandment #7. Ask: *Do you think God's rule is good? Why or why not?*

Let's give our offerings

You will need a basket or plastic container to pick up the offering.

Have the group sit in a circle. Show the children the container with some coins in it. Ask: *Why do we give offerings at church?* (To help the church tell others about Jesus, to help others.) Now we will pass the plate or basket around and put in our offerings.

When the plate passes in front of you, be very obvious and take out coins instead of putting money in. Then ask the children to pass the plate a second time and take out more money again. You will hear some children begin to comment.

Say: *Why is it wrong if someone takes money out of the offering?* (That's stealing, the money belongs to God and the church). Place the money back in the plate.

Say: *In today's lesson we will talk about what God said in his Word about stealing and lying.*

BIBLE STORY

Naaman was an important man who worked for the king. He lived far from Israel, and had an Israelite servant who worked for him and knew the true God. Naaman got very sick with a horrible disease that affected his skin and caused sores all over his body. It was called leprosy. Naaman had treatments but none had helped him. It was getting worse!

One day, the servant spoke to Naaman's wife and said, "Elisha, the prophet of God, can help your husband. He is in Israel. He should go see him!"

Naaman went to Israel and visited Elisha. The prophet knew what the general should do to be healed by God.

Naaman did what the prophet told him and his leprosy disappeared. His skin was like new, all the sores were gone! He was so happy!

"Thank you, thank you," he said to Elisha. "Now I know that there is no God in the whole world like the God of Israel. Please accept these gifts in appreciation."

"No," Elisha answered. "God healed you, I didn't. I will not accept it!"

"Go in peace," Elisha said to Naaman.

Gehazi, Elisha's servant, had been listening. "I can't believe that Elisha didn't accept anything from this Syrian Naaman! He had beautiful clothes and gifts of silver. Elisha should have accepted something!" he thought.

The servant continued thinking. Finally he decided what he would do. "I will run after Naaman and ask him for a gift and keep it for myself."

Gehazi began to run. In the distance, Naaman saw him approaching and turned to find Elisha's servant.

Naaman asked, "Is everything all right?"

"Yes, everything is fine," said Gehazi. "But Elisha has a message for you. There are two young people who need your help and he wants you to give me the silver gifts and the robes."

"Very well!" said Naaman. "I will give you the gifts for Elisha."

Gehazi departed from Naaman with the gifts. He pretended nothing had happened.

"Where were you, Gehazi?" Elisha asked him.

"What do you mean?" he replied. "I didn't go anywhere."

Elisha shook his head sadly and said, "I know what you did, Gehazi! You lied and you stole. You also sinned against God. You broke his commandments."

Gehazi ducked his head, shamefaced. Elisha had discovered what he had done.

"Now you will be punished for your sin! Elisha said. "You and your children will have leprosy, in the same way that Naaman had before he was healed."

And so it happened. Gehazi had to learn very sadly what it means to break God's commandments.

ACTIVITIES

"What did you hear?" Review

Take a moment to review the story. All the children will sit in a circle. You will begin by asking a question to the first child to your left. They will answer the question, and then will ask the person to their left, "What did you hear?" (In relation to the biblical story). And each child continues the story around the circle.

You will say: "I heard that there was an important man, that he was a military man."

Then ask: "What did you hear about it, Elisa?"

Elisa will say: "His name was Naaman."

Then, Elisa will ask: "What did you hear, Mario?"

Mario will say: "Naaman had a servant."

And in that way, they will continue to tell the bible story. If any part is missing, you will ask: *Was something missing?* Let whoever knows what is missing include it in the story. Go back to the place where the story was and ask: *What did you hear?* And continue the story.

End with questions that may be general or repetitions of the story.

Memorization

What did Gehazi do?

You will need: markers, 2-leg paper hook, scissors, paper clip hook.

Help the children do the activity sheet from the student book, lesson 20. Ask them to color the figures and answer the questions. Give them time to complete the game.

Ask the children to glue their Roadway to the Ten Commandments on some thick cardboard or posterboard. If there is enough time, allow them to play the game. Tell them that they can play at home and tell their family why it's important to obey God's commandments.

Before finishing the class, ask them to say three times or more the two commandments, "You shall not steal. You shall not give false testimony against your neighbor." (Exodus 20:15-16).

To end

Pray for the children to be obedient to the Ten Commandments of the Lord.

You can sing at the pace you like the following chorus. Repeat it several times, faster and faster.

"I promise you, Lord,

I won't lie and I won't steal

I promise you, Lord,

I'll obey your commandments."

Say: We are all responsible for not lying and not stealing, whether we are children or adults. God has the power to forgive us and keep us from falling.

 Notes:

72

Greed is dangerous

Biblical References: Exodus 20:13-17; 1 Kings 21:1-29

Lesson Objective: To help children understand what greed is and to be happy with what they have.

Memory Verse: *Obey the Lord your God and follow his commands and decrees that I give you today* (Deuteronomy 27:10).

PREPARE YOURSELF TO TEACH!

Children have an attitude that's influenced by a consumer society that says "more, more, I want more." Advertisements bombard children with creative, fast, colorful and very attractive images. Everything to make them want the latest products on the market. Advertisers want children to want the new toy, electronic game, fashionable clothes or the latest computer. Most children, adolescents and young people, as well as many adults, are consumed by unbridled desire to have more, larger and better quality.

This lesson is God's response to the desire to have more, more and more. He commands us to be happy with what we have. He also warns us that coveting what we can't have can lead us to sinful actions.

During this lesson, help the children focus on God and everything he gives them. Tell them to look at him, to remember his commandments and thank him for all the good things he gives them. It's possible that this doesn't satisfy their desire to have the most beautiful and modern, but it will lead them to think or to have the idea that God has better things in mind for them than what the world can offer them.

BIBLICAL COMMENTARY

"You shall not covet" (verse 17). It was with this last commandment that the Israelites were terrified once more in the presence of almighty God. In fact, they pleaded with Moses, "Speak to us yourself and we will listen. But do not have God speak to us or we will die" (v. 19). The Israelites were afraid to be in the presence of their Creator.

Moses had become the mediator between God and the people. God spoke to Moses and then Moses gave the message to the people. This role of mediator was carried out by many leaders throughout the history of Israel. Moses, Joshua, the judges, the prophets, kings like Saul and David, were all important to God. The last and perfect mediator was Jesus Christ, his Son.

The covenant between God and his people was established with the giving of the law. The Ten Commandments are God's rules to live in a right relationship with him and with one's neighbor.

The promises were made and the terms of the contract established. He would be the only God of Israel; He would be their guide, protector and leader if they lived in obedience and loyalty to him.

The rules were there, but could people obey them? Unfortunately not. Through the history of Israel we see many examples of disobedience. There were times in which all turned their backs on God, and others in which a single individual sinned and led a whole nation to do so.

In each case, we see the evidence of God's justice and grace.

Read 1 Kings 21:1-19. The story of Ahab is an example of how greed leads to sin. Ahab was the King of the north, of a divided Israel. As King, he was responsible for being the mediator between God and his people. But Ahab didn't take this responsibility seriously. He used his monarch role to get what he wanted and not to do his best for the people.

One day, Ahab saw a beautiful vineyard and wanted it for him. Not only did he admire the vineyard, he was willing to do anything to get it.

Ahab allowed the owner, Naboth, to be killed, in order to obtain the vineyard. And thus he broke two commandments: the one of "not coveting" and the one of "not killing."

God sent his prophet, Elijah, with a message for Ahab. How many times when we refuse to listen to God does he send others to bring us back and make us understand what he wants from us? Ahab learned that even he, who was the King, must obey God. And now he would be held responsible for his sin.

In our society, we're told that there's no definite or absolute, that good or bad is only a matter of opinion. In our arrogance, we believe that God doesn't see our sins or at least overlooks them. But it's not like that. The God who gave the Ten Commandments as rules for life is the same creator and sovereign God of the universe. We can't break his rules and do what we want. We must decide to live in obedience to him. And we can do that if we reestablish our relationship with God, through Jesus Christ.

How did Ahab's story end in today's passage? Ahab humbled himself before God. In 1 Kings 21:29, we see again that the grace of God extends to those who humble themselves in obedience. God forgave Ahab and didn't punish him immediately.

LESSON DEVELOPMENT

Receive your students with affection and ensure that the classroom is clean and tidy when they arrive. Ask them if they obeyed the Lord this week and if they were able to keep the commandments learned up to today.

Important words

Before class, write the word "GREED" to add to the rest of the important words in the mural.

On 5 cards of posterboard of 15 cm. x 15 cm write the word "greed", each letter separately. Hide the letters in various places in the room. Ask the students to look for the cards, bring them to the table, and put the important word together.

Say: This is our important word today: GREED, means really wanting something that doesn't belong to us. God says that's wrong. We must be happy with what we have. Everything we have is a gift from God for us.

Statutes: "Have you wished?"

Ask the students to form a circle. If the classroom is small, you can do it in the yard.

Ask them to walk slowly to the beat of music, of a bell, or of clapping without breaking the circle until the sound stops. At that moment, they must stop walking and you will walk around the circle and touch a student's shoulder. Ask them: *Have you wanted something with all your heart? What was it?*

Continue the game until everyone has told what they want. If you wish, you can also tell what you have desired or want.

Explain that it's okay to want something that we like. The trouble is in wanting something so much that it leads us to break the laws of God, that is, the Ten Commandments. That's greed.

BIBLE STORY

King Ahab coveted Naboth's vineyard

"What a beautiful vineyard!" Ahab said. "Look at all those grapes, what lovely clusters! They look delicious! These lands are perfect for my vegetable garden!"

The more he looked at the vineyard, the more he wished it was his. "That vineyard has to be mine. I'm the king, I must have the best lands," he told himself.

Then he went to see Naboth, the owner.

"Hello, Naboth," said Ahab. "I need to talk with you."

"What's going on?" Naboth asked.

"I like your vineyard. Actually, I love it, so you have to give it to me. You can have another one if you want. I'll let you choose the one you want."

"No thanks," said Naboth. "That vineyard has belonged to my family for a long time and I will keep it for my children."

This made the king very angry and his face reddened by the anger he felt.

"Who do you think I am, Naboth?" The king scolded. "I'm the king, and I want that vineyard!"

The king returned to the palace and locked himself in his room. He went to bed, he didn't get up, he didn't eat or drink and he was still angry.

He continually thought more about the beautiful vineyard. "It's perfect," he thought. "It must be mine. I want it for myself. I'm the king." He complained so much that Queen Jezebel got tired of listening to him. One day she decided to talk to him.

"Why don't you eat?" she asked. "What's your problem? Why do you grumble and grumble?"

"I'm angry and sad," the king said. "I want Naboth's vineyard and he doesn't want to give it to me. I offered to pay him and he said he wouldn't accept it. How can he be so selfish?"

Jezebel frowned when she heard the king. "Don't act like a baby. Aren't you the king of Israel? Get up, eat, be glad; I'll get you Naboth's vineyard," said the queen.

And she made a terrible plan. She pretended to be King Ahab. She wrote letters and sealed them with the royal ring. Everyone believed that Ahab had written them.

The king wasn't worried about what his wife was doing. The only thing that mattered was getting the vineyard from that man at any cost.

"Prepare a special meal and invite Naboth," the queen wrote. "Give him a special seat, then say that the guest said bad words about God and then kill him."

The leaders did what the queen had written. They invited Naboth to a special meal.

"Sit here," they told Naboth. "We have this special seat for you."

Naboth sat down. Then two wicked men pointed to Naboth and shouted, "He spoke evil of God!"

Everyone agreed that Naboth should die. They killed him and sent a message to Queen Jezebel. "They stoned Naboth and he died."

Jezebel was happy. She quickly went to tell the king that Naboth had died. The king went happily to the vineyards.

Ahab rubbed his hands like a happy child with his favorite toy. "These vineyards are mine now!" He picked up some dirt and let it slide gently between his fingers, feeling the taste of victory.

While Ahab was celebrating, God spoke to Elijah, his prophet.

Ahab killed Naboth and is taking over his property. Go where he is," God said to Elijah.

Elijah found the happy king in his new vineyards.

"God is very angry with you," said Elijah. "You have sinned, you broke his commandments! You disobeyed God! God will take everything from you and you will die!"

Suddenly King Ahab realized his wickedness and was very sad. "How could I have done this terrible thing?" he cried.

Ahab knew that he had sinned. He knew he had done the wrong thing. Weeping and wailing, he repented and dressed in old clothes, and asked God to forgive him.

God knew that Ahab was repentant. So he forgave him, but told him that his children wouldn't be kings. Ahab learned that he couldn't break God's laws without paying the consequences. He understood how important it is to obey God.

ACTIVITIES

Bouquet of Contentment

Give your students the activity sheet from the student book, lesson 21. Follow the instructions to do the bouquet.

You will need: scissors, sticks or green wires, large disposable cups, sand to fill the cups, tape and glue, for each child.

Say: *This is a bouquet of contentment. Beautiful flowers are a gift from God. Whenever you see a flower, stop to thank God for all the beautiful things He gives us.*

Ask them to read each sentence that appears on the flowers:

- ✘ Be content with what you have.
- ✘ You shall not covet.
- ✘ Say no to greed.
- ✘ But if we have food and clothing, we will be content with that.
- ✘ Thanks, God.
- ✘ Happy

Take this bouquet of contentment to home. Put it in a place where everyone can see it. Every day give thanks to God for what you have. That will help you remember that we should be content and happy, and thank the Lord for not coveting what others have.

Memorization

"You shall not covet" (Exodus 20:17). Ask the children to repeat this verse several times.

Since this is the last lesson of the month, do a special activity to review the Ten Commandments. Put the children in a circle. Let them pass a small light ball. Start soft music. When the music stops, the child holding the ball in his hand should say the memory verse. Put the music back on. The next child who holds the ball in his hand when the music stops should say Commandment #1, and so on. If there are children who don't remember the commandments, others can help them, or you can do so through keywords.

To end

Let the children have a light snack (fruit, cookies, sweets) as a "reward" for their attendance and participation in learning the Ten Commandments.

With their eyes closed, direct a prayer with all children participating in it. Everyone can say short phrases like: "I thank you Lord for my mom". "I thank you Lord for my dad." (Keep giving thanks for all the things that God gives us: health, family, siblings, work, school, toys, friends, teachers, pastors, trees, flowers, animals, etc.)

End by praying for the children - that the Lord would help them to be happy and grateful, instead of coveting things that others have. Thank the Lord that the children have learned the Ten Commandments and ask him to help them remember the laws that He left us to do and be happy.

Encourage them to thank the Lord during the week instead of complaining.

Sing an appropriate chorus about happiness, contentment or gratitude.

Year 3
Introduction – Unit VI
GOD IS UNIQUE AND POWERFUL

Biblical References: Numbers 13:1-14:42; Numbers 27:12-23; Joshua 1; Joshua 3-4; Joshua 6; 14:6-15.

Unit Memory Verse: *The Lord your God will be with you wherever you go* (Joshua 1:9b).

Unit Objectives

This unit will help the elementary students to:
- ✗ Lose fear and trust in God.
- ✗ Have courage to confront difficult situations.
- ✗ Realize that when they obey God, He helps them.

Unit Lessons

Lesson 22: Go forward without fear.

Lesson 23: Go forward with courage

Lesson 24: Go forward in obedience

Lesson 25: Go forward with God's power

Lesson 26: Go forward with God's promises

Why Elementary Students need the teaching of this unit:

Fear, lack of courage to face some things, and disobedience are common in elementary students.

That's why, according to the approach and the dynamics that you have in your class, you can allow them to feel free of their small burdens, which can be very harmful to them.

May they come to understand that, although invisible to human eyes, God is with them everywhere. This will help them overcome a "ghost" that scares them a lot: feeling alone, away from home or helpless.

In addition, they will learn, not in just one day but eventually, that being close to God will make them happy, and that when they obey Him, He will take care of them in situations that generally cause them insecurity.

It's important for your students to know that God is a friend who is always on their side.

Go forward without fear

Biblical References: Numbers 13:1-14:42

Lesson Objective: That the children will learn what it means to trust God and obey Him, and believe that He will give them the courage to do whatever He asks them to do.

Memory Verse: *The Lord your God will be with you wherever you go* (Joshua 1:9b).

PREPARE YOURSELF TO TEACH!

Children have many fears. They often fear animals, darkness, unknown people and new experiences. According to their personality, children express their fears in different ways: screaming, crying, clinging to the adult or acting with reluctance. One of my little friends never tells me exactly, "I'm scared when I'm away from home." But he constantly asks me, "Are we far from the ice cream shop? What are we going to do now? How far is my house?"

This lesson will show the child that sometimes, even adults feel fear. But trusting God makes the difference between being brave or fearful. People who trust in God believe in His goodness and love for them. They believe that He is greater than everything and everyone. They confidently trust that He will help them do whatever they are asked to do.

This level of trust isn't built in one day. But the lessons of this unit are important bricks for the construction of those truths in children. It's not that God only tells us to trust him, but through the Scriptures he shows us who he is, what he is like, how he keeps his promises, and how he has previously helped people.

Be sure to share with your students how God came into your life. Your testimony, along with the Scriptures, is another brick to build the faith of children.

BIBLICAL COMMENTARY

The story of the rebelliousness of the Israelites in Kadesh-barnea illustrates the truth that's mentioned in Hebrews 11:6: "without faith it's impossible to please God." God faithfully led his people away from slavery, established a covenant with them, and miraculously provided sustenance for their needs. And the time had come to enter the promised land: Canaan. But because of their unbelief and rebellion, that generation of Israelites lost their inheritance in one of the worst disasters the bible tells about.

This incident happened about 14 or 15 months after the Israelites left Egypt. Moses sent 12 leaders on a spy mission to discover what opportunities and challenges Canaan presented. It took the spies 40 days to travel back and forth through the distance between the desert and Canaan, which was about 402 km. When they returned, they admitted that it was a good land, which was evidenced by the fruits they brought.

However, we can discover the first clue to this problem in 13:27 when the spies say, "We went to the land to which *you* sent us ..." (emphasis added). Prior to this, Canaan was constantly referred to as a precious gift from God (see v. 13:2). The spies' phrase in v. 27 reveals their negative feelings towards that land.

The spies' problem was that they focused on the negative. Many of the Canaanites were known for their exceptional size and strength. And Hebron was a very well fortified city. However, God repeatedly promised his people that he would give them the land of Canaan.

Joshua and Caleb did their part by focusing the people's attention on the promises of God (13:30 and 14:6-9). However, the unbelieving spies only became more rebellious and gave a "bad" report. That word means that their comments weren't only negative, but also exaggerated and false. Their terrible speech produced sudden fear. The Israelites demanded to return to Egypt and threatened to kill Moses, Caleb and Joshua.

The sad irony of this story is that what the Israelites predicted would happen to their children if they went to Canaan was what really happened to them because they didn't believe in God's power.

Finally, God forgave his people and kept his covenant with them. However, he left them to face the consequences of their actions. Those consequences affected both the innocent and the guilty. Joshua and Caleb, being righteous men, had to suffer the privations of living in the desert for another 40 years instead of enduring only a few weeks. But, finally, only the children of the murmuring Israelites could enter.

God expects his people to trust him. As he did with the Israelites, he offers us enough evidence of his love, strength and ability to develop our faith. However, in the end, the choice is always ours. We can decide to trust in God, taking into account our previous experiences with him, or to doubt and rebel. Trusting is difficult. But as history shows us extensively, not trusting is even worse.

LESSON DEVELOPMENT

Prepare in advance the teaching materials you will use for this lesson and try to have your classroom ready before your students arrive.

Remember to welcome visitors and collect their info to contact them during the week.

What are you afraid of?

Before class, place a tablecloth or plastic wrap on the table.

In class, give each child dough or play dough (see recipes at the beginning of this book). Ask them to make a figure that represents an object or situation in which they are afraid. Let them show you what they made and explain their creation.

Ask: *What do children do when they are scared?*

All people feel afraid sometimes. Sometimes, feeling fear is good. It helps us protect ourselves from danger. But other times, it prevents people from doing what God wants them to do. In our story today, people were afraid. Let's see what they did.

BIBLE STORY

Don't worry

This is a simple story to illustrate. Look for figures of biblical characters in the student book, make photocopies of Moses, Aaron, a crowd, color them and stick them on a background of bunches of grapes. While telling the story, stick the figures to the background with flannel or tape. Children can also make a large mural with vineyards, grapes, and fruit trees. Then they can attach the figures of the spies on it.

"Moses," God told him one day, "send some men to Canaan to explore the land I will give you."

Moses called 12 leaders, "Go to Canaan," Moses said. "Explore the land and discover if it's good or bad. See what the cities are like and if the land is good for growing food. Bring back some of the fruit that grows in Canaan."

The 12 men went to Canaan immediately. For 40 days they explored the whole land. There they saw dry and desert places, fields of mature grains, and fast-flowing rivers. A lot of good fruit grew there. The spies took figs and pomegranates, and cut a huge bunch of grapes. It was so big that they had to carry it between two men. Forty days later they returned to report to Moses.

When they arrived, they showed Moses, Aaron and all the people the fruit they had brought. Then, 10 of the spies began to say, "Canaan is a good land. Look at the beautiful fruit! However, the inhabitants of Canaan are very large and strong. They live in cities with thick strong walls.

"We shouldn't worry about that," said Caleb, another of the spies. "I think we could go now and take the land. We can do it!"

"Don't!" the others shouted. "We can't attack those people because they aren't just big, they're giants! They're going to smash us like locusts!"

The Israelites were beginning to get upset. "Oh why did we come here?" they lamented. "God will let them kill all of us. Enemies will take our wives and children

captive. We should go back to Egypt. Let's choose a new leader to take us back."

Moses and Aaron fell to their knees with their faces on the ground. The people were dishonoring God by saying so many bad things about him. What would God do? Joshua and Caleb tore their clothes to show how disgusted they were.

"Don't talk like that!" shouted Joshua and Caleb. "The earth is good and we must trust in God. Don't frighten the people. God is with us. We can take the land!"

But the people didn't want to listen to them. They were so scared and angry that they even wanted to kill Moses, Joshua and Caleb.

Suddenly, God appeared to them as a bright cloud of light! He was also angry.

"Until when will these people continue without trusting in me?" God asked Moses. "I will destroy them and start a new nation with your family."

"No God, please, don't do that!" Moses begged. "You brought us from Egypt and everyone in Canaan knows that. You are kind and forgiving. Please forgive these people even though they have done such great harm!"

"I will forgive them, but I will not let any of them enter Canaan. They saw all the miracles that I did in their midst, but they didn't trust me or obey me."

Tell this message to the people: "They will live in the desert for another 40 years. This represents one year for each day that the spies explored the land. Everyone who is 20 years old or older will die, except Joshua and Caleb, who trusted me. Your children will one day live in Canaan, but you will not."

When Moses told the people what God had told him, they were very sad.

"We have sinned," they said. "Therefore, now we will go to the land that God promised us."

"Don't do that!" said Moses. "It's too late for you to go to Canaan."

The 10 spies who didn't trust God died soon after. Only Joshua and Caleb lived. And they had to wait 40 long years. But they knew that God would keep his promise and take them one day to the land of Canaan.

Tell the children: *Joshua and Caleb believed in the promise that God would give them a new home. They trusted God and wanted to obey Him. God wants us to trust him and obey him. We shouldn't be afraid to do what God wants us to do.*

ACTIVITIES

A maze of feet

Give the children the activity sheet from the student's book, lesson 22. While doing the maze, they can repeat the bible memory verse.

78

Ask review questions about the spies' trip, the attitude of the Israelites, God's punishment, etc.

Word Search

Ask the children to work on the Word Search from the activity sheet and then complete the sentences with the words: "trust", "obey", "God", "me" and "courage".

The two activities will give you the opportunity to review the lesson with appropriate questions prepared by you in advance.

"Trust and Obey"

Make a set of cards with the words "Trust" and "Obey" for each child. The letters of the two words must be wide enough to be filled, painted and / or decorated. Write them on 15 cm x 30 cm cards. Bring colors, paints, brushes, markers, crayons, seeds, beans, corn, rice, paste, small fruit stickers, etc. Ask the children to decorate the words as they like. While they are working, take the opportunity to ask them questions about the lesson and to explain the meaning of those words.

Memorization

Sort the verse

After repeating the memory verse several times to memorize it, write it on the board in a disorderly way. Then, ask the children to go to the board and write the text in the right order. Give the opportunity for all children to participate by writing the text. Those who don't know it can repeat it with the help of children who have already learned it.

To end

In class, sing 2 or 3 choruses that talk about being afraid and trusting in God.

Say: *Trusting and obeying God isn't always easy. But God will help us, just as He helped Joshua and Caleb.*

Tell them to mention reasons for thanking God and prayer requests. Pray for those requests. Ask the Lord to help the little ones learn to trust him and obey him as Joshua and Caleb did.

 Notes

Go forward with courage

Biblical References: Numbers 27:12-23; Joshua 1.

Lesson Objective: That the children know that, just as God gave Joshua the courage to be the leader of his people, he will also give them the courage to do whatever he asks them to do.

Memory Verse: *The Lord your God will be with you wherever you go* (Joshua 1:9b).

PREPARE YOURSELF TO TEACH!

This lesson has two possible applications for children.

First, the bible story shows us how God strengthened Joshua to make him the new leader of the Israelites. He commanded Joshua to be strong and brave. Then he endowed him with those qualities with the promise that he would be with him and make him successful.

God will not ask the children to become leaders of the nations. But sometimes he wants the little ones to do some things that require courage. For example, in this era it takes a lot of courage to face a friend and tell him he is making a wrong choice. This lesson will assure the child that God is on his side, helping him do the right thing.

Second, it will help the children to respect and obey their leaders. Unfortunately, the authority figures that children have today are men who mock and disobey. On a daily basis, television shows show parents as unwise people or even worse. Possibly, older siblings speak disrespectfully about their teachers or those who exercise authority. This lesson will show children how God's children should treat leaders: with respect and obedience.

Ask God to help the children learn and remember the Bible stories you teach them. God gave us these stories so we can learn what he is like and help us build our faith.

BIBLICAL COMMENTARY

Read Numbers 27:12-23. The expression "passing the torch" evokes memories of the Olympic competitions in which a lit torch is passed from one runner to another. It also refers to the transfer of leadership from an old leader to the next generation.

Moses' 40-year leadership of the Israelites would soon be over. Because of his disobedience when bringing water from the rock for the people in the desert (Numbers 20:1-13), God denied him entrance to Canaan. However, Moses saw the land from Mount Nebo before he died.

Joshua was the man that God chose as the new leader. He had really demonstrated his courage and faith in God. He had served as Moses' assistant during the 40 years in which they had wandered in the desert.

In a special ceremony, the transfer of Moses' leadership to Joshua was made public. In biblical times, the laying on of hands indicated that one person became a substitute or representative of the other. This practice was also followed by the transfer of the blessing to the other person or of sins to a sacrificed animal.

Joshua would be, in many ways, a leader like Moses. However, there were also important differences. Moses had spoken face to face with God. Joshua's dealings with God were through Eleazar the priest, who had sought Jehovah's direction through the Urim and the Thummim. Those were special stones that were used to determine what God's point of view was.

Read Joshua 1. As this chapter begins, Moses was dead and Joshua assumed total leadership of the people. The chapter points out several things about his leadership:

1. Joshua's leadership was a position of responsibility. Moses had brought the people out of Egypt; Joshua was in charge of taking them into Canaan.

2. Joshua wouldn't lead them alone. God had once again promised that He would give the land to the people. While they would have to fight to win it, they could only do it knowing that victory was assured. God also promised that he would be with Joshua as he had been with Moses in every situation (v. 5-9). The command given in verse 9 emphasizes that point. "For the Lord your God will be with you wherever you go."

3. Joshua would need great faith and great courage, both necessary characteristics for both a military and a spiritual leader. On three occasions God commanded Joshua:, "Be strong and be (very) brave" (v. 6,7 and 9). Twice this command was in reference to taking over the land of Canaan. But in verse 7, God told him: "Be strong and very courageous. Being careful to obey all the law my servant Moses gave you."

J. Gordon Harris says: "When leaders faithfully seek to do God's will, they discover that God has prepared the way to success."

While teaching your children, you can also count on God, knowing that he will fulfill the promise of Joshua 1:9.

LESSON DEVELOPMENT

Prepare in advance the teaching materials you will use for this lesson and try to have your classroom ready before your students arrive.

Remember to welcome visitors and collect their info to contact them during the week.

Follow the leader

Take the children to the patio or to a large open room where they have room to move. Choose one of the children to be a leader. Tell the children to do everything the leader does. Explain that they can walk, run, jump, jump on one foot, etc. The leader can also make gestures with their hands or any other movement with their body for the class to follow. After a few minutes, change and let another child be the leader. Continue the game until most have been the leader.

Have the children sit in a circle and discuss the game.

Say: *Sometimes it's hard to make people follow us. Today's Bible story tells us how God called a leader to do a difficult task. Let's find out what he was commanded to do and what God promised him.*

Review of the biblical story of the last class

Ask for a volunteer to tell the story of the last class. If the child forgets or omits any detail, another can raise his hand, or go to the front and stand next to the child who is speaking and say: "I remember that: ..." and tell the part that he omitted or forgot. Once they finish remembering the whole story (you can interrupt by asking appropriate questions from the last class, so they remember), say: *Last week we learned that Joshua and Caleb were the only two spies who obeyed God and entered Canaan. This week we will hear more about Joshua. I wonder what happened to him later.*

BIBLE STORY

God's Courage

Moses had aged a lot. He knew that the time of his death was approaching, and he was worried about the people of Israel. They had been wandering in the desert for 40 years. Soon they would have to enter the new land that God had promised them a long time ago.

Then Moses said to God, "These people are like sheep. They need someone to guide them or they will continue to wander."

The Lord answered him, "Joshua is the right man for that task. He trusts me, and he obeys me. He will be a wise leader. Have Joshua go with you and the priest, and stand before the people. Put your hands on him and show the people that you are putting Joshua in charge of them."

"I'll do what you tell me," said Moses.

Moses gathered all the people together. And with Eleazar the priest, they stood before all the people. Moses put his hands on Joshua and named him as the new leader of the people.

Soon Moses died. Not long after, God spoke to Joshua.

"Joshua," said God, "you must lead the people through the Jordan River to the new land that's called Canaan. I will keep the promise I made to Moses that I would give this people the promised land. I'll be with you. I command you to be strong and brave; Don't fear or be dismayed, for I Jehovah your God, will be with you wherever you go."

Joshua gave the order to the people to prepare to cross the Jordan and go to the new land. Would the people obey? For many years Moses had been their leader.

However, all the people agreed to obey Joshua as they had obeyed Moses. They trusted and believed that God was with Joshua just as he had been with Moses. Anxiously the people waited for Joshua's next orders. Soon they would enter their new land.

After the story, play tic-tac-toe (three in line). Draw on the chalkboard a tic-tac-toe grid (3 horizontal squares x 3 verticals). Divide the class into two teams. Prepare questions in relation to the story just told. Ask the first group a question. If they answer it correctly, tell one of the members to put an X in the square that the team chooses. Then ask the second team a question. Let the team draw an O if it answered correctly. If the team responds incorrectly, it loses its turn and it's the other's turn to play. Continue playing until one of the teams forms a line of 3 crosses or circles vertically, horizontally or diagonally, or when the 9 squares are filled, in which case the one that has filled the most squares will be the winner.

ACTIVITIES

Do these activities to help students connect the biblical truths with their lives.

Follow the leaders

Say: *God chose Joshua to be the leader of his people. The people promised that they would obey and follow. Who are the leaders we must obey today?* (Parents, teachers, pastors, grandparents, government people, etc.) *What should we do to respect them?* (Obey them, be kind, pray for them.)

Give each child a cardboard plate. Tell them to draw the face of one of the leaders they should follow or obey. Let them decorate the plate by drawing the face with markers, and then gluing strings or yarn to make the hair. Tell each person to glue a wooden stick (ice cream stick, popsicle stick, etc) on the underside of the face to hold it. When they are finished, ask them to take turns holding their "face" in front of their face and telling the rest of the class whom they drew.

Ask each child: *What things can you do to respect this leader? How can you follow him or her?* Let the children share their ideas.

Say: *We obey God by respecting and obeying the leaders he placed in charge of us. Being a leader isn't easy. But we can help them by praying for them.*

Marching together

Before class, make or borrow percussion instruments that the children can use.

In class, pass out the instruments. Play a musical theme with enough rhythm. Tell the children to march around the room accompanying the music with their percussion instruments, clapping or whistling. While they are marching, stop the music several times. When stopped, say:

Teacher: - Who gives us courage?

Students: - God!

Teacher: - Who should we trust?

Students: - God!

Teacher: - Who should we obey?

Students: - God!

Continue playing, marching, and proclaiming as time permits. Each time they finish making one of the proclamations, play the song again.

Then say: *Today we learned that Joshua went ahead with courage. When God asked him to be the leader, Joshua trusted him and obeyed him. The Lord gave Joshua the courage he needed to be a good leader. Likewise, He will give us the courage to face the difficult situations that we face.*

Memorization

Funny footprints

Before class, make or find a picture of a small footprint and photocopy 11 for each child. Print Joshua 1:9 - enough for each child to have a copy.

In class, give each child 11 footprints and one sheet with the verse. Tell them to cut out the verse with the 11 words separated into 11 pieces of paper, and then glue each word on one of the footprints. Allow them to practice putting the prints in order, so that the verse is correctly assembled. Then tell them to mix up all the footprints and stack them all together in front of them. When you give the signal, tell them to start ordering them as quickly as possible until the verse is assembled correctly. The first child who gets it done will lead the group to say the verse. Do it several times.

Give each child an envelope or plastic bag to keep their footprints. Let each one write his name on the envelope. Save them for use the following week.

Tell them: *This verse tells us that God will be with us wherever we go. It's a special promise for people who are trying to do what God asks them to do. In our bible story today, Joshua received a special task from God. And we saw how he could do it and how the Lord encouraged him to have the courage to do it.*

To end

Say: *Think of situations in which you need to have courage to do the things that God wants you to do.* (Let the children respond and tell everyone.)

What can we do when we need courage to do something?

Many times children may not have too many ideas. Give the children the activity sheet from the student book and ask them to follow the instructions.

Give them crayons or red and green markers. Let them complete the page and discover the word "Pray".

Say: *When can we pray?* (Anytime we need God's help). *Remember that we can talk to God at any time, anywhere and about anything.*

Tell them about an experience in which you asked God to give you the courage to do something he wanted you to do. Tell them how God helped you.

Ask the children to complete the activity sheet entitled: "Who is he?"

Finish the class by praying for their requests (for courage to face difficult situations) and other needs the children have. Ask God to help them to remember to pray whenever they need courage.

When the children leave, make sure they take their crafts.

Go forward in obedience

Biblical References: Joshua 3-4.

Lesson Objective: That the children will know that God will honor them when they follow his instructions, and that he will make them brave when they dare to obey him.

Memory Verse: *The Lord your God will be with you wherever you go* (Joshua 1:9b).

PREPARE YOURSELF TO TEACH!

Bible characters, even those who were involved in stories of miracles, may seem boring to children compared to characters in cartoons. Some of the children, especially the youngest ones, have difficulties differentiating fantasy from reality. One of our goals as teachers is to help them realize that the stories in the Bible are real. When your students name a television superhero, remind them time after time that the character isn't real, but that the characters in the Bible were real.

Today's Bible story tells us how God used his power to help those who trusted and obeyed him. Children live in an uncertain, often terrifying world. They need to know that the God of the universe cares for them and has the power to help them.

In your teaching, emphasize that God knows and wants the best for us. Believing this will establish the foundation for trust and obedience.

This month's lessons are focused on trust in God. Joshua and Caleb trusted him when others did not. Joshua trusted that God would help him be the new leader. Joshua and the Israelites trusted that God would help them cross the Jordan River - even with its banks flooded - and take them into Canaan. Examples of these Old Testament heroes can help first and second grade children know that they can also trust and obey God.

BIBLICAL COMMENTARY

The 40 years of wandering in the desert ended. God led Israel to the banks of the Jordan River. The plans for his people were the same as before: they would go to Canaan and own the land that he had promised Abraham a long time ago. Obeying the divine mandate wouldn't be as easy as it had been 4 decades ago. And it could still be harder now, as the banks of the Jordan River are overflowing.

Under Moses' leadership, God had given Israel a cloud and a pillar of fire to guide them. Now, the ark of the covenant was the visible sign of his presence. The priests went before the people, carrying the ark as a symbol of the presence of God who went before them showing them the way.

After arriving at the Jordan and establishing camp there, Joshua waited three days until he received more instructions from the Lord. Finally, he told the people to prepare because God had said it was time to get going. Sanctification would prepare the people to be witnesses of the powerful action of the Creator. It would show them their dependence on Him. Only when we go to God and depend on him can the Lord do great wonders through us.

After sanctification, the people were ready to cross the Jordan. As soon as the priests who carried the ark stepped into the water, the river dried up. The priests stood in the middle of the riverbed while the people crossed over dry land. After all had passed, Joshua called a person from each of the 12 tribes. He told them to take a stone from the bottom of the riverbed where the priests were standing. With those 12 stones they built an altar. That was for the people to remember the great power of God and how He used that power to help them when they followed his instructions.

LESSON DEVELOPMENT

Prepare in advance the teaching materials you will use for this lesson and try to have your classroom ready before your students arrive.

Remember to welcome visitors. Collect their information and don't forget to visit them or call them during the week.

Do these activities to help the children focus their attention and prepare them to learn the biblical truth of today.

Follow the instructions

Before class, tape or glue colored paper on the outside of a cardboard box shaped like a cube. Write the following instructions, one on each of the 6 faces of the cube:

✘ Open the Bible to the book of Joshua.

✘ Write your name on the board.

✘ Walk to the door and then return to your seat.

✘ Sing your favorite song.

✘ Shake hands with three people without smiling.

✘ Jump three times with your eyes closed.

In class, tell them: *Today we will see if you know how to follow directions.*

Have the children take turns throwing the cube up in the air, letting it fall to the floor. When the cube falls, they are to read and do the instructions on the top of the cube. Then it is the next child's turn. Afterwards, ask them the following questions:

✘ *Were the instructions hard to follow?*

✘ *Why do people give directions?* (Because they need something to be done in a certain way or for us to learn something.)

✘ *Is it important to follow instructions? Why?*

✘ *What can happen if you don't follow the instructions you are given?*

Tell them: *The instructions of the game that we just did were just for fun, but following instructions is very important. In our bible story today we will discover how important it is to follow the instructions that God gives us.*

Crossing the river

Before class, write the following words on different cards: "swim", "float", "cross over a bridge", "row a boat", "jet ski", "canoe", "boat" and "sailboat" " Put the cards in a small box.

In class say: *Today we are going to play a game that shows us possible ways to cross a river.*

Have the children, in turn, choose a card. Ask each one: *How will you cross the river?*

The child should read what his card says and act out what their card says, without saying a word. Let the others try to guess how that child will make the crossing. (Option: if the number of children in your class is greater than the number of cards you made, suggest that they be grouped.)

Ask: *What do you think people will have to do to cross the river in today's lesson? Listen to the bible story and you'll find out.*

BIBLE STORY

Pass out the activity sheet for this lesson from the student book. Guide the children to cut out and assemble the figures. You will need for each child: pieces of cardboard to glue the figures to and colored pencils or crayons (yellow or gold to color the ark). Once they finish assembling and coloring the figures, they can follow the bible story that you will narrate.

Say: *Today I would like you to help me tell the bible story. I'll tell you when you need to find the specific figure and move it. Our story today is found in the book of the Bible called Joshua. This book tells us about Joshua.*

Last week we saw that Moses presented Joshua before the people as their new leader. Do you remember why God chose Joshua to lead the people? (Because Joshua trusted and obeyed God, and because Moses was old.)

The daring crossing of the river

(Instruct the children to find the figure of Joshua speaking to the people.)

Joshua spoke to the Israelites and told them, "It's time to go to our new land. The priests will carry the ark of the covenant. Follow them, and that way you'll know where to go. Wait and see, tomorrow God is going to do something amazing in our midst."

Soon, all the people would see the power of God in action.

The ark of the covenant was a kind of golden box with two angels with their wings spread out on the top. It was the symbol of God's presence. The priests picked up the ark and carried it, and thus the people would know that God was with them.

(Tell the children to look for the figure of the priests carrying the ark.)

God spoke to Joshua, "Tell the priests to stand in the middle of the river. Tell people not to touch the ark; they must be kept at a distance."

The priests and the people obeyed God and Joshua.

At that time of year, the banks of the Jordan River were overflowing with water. The water was very deep. The priests must have asked themselves, "Why does God ask us to do something that can be so dangerous?" But they decided to trust God and obey Him. What do you think happened? (Allow the children to respond.)

(Tell them to look for the figure of the river.)

The priests put their feet in the water. The river stopped flowing! The water stopped completely! The river bed was dry! How wonderful! The people looked with amazement and could see how the waters stopped running at the moment when the priests obeyed God and entered the water. These people had heard the story of how God had opened a dry road in the middle of the Red Sea when they were escaping from the Egyptians, but they hadn't seen it with their own eyes. Now they were seeing the power of God in action!

The people of Israel crossed the river on dry land. But the priests remained in the middle of the Jordan.

After crossing the river, Joshua continued to obey every instruction that God gave him.

God told Joshua, "Choose 12 men. Tell them to take 12 stones from the middle of the river close to where the priests are. Ask them to carry them to the place where we will stay tonight."

So they did that. Those men went and got the heavy rocks and carried them on their shoulders from the middle of the river, where the priests had stopped, to their new homeland: Canaan. There was one stone for each of the 12 tribes of Israel.

(Ask the children to find the figure of the priests with the ark.)

God told Joshua, "Tell the priests to come out of the river."

The priests obeyed. And then, as soon as the last priest came out of the water, the water started to flow again.

When the people saw what God had done, they honored Joshua as their leader.

"God is with Joshua, just as he was with Moses," they all said.

(Tell them to look for the figure of Joshua with the people.)

Joshua led the people to the place where they would spend the night. There, Joshua used the 12 stones to build an altar.

(Tell them to look for the figure of the 12 stones.)

Joshua said, "One day our children will ask us questions. They will ask us, 'Why are these stones here?' Tell them that God helped us to cross the river on dry land. Tell them they can trust and obey God."

That day the Israelites learned that God's power is greater and more powerful than any person or thing that could exist. God can do all things. He uses his power to take care of the world and people.

We can trust him, even if we don't understand his plans.

Review the story and ask:

How did God show his power to the people of Israel in today's biblical story? (He helped them cross the Jordan River on dry ground.)

What instructions did God give to the people? (That they couldn't touch the ark, that they were to bring 12 stones from the middle of the river.)

Why was it important for the Israelites to follow God's instructions? (To be able to reach the other side of the river and the promised land.)

Tell them: *Trust means obeying God even when we don't understand His plans. Joshua and the Israelites trusted and obeyed, and we can do the same.*

ACTIVITIES

Do these activities to help the students connect biblical truth with their lives.

God's power

Sing an appropriate chorus, which the children know, about the power of God.

Stones to remember

Before class, gather a small stone for each child. They should be large and smooth enough to stick one of these words on them: "Trust", "obey" or "God's Power". Write those words on several sheets of paper.

In class, ask: *Why did God tell the people to build an altar of 12 stones?* (To remind them and their children how God had helped them.)

Give each child a rock. Ask them: *Which of these words would help you better remember this story and the power of God?*

Guide the children to choose "Trust", "Obey" or "God's Power" and stick it on their stone. Tell them: *Our stones will help us remember this story. We can trust and obey God, even when we don't understand his plans and directions.*

Memorization

Fingerprint puzzle

If you didn't do this for lesson 22 of this unit, prepare two sets of cardboard cards in the form of footprints, about 15 cm. long. On each footprint write one of the words of the memory verse. Divide the group in two, and give each one a set of cards. Ask them to place the cards with the text face down on the table and mix them up. Then have them assemble the puzzle / text correctly. The group that finishes first will be the winner. Then ask the children in the winning group to recite the memory verse by heart.

Another way to memorize playing: tape the footprints in order (forming the verse correctly) on the wall or on the board.

Tell the children to read the verse together. Then let one of them remove one of the footprints. Then instruct everyone to repeat the verse, filling in the missing word. Continue this way by asking one child at a time to remove another of the footprints, until they have all been removed and they can say the memory verse from memory.

Those who have memorized Joshua 1:9 will be able to paste the memory verse on their candy jar. After dismissal, the children can take home their story of the crossing of the Jordan River. Tell them to tell the story of God's great power in helping his people cross the river on dry land.

To end

Have a prayer time in which everyone can thank God for helping them. Finish by asking the Lord to help each child obey and trust him.

Go forward with God's power

Biblical References: Joshua 6.

Lesson Objective: To help the children know that the walls of Jericho fell because God did what he had promised; and that in the same way today, we can trust God fully and obey him because he knows what is best for us.

Memory Verse: *The Lord your God will be with you wherever you go* (Joshua 1:9b).

PREPARE YOURSELF TO TEACH!

Learning to trust in God is closely linked to trusting others. Many times adults ask children to do things that they don't understand. If they ask why, the person in authority should help them understand.

This procedure works most of the time. However, there are times when children must trust their elders' decisions and obey them, even if they don't understand them. When a relationship of trust develops with the children, it's easy for them to do what they are asked to do, even if they don't understand it.

When God shows us what He wants us to do, He doesn't always reveal to us why. Obedience at such times may be more difficult, but we still must comply. Help the children understand that they must obey God without fear, because they can trust that he knows and will do what's best for them.

Our bible story is an excellent illustration of this truth. The instructions that God gave to Joshua may seem strange. But, because of their trust and obedience, the walls of Jericho fell!

BIBLICAL COMMENTARY

Read Joshua 6. When the 12 spies returned from Canaan, they agreed on at least one thing: the cities had big walls that made them safe. Archaeological excavations have shown that, in fact, some of the cities built in that place had double walls. It's possible that one of them was the place where our story takes place.

In Joshua 6:1, it says: "Now the gates of Jericho were securely barred". The inhabitants feared the Israelites. No one could enter or leave the city. The citizens of Jericho felt that they were safe from the invaders, but they didn't know that such a strong defense couldn't stop the God of the Israelites.

The destruction of Jericho was important for both religious and military reasons. It was the epicenter of the worship of the moon god. (Probably "Jericho"

meant "the city of the moon.") One of God's constant concerns was that his people would adopt the religions of the Canaanites.

The instructions that God had given to Joshua to conquer Jericho must have been quite strange to the seasoned warriors, but they had begun with His promise: "I have delivered Jericho into your hands" (Joshua 6:2). Armed men went ahead of the seven priests who carried the trumpets of ram's horn. The priests who carried the ark of the covenant followed those who played the trumpets. The rear guard was lined up after them, and then the people were still behind.

The ram's horn emitted a strong and penetrating sound that caught the attention of the people. So the sound of seven of these horns surely alerted the people of Jericho that something was about to happen.

The first day, the people marched around the city without making any sound with their voices. Only the priests blew the horns. This procedure was repeated from the second to the sixth day. On the seventh day, the people marched around the city seven times. Following the instructions God had given them, on the seventh time, the priests blew their trumpets, the people shouted, and ... "the wall collapsed; so everyone charged straight in, and they took the city" (Joshua 6:20).

Strange way to tear down a walled city, right? But it worked because Joshua and the people trusted God. Although they didn't understand how he was going to act, they obeyed his instructions. And because of their obedience, he fulfilled what he had promised.

LESSON DEVELOPMENT

Welcome your students with affection and ensure that the classroom is clean and tidy when they arrive. Before going into today's topic, review briefly the three previous lessons and ask your students to give some examples of how faithful they have been to God.

Children's "trumpet"

Give each child a cardboard tube (this can be from toilet paper or a roll of paper towels). Tell them to decorate it with markers or crayons and write their names on it. Then give each one a square of 10 cm. x 10 cm waxed paper. Help them wrap one end of the tube with that paper, so that it's covered, holding it with an elastic band or adhesive tape. Using a punch, or scissors tip, make four or five small holes in the waxed paper. at the end. Then have the children blow through the open end of the tube so it makes a sound.

Let the children march around the room playing their instruments while they sing a song. Then save the tubes for later use.

Tell them: *Our instruments make a noise similar to that of a musical instrument that had an important* place in our biblical story today. What instrument do you think it will be?

Let's find out what happened.

Important words

Review the new words important to this unit: "admiration", "God's Power" and "wisdom". Write each of those words on the board but with the letters mixed up. Next to the words, draw a straight line. For example: "ropew of dog" _____. Ask for some volunteers who dare to decipher the words (power of God) and write them correctly on the line.

Ask another to identify the second scrambled word (with mixed letters). Have the children write "admiration" in the space they have there. Ask them:

✘   What does the word "admiration" mean?

✘   What happened in last week's Bible story that led the people to feel admiration for what happened when they saw the power of God? (God stopped the river and the people could cross over on dry land.)

Ask the children to now order and decipher the third word: "wisdom."

Ask: *What does wisdom mean?* (Use what we know to do what is right.) *God knows all things. God always does the right thing.* Give examples for each of the important words.

BIBLE STORY

Strong horn sounds and broken walls

Read Joshua 6. *How exciting those days were for the Israelites! They were already in their new homeland: Canaan. They had waited so long, but God had fulfilled his promise to bring them into that land. He had brought Joshua and the Israelites safely across the Jordan River. And now they were ready to conquer the cities.*

Not far from there was the great city of Jericho. It had high and strong walls with large gates. But inside the city, the people were frightened. They had heard many stories about the Israelites and their God.

"I heard that many years ago their God destroyed Pharaoh's army and freed them from Egypt," said a man in Jericho.

"I heard that their God was with them and kept them safe," added a woman.

"And I heard that their God fights for them!" said another man.

The people of Jericho were so frightened that they kept the city gates tightly closed and acted with caution. No one could enter or leave it.

God spoke to Joshua and gave him a plan to conquer the city.

"Do what I tell you and the city will be yours." Joshua carefully listened to every one of God's instructions. *"First, march around Jericho once a day for six days. Seven priests shall carry seven ram's horns before the ark."*

Surely, Joshua was surprised when he heard what God told him to do. That wasn't the usual way to fight a battle. But Joshua believed and trusted God. And God gave him more instructions.

"On the seventh day, you will go around the city seven times, and the priests will blow the horns."

And he continued, "When the priests blow their horns for a long time, the people of Israel will shout loudly! Then the walls of Jericho will collapse, and your army will be able to go straight ahead and destroy the city."

"We'll do what you've told us, Lord," Joshua said.

Then he gathered the people and told them God's plan.

*"What will **we** do?" the priests asked.*

"Take the ark of the covenant and march around the city carrying the ark."

*"What about **us**?" asked the seven other priests.*

"You will march in front of the ark of the covenant and play your trumpets."

*"Tell us what **we** can do," the soldiers replied.*

"Some of you will march in front of the priests. Others will march behind the ark."

"While doing all this, don't shout or say anything. Wait until I let you know. When I give you the order, shout!"

All the Israelites trusted God. They were ready to obey.

"Let's go!" they said to each other.

On the first day, the Israelites marched around the city once and then returned to the camp.

The following days they continued marching.

On the seventh day they got up very early. And they marched around the city again. But that day they didn't stop after going around once. They marched around twice, then three times. Their footsteps grew louder and louder. Then they marched around four, five and six times! Their feet sounded like thunder that shook the ground.

Finally, the Israelites marched around Jericho for the seventh and last time. The priests played their trumpets loud and long.

Suddenly, Joshua said, "Shout, because the Lord has given you the city!"

At that moment all the people shouted!

Boom ... boom, crash, boooom! The walls began to tremble. Crash, smash, craaaack! The earth was trembling! And then ... crash, craaack, boooom! The walls of Jericho collapsed and fell to the ground!

The Israeli soldiers attacked the city. In an instant they had completely defeated their enemies.

That night there was great rejoicing in the camp!

God can do impossible things when we trust him and obey him. The people had trusted and obeyed God. Therefore, he used his power to do the impossible. The walls and the city of Jericho had disappeared!

After the story, perform a review game, using questions previously prepared by you. For example: *How many times did the Israelites march around the city of Jericho on the first day?* (Just one.) *Did the soldiers carry the ark?* (No, the priests.) *On the journey, was the ark behind the people?* (No, it was in front of the people and at a distance.) Etc.

After the game, give the children the instruments they made earlier. If you wish, you can have them build "walls" by stacking small boxes that can be "knocked down". Then, have them dramatize the story by marching seven times around the room or the boxes stacked while playing their instruments. Give them the command to: "Shout!" And have them say, shouting, "Praise the Lord!" Guide them to yell and clap because the walls fell. When the story is over, tell the children that they can take their instruments home.

Remind the children that God can do impossible things when we trust and obey him.

ACTIVITIES

Craaaash ...! Walls demolished!

As soon as the Bible story is over, give the children the activity sheet from the Student book, lesson 25. Ask them to cut out the figures, build the wall and color the scenes, the soldiers and the people. Use this moment to ask review questions about the story you just told.

Bricks of faith

Give each child a piece of clay or dough (you can use the recipe at the beginning of this book). Tell them: In our Bible story today the power of God destroyed the great city with immense walls. Those walls must have been made with very strong bricks. Today we are going to build a brick that will help us remember this story.

Let the children mold the clay into the shape of a thick rectangular brick. Have them engrave the letter "J" on the brick with a pencil or a sharp object.

Tell them: *The "J" in the brick will remind you of "Joshua" and "Jericho." God did something that was impossible for Joshua and the Israelites. And he can also*

do impossible things when we trust him and obey him. Whenever you face a very difficult situation, remember how God helped Joshua and his people. Trust that God will help you, and obey him because he knows what is best for you.

Have the children place their bricks on a piece of aluminum foil or wax paper to dry. Then tell them to attach their name to the waxed paper with tape. The children will take the bricks home next week when they are dry.

Memorization

"Say the verse!"

Before class, place the footprints with the memory verse in a bag or box.

In class, let the children choose a partner. Tell them: **Let's play a memory game!**

Each child will try to say the verse with as few word clues (footprints that contain a word of the verse) as possible. Our verse has 11 words. Each child decides how many words they need to see in order to "recite the verse".

Choose a couple of children to start the game. Have them stand or sit facing each other. One of the children will say: I can say the verse by seeing (5) words. The other child will challenge him saying: I can say it by seeing only (3) words. If the first child thinks he can say the verse with a smaller number of words present, he will continue the challenge by reducing the number. If he sees that he can't achieve it, he should tell his opponent: *Say the verse!* The challenged child should take out of the box the number of fingerprints he said and try to recite it using only those words.

If the child recites the text correctly, give him a small prize, such as a pencil. Then have a second couple of children play the game.

For those who know the whole verse by heart and didn't do it the previous Sunday, they can add the candy picture to their candy jar.

Tell them: *This verse tells us that God is with us wherever we are. God wants us to trust him and obey him. As we saw in our Bible story today, the people of Israel trusted God to perform a totally unusual event. And how beautiful it is to see how the Lord helped them defeat the enemy!*

To end

Have the children tell their prayer requests and reasons for thanks. Tell them: *We can trust and obey God because he knows what is best for us. Thank him for his wisdom and power.*

Pray for the requests and praises of the children. Thank the Lord for helping them trust him and obey him.

Go forward with God's promises

Biblical References: Joshua 14:6-15.

Lesson Objective: That the children understand that God keeps his promises and often works through his people to do that. May their trust in God grow at the same time in his promises.

Memory Verse: *The Lord your God will be with you wherever you go* (Joshua 1:9b).

PREPARE YOURSELF TO TEACH!

Waiting is difficult for children 6 to 8 years old, in part because for them time passes very slowly. I can remember those days when it seemed to me that three years had passed between December 1 and Christmas Day. Reaching second grade seemed like an impossible dream to achieve.

Not only does time go by slowly for children, but for most children of that age, time has little or no value. A week or two ago, I showed the students in my class a Bible that someone had given me as a child. I asked them, "How old do you think this Bible is?"

The first quick response they gave me was, "One hundred!"

In today's story, use this children's characteristic to emphasize the lesson: Caleb had to wait a long time to receive what God had promised him. Most of the parents of the children in your class haven't yet reached the age of 45. Today you will see that Caleb had to wait, wait, and wait; but God fulfilled his promise, as he always does.

We won't always have to wait for such a long time to receive what God promised us. Sometimes the waiting time will be shorter; at other times we'll have to wait longer. But the children of your class will begin to trust that God always keeps the promises of those who boldly trust him and obey him.

BIBLICAL COMMENTARY

Read Joshua 14:6-15. Would you like to have a name whose meaning is "dog"? Probably not. Either way, that's the meaning of our hero's name in our bible story. But regardless of whether the parents knew it or not, they had chosen a name that was very appropriate for their son, Caleb.

Many dogs are known for their devotion and loyalty to their masters, and those qualities characterized Caleb's relationship with God. This story reminds us that his faithfulness was rewarded by One who is known throughout the Bible as the "faithful God" (Deut. 7:9).

The Israelites were dividing the land of Canaan west of the Jordan. Two and a half tribes had taken the plots east of the Jordan. Now the remaining nine and a half were receiving what belonged to them.

During this process, Caleb stepped forward to remind Joshua of the promise God had made to him through Moses (verse 9). Forty-five years ago, during the spy mission to Canaan, Caleb had faithfully given a favorable report about the land. But, although he (and Joshua) urged the people to obey God and enter, they had refused. All adults over 20 years old perished in the desert. But through Moses, God had promised: "Except Caleb son of Jephunneh. He will see it, and I will give him and his descendants the land he set his feet on, because he followed the Lord wholeheartedly" (Deut. 1:36).

We find two ironies in this passage. The first is that Caleb wasn't an Israelite, but a "Kenizzite" - a grandson of Kenaz - who in turn was the grandson of Esau (Genesis 36:10-11). But his loyalty to God had exceeded that of the natural Israelites.

The second has to do with the request that Caleb made to Joshua. He asked for what represented the great challenge that had scared the Israelites 45 years ago. Essentially, Caleb was declaring: "Give me those walled cities full of giants (the Anakites), because with the help of God I will drive them out!" (V. 12).

Joshua recognized the rectitude of Caleb's claim and granted his request. Some scholars believe that Joshua's blessing gave Caleb the spiritual strength he needed to carry out the task of subduing Hebron.

This passage leads us to the following reflections:

1. What we "are" isn't as important as what we "will become" by the grace of God. Caleb, the "dog" (a term that the Israelites ironically applied to non-Israelites), had once been excluded from the promises of God. And he became the first example of what an Israeli "dog" could be: faithful, loyal and courageous.

2. Choice - and not the place where one is born or the environment - determines whether or not someone belongs to the people of God. He chooses us through his anticipated grace.

3. We can count on God being faithful, but we must know how to wait for the right time. Caleb waited 45 years to obtain the land that God had promised him. For some situations, the reward for our fidelity may not even come during our life. However, it will come. Our God has promised!

LESSON DEVELOPMENT

Receive your students with affection and ensure that the classroom is clean and tidy when they arrive. Before starting today's topic, review briefly the four previous lessons.

Letter cube (dice) with important words

Before class, cover an empty cube-shaped cardboard box with colored paper. On each side of the box write the first letter of each of the six important words of this unit: "Admiration," "Courage," "God's Power," "Obedience," "Confidence," and "Wisdom." .

In class, review the important words of the unit. Have children say and define what those words mean.

Show the cube of letters and have one of them throw it to you. Notice what letter appears on the side that is up and name the important word that begins with that letter. Then provide a small definition of that word. Or use that term in a sentence about something that happened in this unit. For example: "Admiration". "The Israelites had admiration at God's power when they saw how he separated the waters of the Jordan River." "Wisdom". "Joshua and Caleb acted wisely when they gave a good report on Canaan."

Let the children take turns throwing the dice to each other. Help them, if they need it, with definitions or sentences. Make sure that each child has played.

Tell them: *Joshua and the Israelites acted wisely by trusting God and obeying Him. God gave them the courage to do what He had asked them to do. God used his power and wisdom to help his people. The people were amazed when they saw what God had done. Our story shows us how Caleb trusted God one more time.*

Promises kept

Before class, prepare a variety of "unappetizing" ingredients: a cup of sand, a heap of stones, a jug of insects, a glass of dirty water, and so on. On the other hand, prepare a delicious snack: cheese cut into cubes, salty crackers, slices of sausages, fruit cubes, potato chips, and whatever you can include. Some drink, glasses and napkins.

In class, say: *Today I prepared a tasty snack for you. I promise you that you'll like it very much.* Put out the "unappetizing" snacks you prepared one by one.

As you put them out, ask: *Do you like them? Why not? But I promised you I would give you a nice snack.*

Allow the children to express their displeasure.

Now put out the real snacks. Ask them: *Do you like this snack more?*

Share the tasty food and allow the children to eat. While doing so, ask them the following:

✘   *How did you feel when I offered you sand, rocks, insects and dirty water as a snack?*

✘   *Why were they disappointing or disliked? (Because you had promised them a tasty snack, but offered them something yucky.)*

✘   *Is it important to do what we promise?*

✘   *How do you feel when someone does what he promised you?*

✘   *How do you feel when someone doesn't do what he promised you?*

Comment: *Someone made an important promise to Caleb, the man of our Bible story today. Let's see if that person fulfilled his promise.*

BIBLE STORY

Go ahead

Read Joshua 14:6-15. *After the Israelites defeated the city of Jericho, they continued into the land that God had promised them. Joshua led the people in many battles against the Canaanites. God helped them overcome their enemies and take the land for themselves.*

Finally, after many battles, the Israelites conquered most of Canaan. Now it was time to divide the land among the tribes of the people of Israel. God had told Moses how to do it. Now Joshua had that job.

One day, Caleb came to Joshua and said, "Joshua, do you remember when, many years ago, you and I were part of the 12 spies that Moses sent to explore the new land?"

"I remember it very well," Joshua replied.

"Well," Caleb continued, "I was 40 years old at the time. When I returned from that trip I told the people that we should obey God and enter the land."

"Yes," Joshua said, "and I agreed with everything you said. You told Moses that the land was good, and that God would help us overcome the people who lived there. You begged us to trust in God and obey Him."

"That's right," said Caleb. "But do you remember what happened next? The other spies gave such a bad report that the people were afraid to follow God."

"Yes, I remember it very well," said Joshua. "That was the reason why we lost 40 long years in the desert!"

Caleb continued, "But I obeyed God with all my heart. Therefore, God spoke to Moses and he made a promise to me. He promised me that I wouldn't die in the desert. He said that when the new land was ours, I would receive part of the land that I walked on, as my property."

"It's true," Joshua agreed thoughtfully.

"The Lord has kept the promise that he made to me 45 years ago when we were wandering in the desert," Caleb said. "Now I'm 85 years old. But I feel stronger than ever. And I'm ready to fight for the land that God promised to give me. If you give me this mountain that God promised me, I will go and conquer the people who live there. And God will help me!"

Joshua replied, "I'm happy to give you the city of Hebron, which is part of the land promised by God. You have been faithful to obey Him. And now I give you the blessing of God."

Caleb didn't waste time. He went to Hebron and defeated the enemies that dwelt in that place. From then on, Hebron belonged to Caleb and his family. God fulfilled the promise he had made to Caleb because he had trusted and faithfully obeyed the Lord.

After the story, emphasize how long Caleb had waited for God to keep his promise.

Tell them: *45 years have passed since God made the promise to Caleb that he would give him the land. How old are you?* Write the children's answers on the board.

Ask them: *How old will you be in 45 years?* Show the children how to use their fingers to add 6 or 7 (their age) to the number 45. Put those numbers on the board.

Ask them: *Does that amount of years seem like a lot to you?* (It's probably difficult for children to imagine such an amount.) Make some comparisons such as: Your grandparents must be (51, 52, 53) years old.

Tell them: *Caleb had to wait a long time to receive what God had promised he would give him. But God did it. God always keeps his promises to those who boldly trust him and obey him.*

ACTIVITIES

Do these activities to help students connect biblical truth with their lives.

The fulfilled promise

Give your students the activity sheet from the student book, lesson 26, so they can read it together with the teacher. It's an appropriate activity to review the biblical story. You can add questions related to it.

Spin spin

Give the children the second activity sheet from the student book. Help them assemble the wheel to play "Round and Round". Ask the children to follow the instructions for assembling the wheel. They will need scissors, cardboard, glue, paper clip hooks and two-legged paper fastener. Then, allow them to turn the clip so that the wheel starts spinning, and they can read the word that comes up when it stops. Instruct them to look for the term or place where the word is in the phrase. Let them write the word in the right place or color it. The complete sentence is: "God keeps his promises to those who trust in him and obey him." Have the children read the prayer.

Tell them: *Caleb trusted God and obeyed him. That's why God fulfilled the promise he had made to him. Sometimes the Lord chooses other people to work for him, to help him fulfill his promises. Who helped God fulfill the promise he had made to Caleb?* (Joshua)

Magnet with promise

Before class, gather magnets with advertisements from your refrigerator, or ask for magnets from friends or nearby businesses. If you don't have enough to give one to each child, use tape to hold the papers.

In class, give each child a magnet, a blank sheet of paper, colors, paints, markers, stickers, etc. Then have them write on the page the following sentence: "God keeps his promises." Tell them they can decorate the paper, cut out the edges, and then glue it to the printed side of the magnet, so they can attach it to the refrigerator in their home.

Tell them: *Today we learned that God fulfilled the promise he made to Caleb. God always keeps His promises. Sometimes we have to wait a while, but we can trust that God will do what he promised. Keep this magnet so that you can remember that the Lord always keeps his promises.*

Memorization

Biblical text career

For this last unit class, children should know the memory verse. Today they can practice a noisy competition.

Divide the children into two groups. It's better if they play in a yard so they can shout without interrupting other classes.

You will stand some distance from the two groups. The first person of each group will run to where you are. When they arrive, they will turn and look towards their group; then they will scream the first word of the verse. If someone doesn't know the word, they must return to the end of their group row. Then the next child from the group will run and they will say the next word of the verse, and so forth. The team that finishes first without error will shout the complete verse with the biblical reference, and will be the winner. You should know who is the last child in each group.

If you wish, and there is time, ask everyone to recite the full verse. Those who didn't stick their candy to their candy jar, can do it this time.

To end

If there is still time, review all the lessons in the unit with simple questions that you prepare in advance. Remind them about the leaders who led Israel to the promised land. How they trusted God and how he never abandoned them.

Finally, this is a good time to pray for the children. Ask the Lord to make everyone brave like Caleb, who was a man who knew how to fight against enemies, but he also knew how to wait for God to fulfill his promises.

Invite your children to the next series of lessons so they can learn the exciting lessons about Jesus.

Year 3
Introduction – Unit VII
We Imitate Jesus

Biblical References: Luke 9:51-56; 12:13-21; Mark 12:38-44; John 4:1-42.

Unit Memory Verse: *Whoever has my commands and keeps them is the one who loves me* (John 14:21a).

Unit Objectives

This unit will help the elementary students to:

- ✗ Learn, through the life of Jesus, to imitate his values.
- ✗ Always choose the path of peace and nonviolence.
- ✗ Know that they are valuable, not because of what they have, but because of who they are.
- ✗ Know that although they are children, they need the Savior.

Unit Lessons

Lesson 27: **Find Peace**

Lesson 28: **Find Love**

Lesson 29: **Find God**

Lesson 30: **Find Life**

Why Elementary Students need the teaching of this unit:

In a time where models worthy of imitation are lacking, this unit has a fundamental importance.

Nothing is more effective for a child who is attracted to harmful examples of television, than to show him the model par excellence: Jesus.

In this four-lesson unit, you will have the opportunity to teach them such important values as peace, love, God's place in their lives and the importance of having the Lord in their hearts.

Elementary-aged children are at an age where they are strongly marked by the values of their schoolmates. We know perfectly well the attitudes and ways of life of today's children who come from non-Christian homes. Hence the importance of these lessons in helping the children imitate Jesus instead of television heroes or characters.

Find Peace

Biblical References: Luke 9:51-56

Lesson Objective: To help the students understand that they should live in peace with others, even those whom they think are their enemies.

Memory Verse: *Whoever has my commands and keeps them is the one who loves me* (John 14:21a).

PREPARE YOURSELF TO TEACH!

As adults, we tend to remember our childhood with nostalgia, forgetting the painful experiences and remembering the good times.

It's through this lens that we imagine our childhood as a happy time, without doubts, worries, or violence. And it's true that most of it was a time without worry, although violence existed and at times fear invaded the lives of many children.

The children whom you teach are aware of the violence that surrounds them. They see it on television, they listen to it on the radio, it appears on the computer, and they hear adults' conversations.

When tragedy strikes, not only adults ask themselves, "Why?" Or "How?"

With this lesson the children will begin to understand that violence wasn't part of God's plan for his children. They will learn from the teachings of Jesus, that God has other goals for his people. He expects his followers to choose peace.

In this story, Jesus chose to move away from the Samaritans rather than confront them. This is so that the children, following his example, will move away from those who seek to fight in the playground, or who say mean jokes, or the adult who ridicules them. Peace is the best alternative to violence; and it's now, when children are small, that we have the opportunity to teach them to respond to violent situations with peace.

BIBLICAL COMMENTARY

The fire threats from heaven remind Bible readers of the encounter between King Ahaziah and the prophet Elijah in 2 Kings, chapter 1. The two stories have important similarities and differences.

The two narratives involve messengers. Jesus sent his messengers to a Samaritan city to make reservations for one night. King Ahaziah sent a messenger to investigate if the false god Baal-Zebub would heal his wounds. God wasn't at all happy with the king's action and gave the prophet a message for him.

Rejection plays an important role in both stories. God felt the rejection of Ahaziah when he consulted a false god, and instructed Elijah to tell the king's messengers that he was the king in Israel and that Ahaziah wouldn't survive his wounds. The messengers of Jesus couldn't find where to stay in the village because the Samaritans hated and rejected the Jews.

The fire of discord was about to break out. Three times King Ahaziah sent his captains with 50 soldiers to try to bring Elijah from where he was and thus kill him. Two of the meetings ended with Elijah asking for fire from heaven, which burned the soldiers, proving that the prophet was indeed the man of God.

The disciples, hearing that they weren't welcome in the city, recalled the experience of Elijah. And they asked, "Lord, do you want us to command fire to come down from heaven ... and consume them?" (Luke 9:54).

Here is the point where the two stories don't match. Jesus scolded his disciples. I can almost hear him say, "Definitely not!" And they continued on their way to another city where they were received.

This story raises an important question: How do we handle rejection when it comes, especially as a reaction to our Christian beliefs? Do we ask God for revenge towards those who do it? There are many psalms we're familiar with where the psalmist does exactly that. Or do we choose the way of Jesus? The way of Jesus wasn't to resist those who reject us (Matthew 5:39), not to take revenge, but to pray for our enemies (5:44), to forgive them the way we want to be forgiven (6:14-15). Of course, Jesus' way is the only way we expect Christians to react. This is how we should live! That is the way we want our students to live.

In this era where violence and revenge are proclaimed, how can we focus on Jesus' non-violent solution in our teachings?

LESSON DEVELOPMENT

Prepare in advance the teaching materials you will use for this lesson and try to have your classroom ready before your students arrive. Remember to welcome visitors and collect their info to contact them during the week.

This activity is to catch the attention of the children and prepare them to learn the truth of this lesson.

Important words

"Followers of Jesus" and "Eternal Life"

You will need: cardboard, scissors and markers. Before class, draw hearts and footprints on cardboard or posterboard to distribute to each child (one for each). The hearts and the footprints can be drawn on 12 cm x 12 cm squares. The children will cut them out in class.

"Followers of Jesus": These are the people who believe that Jesus is the Son of God. A follower of Jesus loves him and obeys him.

"Eternal life": It is to live forever. Those who accept Jesus as their Savior, when they die on earth, will go to live in heaven with him.

Write the words and their meaning on the board. Then tell the children to write the important word on one side of the heart, and the definition on the other side. Also do the same with the footprint and the other important word and definition.

Children will learn these words and their meanings, and then they can quietly tell it to one another in their ears as if it were a secret. Those one who say it correctly will have a prize at the end of the 4 lessons of unit VII. (It can be a pencil, a book with bible verses, stickers, a fruit, etc.)

At the end of the class, children should leave their hearts and footprints in a box or bag to use again in the next class.

Mural of fire

This is another easy lesson to illustrate. You need glue, colors, markers, paintings, magazine clippings of tall buildings, houses and a city; and the children will draw trees, plants and people. In the middle of the buildings and the city, they can paint flames of fire, to illustrate a burning city that represents what Samaria would look like if fire had fallen from heaven as the disciples requested. At the bottom of the mural, write the memory verse: "*Whoever has my commands and keeps them is the one who loves me*" (John 14:21a).

With a mural like that, you can illustrate the lesson very well and make it vivid for your students.

BIBLE STORY

Friendly or unfriendly?

Jesus spent a lot of time teaching people about God's love. He told them how he wanted them to live. He also instructed them on how they should treat others. Jesus helped people and healed them.

The Lord was teaching in Galilee, but one day he had to go to Jerusalem to tell people that God loved them. Jesus knew that interesting things would happen in Jerusalem. One was that his death on the cross was approaching. He knew that the time of his departure to heaven was approaching. And he told his followers, "It's time for me to go to Jerusalem."

So everyone began to prepare what they would need for the trip. One of the disciples asked Jesus which way they would go.

"The fastest way is to cross through Samaria," Jesus answered. "It will take us three days if we go that way."

"But Jesus," said another disciple, "the Samaritans hate the Jews. If we go through Samaria we will have problems."

"We'll go that way," said the Lord. "Samaritans and Jews were both created by God. He loves everyone equally. When we are near the city, someone can go ahead to talk to people. They can tell them that we will not hurt anyone, that we are people of peace."

As they walked towards Jerusalem, Jesus taught them. He wanted his disciples to understand that God wanted them to show love for one another, even for those who are evil or simply indifferent.

They walked until sunset. It was time for them to stop and eat and rest.

"There's a town there," Jesus pointed out with his finger. "Please go and ask if we can spend the night there and if there is food."

Some of the disciples went to the village. A man shouted at them, "You aren't from here; you are Jews. We hate Jews!"

"Look, we're going to Jerusalem," said one of Jesus' followers. "Our group is beyond the entrance to the village. We need a place to stay tonight. Can we stay here?"

"We already know where you are going!" said another Samaritan, "and that's what makes us so angry. You believe that we aren't good enough to go to Jerusalem. Where we worship God isn't good enough for the Jews!"

The Jews thought that the Samaritans were wrong because they offered sacrifices to God on a mountain in Samaria. The Jews thought that the only correct place to offer sacrifice was in the temple of Jerusalem.

The disciples left the angry men and the town. They returned and told Jesus what had happened.

"We can't stay!" they said. "They don't want to have anything to do with Jews!"

James and John heard what had happened.

"Who do those arrogant Samaritans think they are?" they shouted. James and John were known as the sons of thunder because they got angry easily.

"Don't those silly Samaritans know who you are?" they asked Jesus.

"You are more powerful than the prophet Elijah! I know what we will do. Call down fire from heaven! Let the whole town burn; that will give them a good lesson!"

Jesus sighed and shook his head. These two disciples did have a lot to learn about God's love.

"You can't burn people and their homes simply because they are bad," Jesus clarified. "That's wrong. I need people who understand about God's love! Evil actions will not help people understand God's love for them!"

"But what should we do?" asked James and John.

"We'll go to another place, to another city," the Master replied.

That day, Jesus taught an important lesson to the sons of thunder. They learned that God wants his people to live in peace with their neighbors, to show their love, even when others aren't kind.

We can learn from Jesus. We can choose peace and decide to turn away when others want to fight or argue with us.

ACTIVITIES

Friendly or not friendly? Speechless

You will need for each child: picture of praying hands and a picture of a flame of fire, popsicle or ice cream stick about 15 cm, scissors, colored pencils, glue or tape.

Ask them to cut out the flames of fire and the hands that you will have drawn or photocopied in advance. Then they can color them. Then glue or tape the sticks to their pictures.

When you ask the questions, the children will raise their prayer hands or flame depending on what they think the solution is for that situation. Fire for unfriendly, prayer hands for friendly. No one should say a word. Tell them:

1. Jesus listened to his Father, God. Friendly or not friendly?

2. Jesus obeyed God and went to Jerusalem. Friendly or not friendly?

3. Jesus and his followers spoke of the love of God. Friendly or not friendly?

4. Jesus sent some of his followers to Samaria. Friendly or not friendly?

5. The Samaritans hated the Jews. Friendly or not friendly?

6. The Samaritans didn't want to host Jesus and his friends. Friendly or not friendly?

7. Jesus and his friends went to another city. Friendly or not friendly?

8. The disciples wanted fire to fall from heaven onto Samaria. Friendly or not friendly?

9. Jesus wants all people to love each other and not fight each other. Friendly or not friendly?

Memorization

Candy and biblical candies!

Bring a candy for each child, on which they can paste or hang the bible memory verse.

"Whoever has my commands and keeps them is the one who loves me" (John 14:21a).

Have the children take the candy home and practice the verse. They can tell their mom, their dad or a sibling. When they know it by heart ,they can eat the candy. Say: *In the next class you will tell me the verse in secret. At the end of Unit VII if you can say it, you can paste the candy with the verse onto your candy jar.*

To end

Ask the children to cut out, color and complete lesson 27 of the student book. Then pray for them to be bearers of peace among their friends, in their family, and in any place where there are difficult situations.

Ask the Lord to keep them from evil. Encourage them to return to the next class.

 Notes:

Find Love

Biblical References: Mark 12:38-44

Lesson Objective: That the students, as followers of Jesus, can give what they have because of their love of God and not for other people to see them.

Memory Verse: *Whoever has my commands and keeps them is the one who loves me* (John 14:21a).

PREPARE YOURSELF TO TEACH!

Children live in a world that teaches them to try to be the best in everything. As they grow, they learn that success is measured by what others think of them and by the amount of money and possessions they have in life.

This lesson will give you the opportunity to show them that there is a different and better way: the way God wants it to be. They need to know that God's opinion is what really counts. And that He likes it when they show love to him and others.

They should know that God doesn't care how much money they have or how much they have earned. God cares about how their hearts and relationships are with him and with others.

Help your students discover ways to demonstrate their love for God. Then they can make a promise to love and honor the Lord above all things.

BIBLICAL COMMENTARY

How do you feel when you are near a person who thinks they are very important? Do you know what I mean? I'm talking about those people in smart clothes who say, "look at me!"

And what about that other one who makes you notice the expensive watch they're wearing? Or the one who drives a late model car and lives in a mansion?

I know how you feel: very uncomfortable! Personally I feel even embarrassed when I'm around people who show off their fortune.

The above reminds me of a successful businessman who wanted to show off his wealth to his colleagues. So he went and bought a new car, which he paid for ... in cash.

The next morning he drove his car to work. He parked in front of his office. The moment he opened the door, a truck hit him on his side, tearing off the car door and amputating the owner's arm.

The police arrived immediately and the injured man began to shout, "Find the driver of the truck! He ruined my new car and embarrassed me in front of my colleagues! This is terrible!"

The police officer replied, "Sir, we'll try to find the other driver! But first, we need to assist you! Don't you realize that with the impact you lost your arm?"

The rich man looked at his bloody body and exclaimed, "Oh no! Where is my expensive watch?"

That was a man with messed up priorities!

On the contrary, there are many people who help and give their money and time for others to be happy. There are people who invest in schools, churches, hospitals, or scientific research so that other people can have improved health or are healed of previously incurable diseases. They are modern examples, as was the widow whom Jesus named. She gave everything she had; she didn't give a percentage, nor what she had left over; she gave everything. The widow gave all her coins and was in complete dependence upon divine care. She gave because she loved her God. She wasn't the kind of person who expected to be seen and admired for what she owned or had done.

Paul wrote: "Remember this: Whoever sows sparingly will also reap sparingly, and whoever sows generously will also reap generously. Each of you should give what you have decided in your heart to give, not reluctantly or under compulsion, for God loves a cheerful giver."(2 Cor. 9:6-7).

Giving with the heart is the result of the love we feel for God and for our neighbor.

LESSON DEVELOPMENT

Prepare in advance the teaching materials you will use for this lesson and try to have your classroom ready before your students arrive.

Remember to welcome visitors and collect their info to contact them during the week

Let's collect the offering

Ask the children if they know why offerings are collected in the church, and what they are used for. Allow them to give their opinions. Clarify the wrong ideas, like that the offerings are all for the pastor. Explain that some offerings are for missions, for the Word of God to be preached in other countries, for expenses for the church building, for pastoral salary, etc. Then tell the children that they will collect the offering. One child can do it and another pray a prayer of gratitude.

Then ask them how they felt when they gave an offering. Ask: *Did anyone want your classmates to see what you gave. If so, why did you want to be seen?* This will be a good practical lesson to do the introduction to today's lesson.

A gift of love puzzle

Ask the children to cut out the circles from the activity sheet from the student book, lesson 28. Then stick them on cardboard or posterboard. Tell them to cut out the figures and color them. On the other side of the wheel, instruct them to draw a way in which they can show their love to God. Provide a bag or envelope to take the pieces home.

BIBLE STORY

A great gift of love

"They believe that they dress very well with their expensive clothes," Jesus said. "They believe that it's very good to make everyone else look at them. They like to draw attention when they sit at the front during times of worship. They also wait and look for the best places at parties. They try to show that they love God and that they obey Him, but the truth is different. They only show love for themselves. Their prayers out loud are only to be heard by others, but not for God to hear them."

"That does make sense to me," said a woman. "If I pray to God and hurt others, that isn't showing them that I love them."

Then Jesus sat down. Nearby, he could see the container for the offerings. He looked around, and saw that people were passing by and putting in their offerings.

A rich man, who seemed very important, came to give his offering. He made sure that people noticed him. He put in a large quantity of coins and looked around with great pride. He wanted people to see how important and generous he was.

Jesus continued to observe other rich people who did the same putting on a great show.

They felt very proud. No doubt, none of them thought of God.

Then, Jesus saw a very poor widow who approached silently. The woman didn't look at anyone. She walked with his head bowed down. She looked ragged, with patched and torn clothes. Her husband had died. All she had were only two coins! Jesus smiled when he saw her approach and give God everything she had.

"Look," Jesus said to the people who were with him. "Look at that quiet woman."

"But she had almost nothing to give to God," said the apostles.

But Jesus answered them, "I want you to remember this important truth: that poor woman gave God much more than all those rich people gave, because she gave all she had. They gave from their excess, from what they had left over, but this poor woman put in everything she had to live on."

God doesn't want us to give for other people to think we are good. He wants us to give everything we can because we love him, not because it makes us feel important.

In the end, the followers of Jesus understood what he was teaching them. Now they understood that God is interested in us loving him and loving our neighbor, and not in being seen. This was an important lesson at the temple.

Today we can learn something very special. We must give the best we have because we love God, not because we want others to see us and think we are good and important.

This is a good opportunity to pass the offering if you didn't earlier. You can say, "Jesus taught very important things. Today's Bible story teaches us that the important thing isn't how much we give to God; what is important to him is why we give it. He wants us to give our best because we love him."

ACTIVITIES

Practical task: "Gifts of love"

One or two weeks before class: Ask your students to use their own money to buy ¼ kilo, ½ kilo or 1 kilo of any non-perishable food to place in 1 or 2 bags or boxes to give to others. Prepare the boxes (they shouldn't be very large). You can cover them with wrapping paper and put a large label that says: "Our gift of love."

Ask the pastor or the parents of the children if there is a needy family to whom your class can give the boxes.

Clarify that those who can't bring a gift shouldn't feel bad. Those who can bring more than 1 kilo don't have to feel proud (or important). Emphasize that we will bring those gifts because we love God and the people.

Children can make two large cards of 30 cm. x 25 cm. Each one that says: "Our gift of love for you, God bless you! From: the Elementary Sunday School class." Ask them to decorate the cards with stickers and colors.

Everyone, even the teacher, can sign the cards. The gifts can be sent, or the teacher and 2 or 3 students can take them personally to the family in need.

Lost and found coins!

Hide 2 coins of little value in the classroom. Ask the children to find them. The first two who find them can keep the coins and take them home to give to two friends. Then tell them to tell their friends about today's Bible story.

Memorization

Copy or draw the front of different coins of your country's money. Make them on cardboard or posterboard of about 10 cm. diameter in size Paint them gold, silver or copper. On the back of the coins, write one of the words of the memory verse. Hide them all over the room. Before beginning the search for them, write the verse on the board and practice it several times. Ask the students to look for the 14 coins, including the biblical reference: "*Whoever has my commands and keeps them is the one who loves me*" (John 14:21a). When the children find the coins, they should run and place them on the table in the right order to form the memory verse. Those who didn't find any coins can help to arrange the words on the table. Save the coins for memorization and review in the next class.

To end

Ask the children how they felt about giving their love gifts and using their own money to buy the food products.

Place the group in a circle. Ask them to start praying for their partner on their left. Everyone prays for the next child. When it comes to the teacher, he/she will pray for the little one on their left and for the whole class, so that they will be loving children who do the Word of God, eager to love the Lord and their neighbor without being seen by others. Thank God for the love the children showed when they gave their savings and brought food for people in need.

Lesson 29

Find God

Biblical References: Luke 12:13-21

Lesson Objective: That the students know that it's bad to be greedy and selfish, and that God can help them love Him more than earthly things.

Memory Verse: *Whoever has my commands and keeps them is the one who loves me* (John 14:21a).

PREPARE YOURSELF TO TEACH!

Television and other advertising sources are designed so that we want to spend more. Its goal is to make us believe that the products we see, hear and read about are necessary for us to be happy.

Advertising isn't only directed at adults. Have you seen children's programs on television? Do you hear the types of advertising on the radio? There's no doubt that they are made to attract children, because advertisers know that many children have money to spend, or that they can ask their parents.

Jesus teaches us a different way of looking at what we want. He teaches us that possessions and riches don't lead to happiness; that true happiness is found through a deep relationship with God. Children today need to hear that the Lord has much more for them than material possessions and riches. He has eternal life in mind, and they have to make a decision. Children can choose God first, no matter what others do or say.

BIBLICAL COMMENTARY

It's difficult to pretend that children who grow up in high society understand the meaning of the parable of the rich and the poor. On the contrary, it will be easier for children who are in contact with a wide variety of needs to understand the this story. Anyway, the point

that Jesus emphasizes in these verses is crucial to living in the way that pleases God. Our society becomes crazy to consume. In this particular case, Jesus calls attention to the rich fool who savors and depends on his fortune. This is a good time to guide your students to have Christian attitudes towards other people and toward possessions. Here we present five perspectives that can help you present this lesson.

Toys and things. There isn't anything wrong with having the right tools to do a job. Nor is it bad to have fun, which allows us to distract ourselves from our tasks. But if we start to value ourselves as people according to the amount of toys or material things we have, we will pay a very high price. Toys and things will occupy our time and attention. If they are the most important things to us, that will lead us to neglect our spiritual life, and the problems will begin to interfere with both our inner life and our relationship with others.

Me and always me! The rich fool in Jesus' story made the mistake of thinking that his riches were all he needed to do well in life. He believed that he had produced all the harvests by himself, completely forgetting that his possessions were a gift from God to him. He became the center of his own world. The same can happen to us if we constantly feel the need to be "first ...me and always me".

More ... I want more! There is something strange about this aspect of accumulating more and more. For some reason, "more" is never enough. Most people who get involved in materialism are never satisfied. They believe that "one more thing" will make them happy. They don't realize that having "more and more" is a vicious circle that never ends.

Fun and more fun! Some mistakenly believe that the purpose of life is pleasure. Pain and problems are seen as interruptions in achieving happiness. Things often become more complicate, and lead the person further and further away from God, when pleasure is attached to possessions. The thought is: "the more toys I have, the more fun I will have". But the joy doesn't last long.

Where is God? Concentrating on himself and his riches, the rich fool turned into a perfect atheist. He eliminated God from his life. That same danger exists for us today and always. If our purpose is to gain possessions and have pleasure, we will be trying to satisfy our egoistic desires. The basic question on which our destiny depends is: will we live only for ourselves, or will we choose God and his ways?

This week as you inspire your students, pray that they will see and understand the truth that God wants to teach them.

LESSON DEVELOPMENT

Receive your students with affection and ensure that the classroom is clean and tidy when they arrive. Before starting today's topic, briefly review the two previous lessons. Ask the children how they did during the week and if they have prayer requests.

Choose an activity that helps the children understand the lesson.

Let's search the Bible!

Each classroom should have a number of Bibles for the children who can't bring their own.

Ask them to sit in a circle. You will stand, outside the circle to start the game / activity. All children will have their Bibles closed. Begin to walk around them. At one point, stop and say the unit's scripture: John 14:21. Tell them not to open their Bible until you say: now! When you say: now!, the first child to find the verse will stand up and read it aloud. Then you continue walking. All children will have their Bibles closed. Now you say the reference from today's story: Luke 12:13-21. Then say: now!

The first child who finds it will read the Bible story or the most important verse, such as Luke 12:15. Repeat the game while there is time or interest.

This activity will help the children in the use of the Bible. If there are new children or those who don't know how to use it, practice for a few minutes before the activity.

Important words

"Followers of Jesus" and "Eternal Life"

You already have the hearts and footprints for this activity, made in lesson 27.

"Followers of Jesus": These are the people who believe that Jesus is the Son of God. A follower of Jesus loves him and obeys him.

"Eternal life": It is to live forever. Those who accept Jesus as their Savior, when they die on earth, will go to live in heaven with him.

Write the words and their meaning on the board and ask the children who don't have the hearts and the footprints to copy what you wrote.

Children will learn these words and their meanings and then they can tell it to each other in their ears as if it were a secret. The one who says it correctly will have a prize at the end of the 4 lessons of unit VII (it can be a pencil, a small book with biblical portions, a page with figures or stickers).

At the end, children should leave the hearts and fingerprints in a box or bag to do the same in another next class.

BIBLE STORY

The man who wanted more and more

Many people gathered next to Jesus.

"Listen to what he says," someone suggested.

"It seems he knows God," said another.

"He's a great teacher," clarified a woman who was among the crowd listening to what Jesus taught.

But there was one man among them who didn't have a happy face. "Maybe I can get Jesus to talk to my brother so that he will share the inheritance with me," he thought. He was the youngest brother. The law said that his older brother would receive the inheritance. The young man had some money but it wasn't enough. He wanted more! "It's not fair!" he told himself. "Master," the young man called to Jesus. "Tell my older brother to give me the inheritance money," he continued. "It's not fair that he should have more than me. It's me who should have more."

"Young man," Jesus replied. "I'm not a judge. It's not for me to make your brother give you the money."

The young man looked at him and frowned. This situation wasn't working out as he had hoped. His brother wouldn't listen to him. But he would give him more money if Jesus interceded for him.

Jesus looked at the young man. He knew he wasn't happy with his answer. Then he looked at the crowd. "This is an excellent time to teach them a parable," Jesus would have thought.

"Let me tell you a story," continued the Master.

Jesus knew that the young man, and others, needed to hear the story.

"This is the special story of a rich man. The rich man was a farmer. He had grown a lot of grain in his fields. There was a year in which his grain production was abundant and of very good quality. The harvest was so great that the man had nowhere to put it all."

"What will I do now?" the farmer asked himself. "I don't have enough granaries to store the harvest."

(Pause the story to ask the following questions:

- *Who made the grain seeds grow?*
- *What must the farmer say to God for having harvested so much healthy grain? (Thank you Lord.)*
- *What do you think the farmer should have done with all the grain he harvested? (Help the needy who had no food.)*
- *What do you think the farmer did with the grain he couldn't store? (The answers will be different.)*

Let's see what the Bible tells us about the farmer.

In the farmer's village there were many people who didn't have enough food. But the farmer didn't care. He started making other plans.

"This is what I will do," he said. "I will destroy my small granaries and build bigger ones and I will keep the whole harvest for myself."

"The farmer was very happy with his idea," Jesus continued. "The very foolish man destroyed his small granaries and built bigger ones and sat down and thought: 'What a beautiful life I have! I'm so strong and healthy! My life will be very easy for many years. I will have a lot of food! The truth is that I did a good job! Because of my ability. I'm the most important!'"

"God heard the man," Jesus continued with his story.

"You are a fool," said God. "You forgot about me. You forgot to love me. You forgot that everything you have comes from me. You will die this very night, and do you think that your barns and crops will come to your aid?"

The crowd was shaking their heads.

Jesus then said, "That night the fool died. He couldn't take his grains with him. He couldn't use his crops. Before dying, the farmer learned a great lesson. He learned that he should put God first, that he should have trusted him to take care of him, that he should have thanked the Lord for all the good things he gave him. And that he should have used what he had to help others in need.

Jesus wanted the people around him to learn and remember that they should love God more than anything in this world. All of us can learn that lesson. We can decide to put the Creator first. We can decide to love God more than money, or material things, or even people.

ACTIVITIES

Mural: "I can live like Jesus"

Prepare a large poster for the children to work on that will stay hanging in the classroom for several weeks.

In the center write in wide letters that can be filled in and decorated: "I can live like Jesus." Ask the children to bring some grains / seeds from home: corn, rice, beans, etc. During the class, they will paste the different grains that they brought inside the letters. It will be very nice if they are grains of different colors.

Bring figures or photos of people doing a good deed or sharing / serving in some way. They can also be drawn / painted by the children. Around the words filled with seeds, they can paste and then comment on the figures / photos. Guide them with questions about the subject of the lesson.

"Give God first place." Decoration

Give students the activity sheet from the student book, lesson 29. Ask them to draw a picture of themselves in the circle or to put their name on it. While drawing, ask them as a review: *How can you put God first?* (Talking to him, learning from him and his Word, following Jesus in obedience, showing his love through words and deeds.) Ask the children to connect the dots to draw the figure on the back of the page. Ask them: *Who didn't put God first? What important thing did you learn today?*

Help them assemble the decoration by following the instructions on the same page. Ask them to take it home and tell someone today's story.

Say: *You can decide to live as Jesus teaches, putting God first. What is most important, God or money? A video or God? Who is more important, their parents or God? God is more important than any person or thing. He gives us good things. He gives us our parents to love us and we love them. But he is the only God. We must love him more than anything else.*

Memorization

Use the coins from the previous class to emphasize the Bible verse. Hide the coins throughout the room. Before beginning the search, write the verse on the board and practice it several times. Then ask the students to look for the 14 coins, including the biblical quotation. 1. Whoever, 2. has, 3. my, 4. commands, 5. and, 6. keeps, 7. them, 8. is, 9. the, 10. one, 11. who, 12. loves, 13. me, 14. (John 14:21a).

When the children find the coins, they should run to place them on the table in the right order to form the memory verse. Children who didn't find anything can help put the verse on the table.

To end

Ask each child to pray, repeating these words:

"Jesus, I want you to help me so that you have the first place in my life. I don't want anything like T.V., sports, my friends, or anything else to be in your first place."

Pray for your students to know how to always put God in first place.

Find Life

Biblical References: John 4:1-42

Lesson Objective: That the students understand that salvation is for everyone who believes in Jesus and receives Him as their Savior.

Memory Verse: *Whoever has my commands and keeps them is the one who loves me* (John 14:21a).

PREPARE YOURSELF TO TEACH!

Recently someone asked me, "Don't you think that people love better those with whom they feel comfortable?"

This made me think and observe the people that are around me in the church I attend. I noticed a great resemblance between all of them, but I also noticed several differences.

After thinking about that question, I realized that I didn't agree. I don't believe that God has called us to form select groups and to distance ourselves from those people who are different from us.

In fact, I believe that this bible story teaches us to do the opposite. Jesus teaches us to look beyond those with whom we feel comfortable. Jesus wants us to offer the gift of salvation to all who need to know Him. Children are often extroverted when it comes to talking about Jesus and their faith. They love Him and want others to know Him.

Encourage your students to think beyond their family and friends in the church. Help them think of people who need the Lord.

Then, start praying with your students for those people. As a teacher, you can help deepen their relationship with God in two ways. First, give them the opportunity to know Jesus as their personal Savior. Second, help them by offering them the tools they need to tell others about God's gift: eternal life.

BIBLICAL COMMENTARY

This question is for you: Who can be a Christian? At first, this may seem like a simple question with a simple answer. You will say: Everyone, of course.

Then let me ask you something else: Which person will find it more difficult to become a Christian? Someone with impediments or barriers, whether real or imagined, will have difficulty accepting the Lord.

In his conversation at the well, Jesus broke down two barriers that his society had raised. First, he dissolved the differences between those who were "chosen" and those who were "rejected." The Jews, "the chosen race," rejected the Samaritans. The Scriptures say: "For Jews do not associate with Samaritans" (John 4:9). Jesus paid no attention to that belief. He hadn't only associated with Samaritans, but used them as an example worthy of imitation by the Jews.

In the second place, Jesus broke a taboo by talking to a woman. It wasn't acceptable for Jews, and Jesus was a Jew, to talk to an good Samaritan woman (although the Jews doubted there was such a thing), but it was even worse for him to talk with the woman he talked with. She was even despised by her own society because of her marital problems.

In the eyes of Jewish culture, this woman was totally unacceptable. But still, Jesus saw her as someone who was worthy to hear the Good News he had for her. He discussed every objection the woman made to him, and patiently broke down each of the barriers that she had about the Messiah. Finally, she believed, and many more believed in the Lord because of her testimony about Jesus.

This is a story with a happy ending, although at first, the walls had to be demolished. This then brings us to another question: Who isn't able to receive salvation today?

Before you answer "nobody" and dismiss the idea, think about the barriers that people must face these days.

For some, their race is a barrier, either to speak or hear the Gospel. Skin color and cultural differences can be hindrances to evangelism.

In the pluralistic cultures of today, almost every human being has different opinions. On many occasions the diversity of ideas is a barricade for evangelism.

Some think and act as if those who belong to a political party different from theirs are not true Christians. Closed minds are real barriers.

People of different religions have trouble understanding each other. If we don't know what Muslims, Hindus or Jews believe, how can we preach to them the Gospel of Jesus?

And what about the circumstances of life? Do we tend to despair because some are too poor, or too addicted, or too hopeless to be Christians? If so, we must tear down those walls.

John 3:16 doesn't recognize the barriers that humans raise. There is no exclusion in "everyone". Everyone, regardless of their circumstances, is worthy to hear the Gospel, and have the opportunity to believe.

LESSON DEVELOPMENT

Receive your students with affection and ensure that the classroom is clean and tidy when they arrive. Before starting today's topic, review briefly the three previous lessons and ask your students to talk about how they have been faithful to God during this month that's about to end.

101

Fresh water

If possible, before the class have some activity for the children to run or jump; that way they will be thirsty.

In the class you will need: jars with cold water and glasses. Place the jar with cold water on the table. Hide the glasses.

Ask the children if they want a drink of water. Point to the jar. Invite those who are thirsty to drink. The children will discover that there are no glasses. Ask: *What do you need to drink?*

Bring the glasses and serve the water to the children. Ask: *When is it good to have water nearby?* (When you are very thirsty or hot.) *How does one feel when he is very thirsty and has no water to drink? Today's story tells us about a time when Jesus sat by a well of water. But he didn't have a container to get the water from the well. Let's see what happened and who gave him water.*

Important words

"Followers of Jesus", "Eternal Life" and "Living Water"

You will need more footprints and hearts, made on construction paper, for each child (see instructions in lesson 27). Write the words "followers of Jesus" and "eternal life" along with their meanings on the board so that the children can copy them. Make enough hearts and footprints for those who lost theirs and for new children and for the new words. Today they will take the cards home. Hand out the hearts and footprints. Allow time for new ones or those who lost their cards to copy what the board says.

"Followers of Jesus": These are the people who believe that Jesus is the Son of God. A follower of Jesus loves him and obeys him.

"Eternal life": It is to live forever. Those who accept Jesus as their Savior, when they die on earth, will go to live in heaven with him."

"Living water": it's the spiritual water that gives eternal life. The physical water that we drink quenches our thirst, but it's fleeting. The water of God is spiritual and eternal.

Let's see what today's story says about Jesus and the woman at the well.

Tell the children to write the new important words with the definition on the side of their heart or footprint and put their name on it.

Today is the end of unit VII. You can celebrate the end of this unit with the children. Review the Bible stories from Lessons 27 through today, asking questions that you have prepared in advance. You can have small gifts like a pencil, a book with biblical portions, figures or stickers, etc. Give gifts to all children equally. Encourage them to continue remembering the verses they've learned and to continue telling the Bible stories.

BIBLE STORY

Jesus taught in Judea. Many people came to listen to what he was saying. Many believed and were baptized.

The Pharisees didn't like people listening to Jesus.

"This is terrible!" they said. "The followers of Jesus are baptizing even more people than John the Baptist."

Jesus listened to what the Pharisees said and decided to go to Galilee.

Together with his disciples, they went by the shortest route to Galilee and passed through Samaria.

"Are you sure that this is the best way?" asked one of the disciples.

"We really don't like the Samaritans," added another.

"This is the right way to go," Jesus clarified.

Jesus and his disciples walked for a long time. The sun was shining brightly, it was hot, and the road was dusty. At last they came to a village in Samaria. There was a well on the outskirts. Jesus was tired.

"Please go to town and bring us something to eat," Jesus told them, and then he sat down by the well to wait for them.

"Yes, teacher," they answered and his disciples left.

A Samaritan woman approached the well. She carried her water pitcher to collect water. When she passed by Jesus looked at her. He knew everything about her. But above all, he knew that God loved her. Jesus knew that she needed a change of life.

"Would you give me some water?" Jesus asked.

The woman looked at him, very surprised. "This is a Jew," she thought, "but Jews don't talk to Samaritans, especially Samaritan women like me."

"Why do you ask me for a drink?" she asked Jesus.

Jesus smiled at her. "If you knew who was talking to you! I would give you a great gift from God. I would give you "living water."

"How!?" the woman exclaimed. "This is a deep well and you don't have a container to take it out. How will you get that water? Are you older than Jacob? He was the one who made this well."

She didn't know what Jesus was saying. Jesus spoke of eternal life, and not of real water. Jesus replied, "Anyone who drinks of this water will get thirsty again, but whoever drinks the water that I will give them will never thirst again."

"I want that water," the woman exclaimed. And she placed the pitcher to one side. She wanted to know more about God and more about eternal life.

"Go get your husband and come back," Jesus said.

"I don't have a husband," she answered.

"That's true," said Jesus. He knew that she had lived a life of sin. She needed God's love and forgiveness. He told

her several things about her. The woman heard him and asked him questions.

"Lord, it seems to me that you are a prophet. Our fathers worshiped on this mountain, but you Jews say we must worship in Jerusalem. Why?"

Jesus told the woman that one day we will worship God together. She still didn't understand.

"Someday I'll understand," she explained. "The Son of God will come soon and will explain everything."

"I am the Son of God," Jesus told her. "I'm the savior of the world."

Then the disciples returned to the well. They brought food for Jesus. They saw the woman as she walked back to town.

"Come see a man who told me everything I did! He says he is the Son of God," she said to the people in the town.

Meanwhile, the disciples suggested that Jesus eat what they had brought from the town. But Jesus made it clear that he had a better meal, which was to do the will of his Father, God. His task was to preach to all that God loved them.

"You must do the same," he emphasized to his disciples.

Then Jesus and his followers saw that the Samaritan woman was approaching with a large number of people.

One of the men asked Jesus to tell them about the Son of God.

"Please come to our town and tell us about God," the Samaritans said.

Jesus went to the village with his disciples and the people. He stayed there for two days preaching and teaching the people. Many met Jesus, and many received eternal life.

Finally, the other Samaritans told the woman, "We don't believe only because of what you have told us, but because we ourselves have heard and we know that this truly is the Savior of the world, the Christ.

ACTIVITIES

"The ABC's of Salvation"

Give students the activity sheet from the student book, lesson 30.

Tell them and show them how to follow the instructions for this activity. Ask them to mark the sheet with the letters A-B-C. Read each section with them.

Before class, make copies of the following meaning of the colors to use in the moments before the altar call. If you wish, you can make a copy for each child, with the pages of the colors indicated below. On one side, place only the pages with the colors; on the back the meaning of each of them.

Dark color: It means SIN. We have all sinned. We all need God's forgiveness for our sins.

White: FORGIVENESS. We need to tell God that we are sorry for having sinned, and that we are very sad about that. We can decide to not disobey and to not sin. The Lord forgives us. We can decide to love and obey God.

Red: SALVATION. Jesus died on the cross for everyone. Salvation means that we are forgiven by God through his Son, Jesus Christ. We decide to follow and obey God, knowing that he forgives us.

Yellow: ETERNAL LIFE. When we are forgiven and saved, we know that we have eternal life. That's the life that God gives us. It means that we can live for him now, and then in eternal life with the Lord in heaven forever.

Green: SPIRITUAL GROWTH. When we decide to follow Jesus, we are starting a relationship with him. And like any relationship, we want it to grow. We grow in our relationship with Jesus by praying, by reading our Bible, and by coming to church.

Memorization

Write the memory verse on strips of paper. Then glue the strips to sweets or candies. If possible, place the treats in a large clear jar. Children should already know the verse well. Guide them to say it by heart. Everyone can receive as a gift a candy with the verse.

To end

Encourage the children to receive "eternal life" or "living water" and to put Jesus first in their lives.

Pray that they accept the challenge of living as Jesus wants. Talk with the pastor or with the children's pastor, and with the parents of the little ones who accepted Jesus as their Savior. Plan a celebration to thank God for the children who passed from death to life.

Enjoy the blessing of having been an instrument to take the children of your class to the feet of the Lord!

 Notes:

Year 3

Introduction – Unit VIII

THE CHURCH AROUND THE WORLD

Biblical References: Acts 8:1-8,26-24; Acts 10; 11:19-26; 13:1-12; 14:21-28

Unit Memory Verse: *Again Jesus said, "Peace be with you! As the Father has sent me, I'm sending you"* (John 20:21).

Unit Objectives

This unit will help the elementary students to:

- ✘ Know that God founded the Church with the purpose of communicating the Good News.
- ✘ Know that the great work of the church is to proclaim the Gospel.
- ✘ Know that no obstacle can stop the church's growth in the world.

Unit Lessons

Lesson 31: Good News for an Ethiopian

Lesson 32: Good News for a Roman

Lesson 33: Good News for the people of Antioch

Lesson 34: Good News for everyone

Why Elementary Students need the teaching of this unit:

The biblical passages of this unit allow us to show that from the beginning, the Church of Jesus Christ was persecuted and attacked with much hatred. But despite all that, not only has the church survived, it has spread throughout the world.

Throughout history, God has raised up courageous and passionate people who, even at the cost of their own lives, have proclaimed Christ and announced the Good News.

And the most important thing is that as these people fulfilled the mandate of God, the hand of the Lord was with them. His power manifested itself by endorsing his words with signs, wonders and miracles. And many people became followers of Christ.

Your students will learn that the world is very corrupt and that sin seems to dominate everything, but the Church of Jesus Christ remains a reserve of morality and decency which, being supported and led by God, has the power to fight against sin and change lost lives into new and clean lives.

Good News for an Ethiopian

Biblical References: Acts 8:1-8, 26-40

Lesson Objective: To teach the students what it is to be a missionary and how the gospel began to spread.

Memory Verse: *Again Jesus said, "Peace be with you! As the Father has sent me, I'm sending you"* (John 20:21).

PREPARE YOURSELF TO TEACH!

Understanding and accepting people from other cultures is valued in many of today's societies.

Children are encouraged to be considerate of people who are different from them. What a beautiful opportunity to teach our children that this is a Christian principle that was put into practice in the early church! God was the one who established the idea that all people have the same value. It was his idea that Christians should reach out to everyone with the message of God's love.

This lesson is an excellent opportunity to begin creating in the hearts of children a love for the lost of the whole world. Philip teaches us that kind of obedience: reaching out to others to lead them to God.

It doesn't matter who they are or where they are. As happened to Philip, all the children who love Jesus can testify about him.

Help your students understand that when they pray for the unsaved, God listens to them and rejoices. Encourage them to pray for those who aren't saved in their own homes, for their friends, and for people from other countries who don't know the Lord. Join with them in prayer for those people, and for those you have on your prayer list.

BIBLICAL COMMENTARY

Phillip became someone important when the church began to spread to other cities. His work in Samaria was remarkable because of the great conflict between Samaritans and Jews. The Samaritans were treated like Gentiles, although they were part of "the lost sheep of Israel." They believed in a liberator who would save them.

Phillip showed courage and tenacity in going to Samaria, and he was one of the first missionaries of the early church who would carry the message of love and hope to the whole world. In fact, it can be said that Samaria and Ethiopia were the first two geographical areas to which Jesus sent his disciples to preach (Acts 1:8).

Phillip was enjoying a successful ministry in Samaria when he was instructed to leave and begin his journey through the congested streets that led out of the city. It's was as if today someone asked us to go on a road full of cars.

Without asking questions, Phillip went. It's possible that he didn't understand why, nor in agreement with the angel, but he was willing to fulfill his call.

Philip's testimony to the Ethiopian was an important personal work. Christians today can learn a lot from him.

When reading Acts 8, note the following:

✘   Phillip was obedient and went through cultural barriers to be a good witness.

✘   It was God who prepared the Ethiopian's heart to receive what Philip would tell him.

✘   Phillip began to speak from where the Ethiopian could understand him according to his experience. He answered the questions that the man had.

✘   The Scripture was the basis of Philip's testimony - it wasn't his own opinions or knowledge - but what the Word of God said.

✘   Philip emphasized Jesus Christ.

✘   He gave the man an opportunity to respond to the message and testify.

Witnessing through barriers is more than a cross-cultural message. As teachers, we do it every Sunday: an adult moves into the world of children to present the message of God's love. Remember that we must teach, starting from where our children are. Let's listen to their questions and understand their limited knowledge and perceptions. But most of all, let's appreciate their best qualities: hearts full of confidence, curiosity, and openness.

Even the smallest can be instruments in the hands of God to show his love to this world. Many times children are more effective witness than adults because of their ability to love without condition, which is a reflection of God himself in them.

LESSON DEVELOPMENT

Prepare in advance the teaching materials you will use for this lesson and try to have your classroom ready before your students arrive. Remember to welcome visitors and collect their info to contact them during the week.

Good news!

If you can take a cell phone to class, it will be very interesting to use it to start today's lesson. If possible, in advance ask someone to call you at a certain time.

After briefly talking and then hanging up, say: *It was a friend who had Good News to give me. Do you want to hear it?*

Has anyone received good news in the last few days. If so, how did you feel to hear it? (happy, started jumping for joy, etc.).

Important words

Before class, write on a piece of cardboard or posterboard (15 cm x 15 cm) the important word of this lesson: "Good News - the Gospel." Write the meaning on the back: The Gospel is the "Good News" that Jesus died on the cross and was resurrected so that we may be saved.

The second important word is: "Missionary". And on the back write: "A missionary is the person God called to tell the Good News about Jesus to people from other cultures. The church sends missionaries. "

Hang a piece of cardboard or posterboard in the classroom to place the important words of this lesson: "Good news", "Missionary". In the next lessons you can add other terms.

BIBLE STORY

Phillip talks about the Good News

It was a difficult time for the Jerusalem church. The followers of Jesus were being taken to jail. Many had to flee because their lives were in danger. Philip was one of those Christians, and he went to Samaria. I was afraid to stay in Jerusalem, but he wasn't afraid to tell people about Jesus.

"Listen to what I say!" preached Phillip. "I have Good News to tell you!"

The people met to listen. And he told them the wonderful story of how Jesus died for the sins of the whole world. They saw the miracles that God did through Philip. Many decided to follow Jesus. There was great joy in the city.

One day, God sent a messenger angel to Philip. "Go south on the desert road," he said. "It's the road that descends from Jerusalem to Gaza."

Phillip obeyed God. Many people walked on that road.

After a while, Phillip heard the clip, clop, clip, clop of approaching horses. Then the sound of the wheels was heard, and then he could see a very ornate and luxurious chariot. The horses looked very well cared for. Immediately, Phillip realized that this was someone important.

The man was very well dressed and he was reading aloud the prophet Isaiah.

At that moment God spoke to Philip, "Get up close to the chariot."

Phillip ran up to the side of the chariot and asked loudly, "Do you understand what you're reading?"

The man, who was in charge of all the riches of the queen of Ethiopia, said, "No I don't! How can I understand if someone doesn't teach me?"

The Ethiopian smiled at Phillip and invited him into the chariot and asked him, "Who is the prophet talking about?"

Philip told the Ethiopian about the Good News about Jesus.

"The prophet he is talking about the Savior sent by God," Phillip said. "Jesus is that Savior; I know him and you can know him too!"

The two men talked and talked. The Ethiopian's eyes began to shine with emotion, hearing that Jesus loved him.

"Look!" said the Ethiopian. "There is water over there. I would like to be baptized."

(Baptism is a way to show everyone that Jesus has changed your life.)

Phillip baptized the man. As he got out of the water and walked back to his chariot, God suddenly took Phillip to another place. The Ethiopian was surprised and looked around for Phillip. Where had Phillip gone? The man didn't know. But he did know that his heart was full of joy! He jumped into his chariot! All the way back to Ethiopia, he sang praises of gratitude.

"Thank you Lord for sending Phillip! Thank you Jesus because you are my Savior!"

And what happened to Phillip? He continued to travel from city to city, going wherever God sent him. In each place, Philip announced the Good News of Jesus.

ACTIVITIES

The baptism of the Ethiopian

Give the children the activity sheet from the student book, lesson 31, and guide them to cut out and paste the figures of the Ethiopian and Philip. For this activity, you must give each one a large paper plate, colored pencils, and glue. Tell the children to write their names on the work done. This activity will help them think of people to whom they can tell the Good News about Jesus.

Mural of the "Good News"

Get large poster paper or two sheets of construction paper to make a mural with your students, and keep it on the classroom wall for the rest of the unit.

In the middle of the mural draw or paste a map of the world. At the bottom of the poster write the unit verse: "*Again Jesus said, "Peace be with you! As the Father has sent me, I'm sending you." (John 20:21).* Then make lines in all directions, as if they were sunbeams, for children to stick figures or draw people of different races: black, Indian, white, Chinese, indigenous, people of short stature, tall, small children, adolescents, adults, the elderly, well-dressed people, poorly dressed people, etc.

Prepare the following questions, which you can also glue on the mural. While the children cut out the figures from magazines and newspapers and stick them on, ask questions such as:

1. *Is it possible that there are people who don't need the Good News?*

2. *Is Jesus the Savior only for good people?*

3. *Is the gospel only for white people? Or only for black people? Or only for brown people?*

4. *Do very old people need the gospel?*

5. *Do sinners need Jesus and his forgiveness?*

Allow the children to express their opinions on each question. Emphasize the truth that we all need the Savior, Jesus Christ, no matter our age, color of the skin, or whether we are educated or not. Let the children talk about the pictures they cut and pasted.

This mural will help you to review the lesson at the end of the unit.

Memorization

Prepare the memory verse in puzzle form. Cut the silhouettes (you will need 17 cards) of different means of transport, thinking about the means of transportation that the missionaries used in bible times and those used today, such as horses, the silhouette of a person walking, carts, boats, planes, cars, bicycles, motorcycles, etc. Draw the silhouettes on 15 cm x 15 cm cards. Prepare two or three sets. Write on each silhouette one of the words in the memory verse. Take the silhouettes to the class and ask the children to color and cut them out. Be careful not to write the word in the part that will be cropped. Once the children finish coloring and trimming, repeat the whole verse together several times.

Then, divide the class into two or three groups. Mix up each set of cards and place them face down on the table, on the floor, etc. Ask the teams that when you count to 3, they should begin to assemble the puzzle text correctly.

As a reward, the winning team will be the first to leave the room after the class is over.

To end

This is a good lesson for children to feel the need to pray and tell the Good News to others who don't know Jesus. Encourage them to tell their classmates and their families at home about the Lord if they aren't Christians.

 Notes:

Good News for a Roman

Biblical References: Acts 10

Lesson Objective: To help the students understand that God doesn't have favorite people. He loves everyone equally, in every corner of the world, and he wants them to know the gospel of Jesus Christ.

Memory Verse: *Again Jesus said, "Peace be with you! As the Father has sent me, I'm sending you."* (John 20:21).

PREPARE YOURSELF TO TEACH!

Children aren't always exposed to people of different cultures, but when they go to school, that begins to change. In some areas, it's more noticeable than in others. By the time the children reach first and second grade, they begin to notice differences in race, the way people dress, and differences in the behavior of those who are from Christian homes and those who aren't. They also notice the differences of languages, attitudes and traditions. In addition to all that, at this age they begin to receive instruction on tolerance of the secular and to equality, as part of modern culture.

Christian children need to realize that God wants everyone to know the Good News of Jesus Christ. They need to hear that God loves all people, no matter where they live, who their parents are, what race or nationality they belong to, or whether they come from Christian homes or not. The Lord loves all people and doesn't have favorites. He wants everyone to receive him as their Savior. Once the children internalize this truth, they will learn about the importance of reaching others to tell them about Jesus Christ.

BIBLICAL COMMENTARY

This passage tells us about a decisive moment for the church. On it rested the future of Christianity. The actions of Cornelius and Peter contributed to the fact that we Gentiles, who aren't descendants of Jews, could trust in the name of Christ.

God came to Peter's life with a revelation that was the beginning of the changes for the church. He used a devout gentleman to help Peter make an immediate decision. The men from Cornelius were at the door, the disciple had to recognize what God had told him in the vision and had to act quickly.

For the Jews, animosity against Gentiles went far beyond prejudices. It had to do with old laws that stipulated that the people chosen by God should be careful not to be absorbed by other neighboring cultures. The interpretation of those laws varied according to the person who taught them. Peter was fighting with both: the Jewish prohibitions and the new Christian church.

But God caught his attention and guided him in a new direction. We owe a lot to Peter for his willingness to listen and obey the voice of the Lord. How difficult it would be for us today if God had not changed the direction of the church! What would happen today if we tried to change the traditions of our faith that are already established? And if you wanted to move in another direction? Some, without a doubt, would fail. Others would form committees to deal with those issues. And others would respond quickly, as Peter had to do.

Peter had to change his love and commitment for so many traditions and parameters that Jewish law stipulated. He's an excellent example of acceptance and obedience to the Lord.

His deep Jewish roots could have caused a lot of problems for Jesus Christ's plan of salvation. But he was willing to change and accept the great truth of God's love for a sinful world. He had to understand that the sacrifice of Christ was for all humanity through the centuries and not just for a handful of people.

God's plan went far beyond time and space. His plan affected the life of every human being.

Today it's our responsibility to teach children the dimensions of God's love for them and for all others.

Today the little ones must understand that God loves everyone equally and that Christ died for each one in particular.

LESSON DEVELOPMENT

Prepare in advance the teaching materials you will use for this lesson and try to have your classroom ready before your students arrive. Remember to welcome visitors and collect their info to contact them during the week.

Alphabet of countries

If possible, prepare a map of the world before class; if you have a globe, it will also help you. Place the globe on a table or hang the map on a wall. Write on paper or cards the names of countries following the letters of the alphabet, and place adhesive tape behind them to be taped on the board.

A: Albania, B: Barbados, C: Cuba, D: Denmark, E: Egypt, F: France, G: Guatemala, H: Hungary, I: India, J: Jamaica, K: Kenya, L: Liberia, M: Morocco. N: Nigeria, O: Oman, P: Portugal, Q: Qatar, R: Russia,

S: Sweden, T: Thailand, U: Uruguay, V: Venezuela, W: (No country is spelled with W), X : (No country is spelled with X), Y: Yemen, Z: Zambia.

Ask three children to come to the front, pick up a card and then paste it on the board next to the letters of the alphabet that you will already have written in advance.

When the child comes to the front, before affixing the name of the country next to the letter, ask him to say a prayer, for example: "Lord, bless all the people in Albania. Bless those who preach the Good News and the missionaries you send. I pray for all countries whose name starts with the letter A. " And so each child will pray in a similar way for the country he attaches to the board or mural.

Dramatization

This is an easy lesson to prepare as a drama.

Get costumes (towels and sheets) for the children who will represent Peter and the people at Cornelius' house. For Cornelius' costume, you can make a vest with brown paper, and you can cover a piece of wood with aluminum foil to make a sword. If they wish and there is time, children can learn parts of the dialogue between Peter and Cornelius. A third participant can read a short story, previously prepared by you, about the vision that Peter had and what he should or shouldn't eat.

Maybe the children just want to act out the story as you tell it.

BIBLE STORY

Peter gives the Good News

Cornelius was a good and important man in the community. He was a centurion (a commander) of the Roman army. He believed in the one true God. He helped others and was a man of prayer. Cornelius wasn't Jewish, but Gentile.

One afternoon while Cornelius prayed, he had a vision. Cornelius opened and closed his eyes: He saw an angel!

"Cornelius," the angel said.

"Yes sir?" he replied, trembling with fear.

"God is pleased with you," the angel announced. "God wants you to know more about him."

"Yes," Cornelius nodded, excited. Actually Cornelius wanted to know more about God.

"Send one of your men to the city of Joppa," the angel ordered. "There you will find Peter. He will tell you what you want to know."

The angel disappeared. Cornelius immediately sent two servants and a soldier to Joppa. The next day, around noon, they had arrived at the outskirts of the city.

At the same time, Peter was on the roof of a friend's house. His stomach growled. "I'm hungry," Peter thought. But lunch wasn't ready yet. While Peter waited, he began to pray.

Suddenly, Peter had a vision. He saw the sky open and something like a large sheet descended. It was lowered to earth by its four corners. In it there were all the four-legged land animals, reptiles and birds of the sky. Then he heard a voice from heaven saying, "Get up, Peter, kill and eat."

Peter was horrified! Many, many years before, God had told his people not to eat some of the animals like these because they were unclean.

"No, Lord, I can't!" Peter answered. "I have never eaten things that aren't pure and clean."

The voice spoke again, "Don't say that things are impure if God has already made them clean."

Peter had the vision twice more and heard God repeating the same thing.

At that very moment, the men that Cornelius had sent arrived and knocked on the door of the house.

"Is Peter here? they asked.

Peter was amazed at the vision. "What does that vision mean?" he asked himself.

The Holy Spirit spoke to him and said, "There are three men who seek you; go with them."

Peter came down from the roof. "Hi, I'm Peter," he said to the men.

"The Roman commander Cornelius needs to see you now, please," the newcomers said.

Peter began to understand the vision. All his life he had kept away from Gentiles, in the same way that he had avoided eating certain animals. Now God was telling him that the message of salvation was for all people, even Gentiles.

"I'll go with you," Peter said, "but first, spend the night here."

This was a big step for Peter. The Jews didn't invite Gentiles to their homes.

The next day, he went with his three "new friends," and several of the Joppa believers went with them.

Upon arriving at Cornelius' house, they saw many other people gathered there. Cornelius told Peter about the vision.

"We are ready to listen to everything the Lord entrusted to you to tell us," said Cornelius.

Peter looked around and smiled. "This is why I had the vision!" he thought. And he said, "I understand that God doesn't favor some people over others, but that in every nation he loves those who fear him and live righteously."

109

And Peter spoke to Cornelius and the others in his house about Jesus and his love.

"Jesus is Lord of everything," Peter explained. "He died on the cross, but on the third day he rose from the dead and now lives."

Upon hearing all that, Cornelius and those who were with him believed in Jesus. And suddenly, the Holy Spirit came upon them.

"This is wonderful!" thought the Jews who believed. "The Holy Spirit has come upon the Gentiles too." Peter was excited!

"These people can be baptized," he said, "because they believe in Jesus and received the Holy Spirit just like us."

Peter baptized the new believers and stayed with Cornelius for a few days.

Everyone was full of joy. Now Cornelius and his people believed in Jesus Christ as their Savior. Peter and the Jewish Christians learned something new: that God loves all people. The Good News of salvation is for everyone in every corner of the world.

Do you eat that?

During the week, cut out figures of different animals from newspapers and magazines, or ask each child to bring a small toy animal that they have in their home. In class, ask the children to tell what animal it is, what it does, what sound it makes and if they ever ate the meat from that animal. Undoubtedly, some children will express dislike of eating certain kinds of animals. Do some research to find out which animals are eaten in certain countries. For example, in Mexico there are places where a certain type of snake is eaten. Another example may be that the Jews didn't eat pork, since it was considered unclean, but we do eat it.

ACTIVITIES

Puzzle: Good News for a Roman

Give the children the activity sheet from the student book, lesson 32. Guide them to cut out and assemble the puzzle according to the instructions. For each child, you will need cardboard or posterboard of 21 cm. x 28 cm to paste the puzzles onto. While they are working, you can ask them questions about the bible story learned in this lesson.

Important words

"Christian": This is the person who received Jesus as his personal savior. Christians love and obey the Lord.

"Not saved": It's a person who doesn't have Jesus in his heart.

"Salvation/saved": It's what God gave us so that we have a good relationship with him. The Lord forgives the sins of people who feel bad for having disobeyed God. People who are forgiven of their sins are called "saved."

Write all these important words on 15 cm x 15 cm cards and hide them in the classroom. The children who find them will put them on the poster of "important words".

Remember the missionaries

Say: *Peter was a good missionary. He went to Cornelius' house and preached the Good News of salvation. Did Cornelius, his family and everyone in his house become Christians?* (Yes).

Bring to the class the names of missionaries you know about. Write their names on 10 cm x 10 cm cards. You can write their full names and the names of their children, and where they serve as missionaries. Make a mural or poster with all the cards. (Maybe you can get their photos from the World Mission website.)

Each day of class, children can pray for the missionaries.

Urge them to make decorated cards, write notes to the missionaries, place them in envelopes or take photos of them and send them to the missionary family by mail or email. Allow the children to use their creativity for these projects.

Remind the children that the missionaries left their extended families and friends to obey the Lord's call, and that they miss their loved ones and countries of origin. The missionaries are obedient to the Lord. They listen to God's call and the church sends them.

Memorization

If you wish, you can use the same activity from lesson 31 to study the memory verse. But also change it to be consistent with the lesson studied today. You can write the verse on cards, with the silhouette of various animals. Then use the same mode of learning the memory verse.

To end

This is a good time to encourage the children to be like Peter. Obedient missionaries, ready to take the message of the Good News of salvation to their family and friends who don't know the Lord.

Finish with a prayer. The children can pray for the missionaries and you for the children in your class.

Good News for the people of Antioch

Biblical References: Acts 11:19-26

Lesson Objective: To teach the students that in Antioch, the followers of Jesus were called "Christians" for the first time.

Memory Verse: *Again Jesus said, "Peace be with you! As the Father has sent me, I'm sending you."* (John 20:21).

PREPARE YOURSELF TO TEACH!

Children know very well what it means to be or not to be part of a group. They want to dress like everyone else, be the first to buy the new electronic game, or have the most advertised toy. They strive to be accepted, wish to have many friends, and be the most popular at church and school. In the first years of primary school, their friends' opinions are very important.

Many times they feel that they aren't important because they've never done anything "great". Their grades aren't as good, or they're not as popular as other children. This lesson about the anonymous Christian missionaries who started the church in Antioch will encourage them. They will begin to understand that not everyone who does important things is known. They will start to see that living for God and sharing our faith is one of the most important things we will do in our life. Pray that the children in your class will trust God when they talk to people about Jesus.

BIBLICAL COMMENTARY

For the first time since Jesus' resurrection, his followers "intentionally" preached the Gospel to Gentiles who had no ties to the Jews.

The Samaritans whom Philip preached to were half Jews, and weren't popular. Cornelius was a man who feared God, who sought the truth. But in Antioch, no one had asked for the Gospel message. In spite of everything, the persecuted Christians decided to go to a city with a bad immoral reputation to preach the Good News to those who weren't Jews. We don't know who those believers were. There is no record of their names. We only know where they were from and the report of their resounding success. They were common Christians, whose faithfulness opened the doors to the whole world so that Christianity would spread. Their effort was so remarkable that the leaders of the Jerusalem church, upon hearing what was happening, sent Barnabas to investigate.

Barnabas was known as a person who encouraged people. He was a good man, full of the Holy Spirit and of faith.

When he arrived in Antioch and saw the wonderful response of the believers, he knew he needed help. He needed someone to understand these people and their way of being, and to teach them about Jesus. He needed someone to take leadership of the emerging church of Antioch. That man was Saul of Tarsus, who was later known as the Apostle Paul.

For a year, Barnabas and Paul taught the believers in Antioch and preached to those who weren't Christians. The church continued to grow by leaps and bounds. And an important detail was that in those days for the first time, followers of Jesus were called "Christians". The term meant "Christ-ones", or "little Christs," which was originally meant as mockery. In spite of everything, it was a tribute to Christ, since the believers very eloquently preached and lived for the only Christ and Lord.

In our world today, we make an equation between greatness, popularity and riches. We list our achievements and label them; as if listing them would make us better. Unfortunately, today the church often falls into those traps of the world. We also have our leaders, lecturers and popular writers whom people want to hear. We don't often pay homage to the servant of God, not so well known, who year after year faithfully fulfills his responsibilities within the congregation. We all know those servants of the Lord who teach our children, clean our churches, and direct the musical groups, write the Sunday bulletin, or cook for the various activities. We must recognize that their silent labors have an impact on many lives. God chose these kinds of people to take the Christian faith to the farthest corners of the world.

He used a man with a tender heart, someone who encouraged others. Barnabas wasn't afraid to ask for help to establish the church in Antioch. He wasn't afraid that eventually, that person could overshadow him. This passage clearly teaches us what God's heart and plans were like. The "popular" aren't impressed by the Lord, nor those who seek positions to be seen. On the contrary, he looks for those who commit themselves and who faithfully perform their task.

LESSON DEVELOPMENT

Receive your students with affection and ensure that the classroom is clean and tidy when they arrive. Before starting today's topic, briefly review the two previous lessons.

The game of names

Say: *Do you know why you were given the name you have?* (Some children are named after a special family member or event.) *Each name has a meaning. Do you know what the meaning of your name is?* (Let those who know it tell the class. If the children don't know, choose biblical names and teach them what they mean. For example: Dina, justice; Peter, rock.)

After talking for a while about the meaning of the names, immediately move on to the next topic, important words.

Important words

Say: *In our Bible story today, the important word is "Christian."*

Show the word: "Christian." *Who knows what "Christian" means?* (It's the person who belongs to Christ, the Savior.) *It's the person-child or adult-who loves and obeys God.* Allow a volunteer to place the word on the mural of important words.

Ask: *Who can tell me the name of the two people who told the "Good News" in our stories the last two weeks?* (Phillip and Peter). Tape up two cards with the names of Phillip and Peter. Present the card with the name of Barnabas for the class to read. Ask a child to tape the name of Barnabas next to the others.

Present the name "Paul." You can write: Saul = Paul so that the children can become familiar with the two names. Give a short explanation about the name Saul before he knew the Lord, and Paul after he met Jesus.

Paul and Barnabas continued with the work of preaching the Word of God, that is, the Good News. They were true missionaries. Missionary work includes various activities. Some missionaries are preachers. Others work in hospitals as doctors and nurses. Some on computers. There are those who teach people how to live for God. This week we will remember to pray for the missionaries who teach.

Many of us give the Good News to people we already know. But what do the missionaries do? (They talk about Jesus to people who don't know him, in other countries and in other cultures.) *Who knows what "culture" means? It's the way in which people live their lives. Culture includes the foods they eat, the way they dress, the type of houses they prefer, their ideas about God, and other customs and traditions.*

Today's lesson is about people who brought the Good News of Jesus to other cultures. Let's see what happened.

BIBLE STORY

Barnabas and Paul preach the Good News (dramatization of Acts 11:19-26)

(In advance, dress the children who will participate in the drama in the typical clothes of the time. If they don't want to wear different clothes, let them wear their own clothes. Have a copy of the script for each actor to read their part. If they can't read, they can act their part as the reader reads the story.)

Scene 1

Narrator: Stephen was stoned until he died. After that, many believers were put in jail. Others fled from Jerusalem to be safe.

But wherever they were, they taught about Jesus. Some went to the city of Antioch. This wasn't a Jewish city. Most people there were Gentles since they were of Greek origin. But when they heard the Good News, the Greeks believed and received Jesus. Very soon, the Christians of Jerusalem heard the news about what was happening there.

Barnabas and the Christians: (Barnabas reads a message on a scroll, then talks to the Christians in Jerusalem.)

"Listen to this! There's a new church in Antioch that is growing and growing. They say that there are many Gentiles who follow Jesus. Is that true?"

Narrator: The church in Jerusalem sent Barnabas to Antioch to see what was happening there (Barnabas leaves.)

Scene 2

(Athena, Demetrius, and the Christians of Antioch enter, followed by Barnabas).

Athena: Welcome to the city, Barnabas!

Barnabas: It's very nice to be with you here in Antioch!

Demetrio: - It's an honor for us that you came to visit us.

Christians: You are very welcome, Barnabas! Please teach us more about God. We want to know how to love and obey God.

Barnabas: (Speaking to the anxious Christians) "Worship God only. Always put him first. In everything you say and do, obey what Jesus taught."

Narrator: More and more people in Antioch began following Jesus.

Barnabas: (He steps forward a few steps)These Christians are so interested in living for Jesus! I need to teach them more, but I need help. (Barnabas walks out, Athena, Demetrius and the other Christians sit down.)

Narrator: Barnabas traveled to Tarsus. He went to talk to a Jewish teacher named Saul. Earlier, Saul had hated and persecuted Christians, but now he was a believer. Saul's other name was Paul.

Scene 3

Barnabas: (Speaking to Paul) Good morning, friend!

Paul: Good morning, Barnabas! Why are you here in Tarsus?

Barnabas: I need your help.

Paul: How can I help you?

Barnabas: There are many Christians in Antioch. Many of them are gentiles. They didn't know about our God until they received Jesus as their Savior. They need teachers to help them know more about God's love and how they should obey Him. Can you come and help me teach them?

Paul: What a good idea! Let's go right away!

Narrator: Paul and Barnabas leave the room. Paul and Barnabas travel to Antioch.

Scene 4

Paul and Barnabas meet with the Christians of Antioch. Everyone stands up.

Christians: Welcome back, Barnabas!

Barnabas: Hello. I present my friend Paul. He is a teacher who knows the Word of God very well.

Demetrio: (He touches Paul on the shoulder) We're happy that you came to teach us, Paul.

Athena: Yes, we have so much to learn!

Scene 5

(Paul, Barnabas and the Christians are sitting down, Demetrio and Athena are standing).

Demetrius: (Speaking to the audience) For one year, Barnabas and Paul were here in Antioch. They preached to people who didn't know Jesus. They also taught those who didn't believe, like Athena and me.

Athena: We listened and learned how to love and obey God. Soon the people of Antioch began calling us Christians. This word means "one that belongs to Christ."

Demetrio: The people make fun of us. But we are proud to carry this special name. This is the first time that the followers of Jesus have been called "Christians".

Christians: (Together) A Christian is a person who receives Christ as Lord and Savior. Christians love and obey God. The people in Antioch can see that we are like Jesus. That's why they call us "Christians."

ACTIVITIES

What is a good Christian? (say it with mime)

Ask each child to mime (without words) and demonstrate ways to be a good Christian. When a child performs the mime, the rest must guess. You can be the first to start:

A Good Christian is:

- ✘ Friendly (greets other people and shakes hands with a smile).
- ✘ Helpful (helps another person cross the street or room).
- ✘ Giving - generous (give someone something of yours: money, clothes, food, etc).
- ✘ Forgiveness - (someone hits you and you don't retaliate).
- ✘ Obedient (someone asks you to do something and you do it).
- ✘ Goes the second mile (carry shopping bags or sweep the room).

Memorization

You can use any of the silhouettes with the bible memory verse, either the silhouettes of transportation or the silhouettes of animals. Hide the cards all over the room before class. When the time comes, tell the children to look for them. Remember that you must have 17 cards. When the children find them, ask them to put them on the table in order. At the end, everyone will say the Bible verse together.

If there are words that students don't understand, explain what they mean.

To end

Give them time to complete the student activity sheet from the student book, lesson 33. Guide them to complete the missing words (look for them in the word scramble). Then they can color the figures.

Encourage the children to continue telling the Good News, just as Paul and Barnabas did.

Pray for each one so they can tell the message of salvation without fear or shame.

Ask a child to pray for the missionaries who are in countries where they are persecuted.

Good News for everyone

Biblical References: Acts 13:1-12, 14:21-28

Lesson Objective: That the students understand that the church is part of God's plan to bring the Good News to the whole world.

Memory Verse: *Again Jesus said, "Peace be with you! As the Father has sent me, I'm sending you."* (John 20:21).

PREPARE YOURSELF TO TEACH!

Children need to feel that they are a vital part of the community we call the local church. They should know who the local leaders are and relate well to them and to the children's leaders.

The same happens with the missionaries that the denomination sends and supports. Children should get to know them by name and by their photos, and maybe even correspond with them. This particular lesson is a great way to help children understand that missionaries are called by God to go preach the Good News of Jesus Christ. It's the people of the congregation who make it possible for them to carry out the task that God called them to do.

This lesson will help the children understand that the money they put into the missionary offering helps the missionaries to fulfill God's call. Students will learn that when they pray for the missionaries, they are part of God's plan for them and their families.

BIBLICAL COMMENTARY

There is a wonderful secret revealed in these verses. People from different backgrounds can join in a common cause to win men and women for Christ. United by faith in Jesus Christ, they become one and form the Church: the true body of Christ.

In Acts, we begin to see what the mission of the Christian church should be like.

First, the church must recognize God's call to certain people to go and preach the Gospel and teach others the principles of faith. These men and women must be set aside for the work of God, and the rest of the community should give the church's blessing and authenticate their call.

Not only will they receive financial support from the congregation, but they should be remembered in private and collective prayer. In response, the missionaries who are sent must inform the congregations about their work. They must communicate their successes and failures. They must seek the emotional and spiritual support they need.

That was the case of Paul and Barnabas, who were sent by the church of Antioch. These two men traveled the known world of that time, winning the lost, discipling the believers, and encouraging them in their new faith. One of the most significant and far-reaching ministries they had was to establish local leaders among the members of each church.

The two men eventually returned to Antioch and reported how God had blessed their task. They were well aware that they (the sent), and those who sent them (the Christians of Antioch), carried out important roles.

The task of the missionaries we send today is to preach the Good News to those who aren't saved. They should also strengthen and disciple believers and encourage them to remain faithful in the face of adversity. The missionary assignment includes the training of new converts to evangelize their neighbors. With so many religions around the world, many missionaries find it difficult to preach Jesus Christ as the only way of salvation.

Missionaries face great opposition in many countries. It's important to remind the believers of each country how vital it is to testify of the saving grace of Jesus Christ and urge them to have a faithful commitment to the Lord. One of the ways to achieve this is through the organization of leaders for each local congregation.

We must train national leaders to take the leadership of the church in their countries.

Prayer is an essential part of the success of any missionary enterprise. When danger and opposition arise, missionaries depend on the prayer of the people who know them, even if not personally.

LESSON DEVELOPMENT

Receive your students with affection and ensure that the classroom is clean and tidy when they arrive. Before going into today's topic, review briefly the three previous lessons. Talk with the children about the challenges of being faithful to God.

My favorite trip

You will need a small soft ball. Ask the children to sit in a circle. Tell them: *When I throw the ball to someone, they will tell us about a trip they have taken that was very special for them. When they finish telling about their trip, they can gently toss the ball back to me.*

Traveling to different places is what missionaries usually do. They travel to other countries to tell the Good News of Jesus. They work in other cultures than they know. The foods they eat are different. Sometimes, the people of those countries speak a different language and the missionaries must learn it. It's possible that the houses are different from the ones they had in their own countries.

Do you think the missionaries are happy and excited to live in another country and have a different culture? I have a friend who is a missionary. She couldn't take many of her belongings with her to the mission field. She was happy when making plans for her new home. In today's story we will talk about two men who were teachers and missionaries.

Mural of the "Good News"

Gather the students next to the poster prepared for the unit.

Do a review of each lesson. Ask questions related to the figures on the mural and those that are written on the strips and pasted there.

Review of important words

In this lesson there are 5 important words: "Christian", "Gospel / Good News", "missionaries", "non-believers", "salvation/saved".

Assign each word a number. Write cards with numbers from 1 to 5.

Mix them up by placing the numbers down on the table. Ask a child to pick up a card. According to the number, they must say the term or give the meaning of the numbered word.

If the child guesses right, you can give him a small prize or he can leave the classroom first.

BIBLE STORY

To relate and recreate today's bible story, you can get an old blanket and throw it on the floor as if it were a boat. Children should sit on it (boat), and you will indicate that you will be at the helm. When you lean to the right, everyone should lean to the same side. At another time everyone should lean to the left. At times, move simulating that there are many waves. When you perform each mimicry, children should imitate the same movements. Say: *The men of our history traveled by boat. You must do the movements that I do.*

Do you remember the church in Antioch that we talked about in the last lesson? Missionaries are people who tell people what God wants them to do.

Barnabas and Paul were still teaching in Antioch. While the people were worshiping (raise your hand pointing to heaven), the Holy Spirit spoke to them, "Set apart Barnabas and Paul to serve me. I have chosen them to do a special task."

The people of Antioch wanted to do God's will. They prayed and fasted (lean to the right). The Christians placed their hands on Paul and Barnabas and blessed them, "Please, Lord, may your presence be with these men."

They prayed and they sent them off as missionaries. (Lean to the left.)

"This is exciting," Barnabas told Paul.

"Imagine the people who are preparing to listen to the message of Jesus thanks to this trip," replied Paul.

First the missionaries went south, to Seleucia. Then they boarded a boat (move as if there were soft waves) and sailed to the island of Cyprus. They preached the word of God to all. They traveled all over the island.

Paul and Barnabas met Barjesus (cover your face as if frightened). He was an evil wizard and a liar. He worked for the governor of the island and tried to keep the governor from hearing Paul and Barnabas.

"I want to hear what these men teach," the governor demanded. "Be quiet, I want to hear!"

Paul looked into the eyes of Barjesus, the evil man, and said, "You are the enemy of all that's right! You cheat people. You use all kinds of tricks. Will you not cease to upset the righteous ways of the Lord? Now then, the hand of the Lord is against you, and you will be blind and you will not see the sun for some time. (Cover your eyes and pretend that the boat is moving with fury everywhere.)

And so it happened! The evil magician went blind. He tried to find ways to walk, but he couldn't (try to touch things as if he were blind, close your eyes, children should repeat each mimic).

The governor watched everything that happened. He was amazed! (act with much surprise).

"This is incredible!" he said. "I also want to meet this man Jesus."

The governor accepted Jesus and was now a new Christian.

Paul and Barnabas continued their trip (move as if navigating on gentle waves). They returned to many cities where they had been before.

They helped believers to grow in their faith and learn more about God.

"Follow the only true God," they announced. "Do His will."

Paul and Barnabas chose leaders (keep moving the ship gently) in each city they visited to help the new believers.

"Dear Lord," they prayed (close and cover your eyes with your hands), "please help the new leaders and all the believers. Please take care of them. Help them to love you and to follow you."

Then they sailed (move the ship as if there were few waves, but at times as if stronger winds were blowing) back to Antioch.

Then they gathered (open your arms and put them together as if calling people to meet) the whole church, all the members. They should listen to what God had done!

There they informed the gathered believers of all that the Lord had accomplished on their missionary journey

"This wonderful work was done for your sake," explained Paul. "You sent us. God worked through us. Now many people have become followers of the Lord. We did what the Lord called us to do. We gave the Good News of Jesus Christ to many people, in different towns and cities.

Ask questions about the bible story:

1. Who were on that trip? (Paul and Barnabas)
2. Who sent Paul and Barnabas on their missionary journey? (The church of Antioch)
3. What was the name of the magician who went blind? (Barjesús)
4. What did Paul and Barnabas do on that trip? (They visited many cities and taught about Jesus.)

Don't forget that we the church sends missionaries. They go, teach and then return to their countries and give a report. We must help and support them. We must also pray that God will guide the missionary work and that he will take care of those who are in all parts of the world.

ACTIVITIES

Who does God call?

Begin this activity by dividing the class into 2 teams to play the "Good News game". Talk with the students, asking them about the ways and to whom they gave the Good News during these last few weeks. Encourage them to continue talking about Jesus. Tell them: Speaking to people about Jesus is a goal we should have for life. We must never stop talking to people about Jesus.

Hand out the activity sheets from Lesson 34 to the students. Ask them to color the figures and find the two hidden words. Explain: The missionary task is a group effort. Someone must stay to send. And someone must obey and go.

Ask: Who were the ones who sent in today's story? (The church of Antioch). Who obeyed and went? (Paul and Barnabas).

Have the children turn their page over. Have them follow the instructions to find the words and fill in the blanks so they can discover the mystery at the bottom of the page.

Memorization

Divide the class into two groups. One kids from each group will come to the front and assemble the memory verse correctly. The cards with the memory verse will be on the table and the words facing down. When finished, the two children will be able to say the text together. If there are children who don't remember it, others can help them.

To end

Pray for our church that sends missionaries. Also pray for the missionaries, especially those who are in dangerous places. As a teacher, pray for the Lord to call your children to missions.

You can sing an appropriate chorus.

At the end, if you wish, you can bring fruits and cookies to celebrate the end of the unit. Invite everyone to come next week as you begin studying about God's mercy.

 Notes:

Year 3
Introduction – Unit IX
GOD'S MERCY

Biblical References: Genesis 4:1-16; Genesis 6; Genesis 7:1-8:19; Genesis 8:20-9:19.

Unit Memory Verse: *The Lord our God is merciful and forgiving* (Daniel 9:9a).

Unit Objectives

This unit will help the elementary students to:

- ✗ Understand God's immense love for people.
- ✗ Know that God values mercy more than sacrifice.
- ✗ Value God's example: He is a model of compassion and love.

Unit Lessons

Lesson 35: **The sad story of Cain and Abel**
Lesson 36: **A good man in a bad world**
Lesson 37: **God saves Noah**
Lesson 38: **God makes a promise**

Why Elementary Students need the teaching of this unit:

The book of Genesis is fundamental in its entirety. But it has key passages that can help elementary children understand that mercy is one of God's most salient features.

The tragic story of Cain and Abel and the salvation of Noah show His love and justice with great clarity.

Today children learn more easily the culture of "an eye for an eye and a tooth for a tooth"; but God wants them to cross onto the path in front of them and become forgivers.

Make it clear to the students that these stories aren't make-believe but real. And that God is still that way today.

In addition, through these lessons you can teach them that God is merciful, and that he says: "I want mercy and not sacrifice." This means that before rituals, promises and pilgrimages of faith, God wants us to love our neighbor.

The sad story of Cain and Abel

Biblical References: Genesis 4:1-16

Lesson Objective: To help students understand that Cain ignored what God said and let bad thoughts lead him to do bad deeds.

Memory Verse: *The Lord our God is merciful and forgiving* (Daniel 9:9a).

PREPARE YOURSELF TO TEACH!

This seems to be a strange story to tell children in first and second grade, even in these violent times when even youngsters commit murders.

However, this lesson is really about the decision to obey or disobey God. And first and second grade children face these issues.

The context of this story is related to their lives. It's not that the schoolyard or neighborhood streets are terrible places, but there is rivalry between siblings and friends. Children easily become jealous if they believe that another is favored more than they are, either because they get more attention, or enjoy greater approval. These feelings produce strong reactions, such as derogatory names, physical aggression, or other malicious acts.

The emphasis you should give to this class is the following: "It's very easy for bad thoughts to lead us to commit bad deeds." When we allow bad thoughts to settle in our mind, we may end up doing something terrible.

In the same way, it's also true that God can help us and protect us from sin.

Encourage the children to talk to God honestly. And tell them that if they obey him, he will help them.

BIBLICAL COMMENTARY

The phrase "Sin is crouching at your door" (Genesis 4:7) raises two questions:

- Do you have to open the door to sin?
- What happens if we open the door?

The story of Cain and Abel is the story of a murder, which was and is a very serious offense. But observing it from a higher level, this narrative has to do with grace.

The choice is to decide to do good or bad. If we do the right thing, God will accept our efforts, even if they aren't perfect (see v. 7). But if we persist in doing our own will, we run the risk of being "dominated" by sin, that is, falling deeper and deeper into rebellion and bad deeds.

That was the curse that Cain chose. He ignored God's counsel and fell into sin because of his jealousy and anger, which led him to kill his brother Abel. Even so, God didn't abandon Cain, but placed a protective mark on him, to show that his grace is always available while we live here. This should give us some peace of mind in thinking of those who have strayed from the way of the Lord. They didn't go astray to places where His grace can't reach them.

In a way, this story is about the relationship between two brothers. In it, we see more of the character of the "bad" than of the "good". Here we see aspects of our own lives that we know very well. Relationships between brothers (or sisters) can be broken if there is competition between them, or if one is filled with jealousy and anger. How do we act in our family relationships, like Cain or Abel? It's something that we decide.

The story of Cain also has to do with worship. Perhaps Abel's sacrifice was acceptable because he brought the fat portions of the first newborn animals (v. 4). Cain brought some of the fruits of the earth (v. 3). Or maybe there was an attitude problem.

Hebrews 11:4 mentions the offering of Abel in relation to "his faith". Perhaps Abel's sacrifice was a reflection of a loving relationship with God, while Cain's offering was only to fulfill a certain formality.

We can't say with certainty. But it leads us to reflect on the choices we make regarding our worship.

In light of this narrative, we can answer the question of the principle: we are never forced to open the door to sin.

If we do, the consequences are dire, but God doesn't abandon us. As long as we live on this earth, forgiveness will always be available.

The end of the story

I repeat, this narrative is about grace. Here is something we can meditate on.

From the day of that first murder, "you have come to Mount Zion, to the city of the living God, ... to Jesus the mediator of a new covenant, and to the sprinkled blood that speaks a better word than the blood of Abel." (Hebrews 12:22, 24).

This should help us choose correctly, so that sin remains "outside the door".

LESSON DEVELOPMENT

Prepare the teaching materials you'll use for this lesson and have your classroom ready before your students arrive. Remember to welcome visitors and collect their info to contact them during the week.

"Danger or GO"

Before the class, prepare two large posters (like the traffic signs of your country). They can be 50 cm. x 50 cm., of posterboard or cardboard. One sign should read: "STOP - DANGER" (can be made in red and white), and the other: "GO" (can be green).

In class, ask that two volunteers hold the signs. Say: I will read several sentences. In some of them, children have good thoughts, but in others, they have bad thoughts. If the sentence is about good thoughts, they will raise the sign that says "Go." But if it's about bad thoughts, they will raise the signal of "Stop - Danger".

Practice for a few minutes. All children should shout loudly when the "Go" or "Stop - Danger" signs are raised.

- Ana has an old bicycle. Emilia has a new one. Ana thinks, "Why does Emilia have a new bicycle? I hate her!" (Stop - Danger).

- Peter has many toys and John has almost no toys. Peter shares his toys with John (Go).

- Carla wants to do something special and beautiful for her parents (Go).

- Julio bought a huge red balloon. Andrew looks at him from afar and thinks about how he can get close and pop it (Stop - Danger).

- Mary went for a walk with her friends Julia and Cecilia, but she forgot to invite Debora. Debora found out and promised that she would no longer be Mary's friend (Stop - Danger).

- Mrs. Rosa gave her husband a beautiful car. The neighbor Andy is very upset and says unkind things about them (Stop - Danger).

- Julian has a new soccer ball. His brother Paul became jealous and promised to break it (Stop - Danger).

Say: *Why is it dangerous to think like some of these people?* Emphasize that bad thoughts can lead to bad actions, as in the case of Cain and Abel.

Important words: "Sin" and "Obey"

Prepare a posterboard or cardboard to hang on the wall. Divide the poster with a vertical line. On one side write "obey" and on the other "sin".

Write the meaning of obey: To do what God wants us to do. His will is in the Bible, which is his Word.

On the other side write "sin": it's to disobey God and his commandments.

You can bring newspaper or magazine for the children to find graphics or pictures that show scenes of obedience or sin. After they have cut out various pictures, each child should tape/glue them under the correct column. Be sure that the figures are appropriate. Discuss the pictures and their meanings. Practice reading the words and their meaning several times.

BIBLE STORY

Life for Adam and Eve was very different after they disobeyed God. They no longer lived in the beautiful garden of Eden. Their work was hard. Now they suffered from pain and became ill. But God still loved them very much.

Soon, Adam and Eve had children. Eve named the first child Cain, which means "God helped me to have this child." The second they named Abel. Adam and Eve taught the boys about God.

The two grew up healthy and strong. Upon reaching the appropriate age, Cain decided to become a farmer, and Abel decided to raise cattle.

One day, Abel offered a sheep as an offering to God. He carefully chose the best one he had for the sacrifice. Cain also offered an offering. He gave some vegetables and fruits that he had grown.

God was pleased with Abel's offering, but not with Cain's. Why was God not pleased with Cain's offering? The Bible doesn't explain it. But we know that the Lord is good and everything he does is good. Something wasn't right about Cain's offering, or in the way he gave it to God. Cain became very angry with God. But God still loved him.

"Why are you so angry?" God asked him. "If you'll do the right thing, I'll be happy with you. But if you don't do the right thing, you will be sinning. Be careful. It's your choice to do good or to do evil."

Cain heard what God had told him. And he kept thinking about how angry he was. He was angry with God and with Abel. After a while, Cain no longer loved his brother."

One day, Cain told Abel, "Let's go to the field together."

"Okay," Abel agreed.

The two men headed towards the field. While they were there, Cain killed his brother Abel and buried him. Later, God spoke to Cain, "Where is your brother Abel?"

"I don't know!" said Cain. "Is it my job to take care of Abel?"

"I know what you did," said God. "You were very bad. From now on, nothing will be easy for you. You will wander from one place to another."

"Oh Lord, my guilt too great!" cried Cain. "Now people will try to kill me because of what I've done.

Although Cain had done something very bad, God continued to love him and made a promise to him. "I'll make sure no one kills you."

Sadly, Cain left his home and his family. God kept the promise he had made. But surely, many times Cain would have wondered why he didn't obey God and his warning not to do wrong.

ACTIVITIES

Small puppets

Before class, prepare: scissors, glue or tape, wooden sticks or ice cream sticks, crayons. Give the children the activity sheet from lesson 35 of the student book. Ask them to color the little puppets. Help them cut out the figures of the puppets and glue them on flat wooden rods about 20 cm. long by 1 cm. wide, or ice cream sticks. When they have finished, they can act and have the puppets talk about the story of Cain and Abel.

As a review when the story is over, ask the children: *Did Cain have to do wrong and kill his brother?* (No) *Who tried to keep Cain from doing bad?* (God). *What was Cain's biggest mistake, before killing Abel?* (He had bad thoughts about God and his brother Abel).

Bible story illustrated

This will help the children remember the story of Cain and Abel.

Use the following or choose items that you like for the children to use as you tell the Bible Story.

1. Two baby dolls wrapped in blankets to represent Cain and Abel.

2. A stuffed sheep that represents Abel's offering. (Or you can draw a sheep on a piece of paper and glue a stick to it. Use beans or buttons for the eyes). You can also make a puppet with a white sock. Glue on black button eyes. Trim a triangle from a black cloth for the nose and glue it on. Make lips with a piece of red cloth, the ears can be pink fabric. Glue cotton balls to the tail and body.

3. Place some pieces of fruit and vegetables on a plate, to represent Cain's offering.

4. Draw a happy face to represent that God was pleased by Abel's offering.

5. Draw another face but sad. "This is how God felt about Cain's offering."

6. Draw a dark circle (not black), or cut out a circle of brown paper or cardboard, representing Cain's angry thoughts about God and Abel.

7. A card that says: "Don't hurt Cain."

Say: *Each child will have one of these objects. When I mention something that you have in your hand, lift it into the air until I'm done talking about it.*

Once they are finished, place the objects in a basket or box to use them on another occasion.

Memorization

Flags with the memory verse

You will need: poster paper or brightly colored paper, markers, tape, scissors and sticks.

Write the memory verse on the triangle-shaped flags beforehand.

In class, hand out a flag to each child to decorate. Say that they shouldn't color over the memory verse. Once the flags are colored, they should be glued onto sticks about 12 cm. long by 1 cm. wide. Ask the children to write their name on their flag.

Ask them: *What does it mean that "our God is merciful and forgiving"?* (God doesn't punish us as he should for the sins we commit, He is always ready to forgive us if we ask Him.) *When he forgives us, he never remembers our sins anymore. He treats us as if we had never sinned.*

Repeat the memory verse several times. Then they can go out into the yard and march with their flags, repeating it aloud.

Finally, collect the flags. These will remain in the classroom until the last lesson of the unit.

To end

Pray giving thanks for:

✗ Every child in your class.

✗ Their parents and siblings.

✗ Their spiritual lives and their relationship with God.

✗ Their studies.

✗ Because they are good children.

✗ Because they come to church

Pray that:

✗ The children will be obedient to the Lord

✗ They will be good siblings and friends.

✗ They will be good children and students.

✗ They will have good thoughts towards God and others.

A good man in a bad world

Biblical References: Genesis 6

Lesson Objective: To help the students know that Noah decided to obey God, even when no one else did.

Memory Verse: *The Lord our God is merciful and forgiving* (Daniel 9:9a).

PREPARE YOURSELF TO TEACH!

When I was a girl, the pressure of the group didn't affect me much until I got to 8th grade. But as the years have passed, the age of pressure on children has gotten lower and lower to now it's the years before adolescence. At present, children of six and seven years, and even smaller, are greatly influenced by their peers.

One of the reasons is that they spend more and more time with other children their age. With the arrival of nurseries and kindergartens, children begin to be influenced by their peers, practically from when they are born. Since many children spend between 4 to 12 hours per day with other children, they worry more about what their classmates think and approve of.

Today's lesson finds elementary children with this reality in their unique and particular situations. It's never easy to be different from the rest of the group, especially these days. And with the corruption of basic moral values of society, children have to deal with choices that we didn't have to make years ago. As you prepare the next three lessons about Noah, immerse yourself in the scriptural passages and story.

Ask God to help your present Noah in such a way that your students admire him and want to act like him. Noah stood alone in front of a world of sin and violence. Pray that your students will learn to trust the Lord enough to do the same when necessary, in the classroom, on the playground, in their neighborhoods, or wherever they proclaim that they are children of God.

BIBLICAL COMMENTARY

In any story where judgment fell on people in rebellion, it's easy to see God as a harsh judge. In this story about the flood, it's easy to see God as the one who killed the wicked and saved a few righteous.

If we look at it that way, we'll overlook what the Scriptures describe: "The Lord regretted that he had made human beings on the earth, and his heart was deeply troubled" (6:6).

Only a God who loves so much can feel so much pain for the evil person.

God's pain wasn't because he created man, but he suffered because the people he loved refused to restore their relationship with him.

Therefore, the anguish of the Creator was because of the wickedness of mankind. Humanity had gone astray. That situation was followed by a period of cleansing and forgiveness, which was an act of love, not revenge.

This story has a parallel with the conversion of a person. When the person's heart is filled with pain due to his mistakes and sins, and he seeks God to help him, God responds with forgiveness and transformation. In his mercy, he cleanses the chaotic world created by the wandering heart.

In biblical history, we see that not everything was destroyed by the universal flood. The branch of the olive tree is the first proof that vegetation had survived. When Noah and his family left the ark, they had the forests and fields available to rebuild their lives.

By cleaning the human heart, God didn't destroy the framework of the old creation. People remain human after their conversion, but with the new opportunity to rebuild on the foundation already provided.

The story of the flood emphasizes that each individual is responsible, regardless of what others do or have done. Noah was the only "righteous man, blameless among the people of his time, and he walked faithfully with God" (v.9). This doesn't imply that Noah had never sinned. Like all of us, he was the recipient of a fallen nature, which was the result of the sin of Adam and Eve; although Noah loved and obeyed God with all his heart.

Noah could have been like everyone else, but it wasn't like that. He had the courage to be different from the rest of the group, a quality that God rewarded. This is a difficult point for adults to accept, how much more then it is for children. The power of the crowd or what we know as "the group phenomenon" is hard to resist.

When everyone in the group does something, it's difficult to do something different, especially when "doing that something" is the right thing to do.

Noah is an example for us and the children that following God is always the right thing to do, regardless of whether others do it or not.

Here's something to think about, not just for this lesson, but every time we're in contact with students: How can we, as teachers of children, influence our students to trust God in such a way that they are willing to obey Him when their friends tell them to do the opposite?

LESSON DEVELOPMENT

Prepare in advance the teaching materials you will use for this lesson and try to have your classroom ready before your students arrive. Remember to welcome visitors and collect their info to contact them during the week.

Can I enter the ark?

You'll need: posterboard or cardboard, scissors and markers. Before class, write on 10 cm x 10 cm cards the names of animals that are easy for the children to recognize, for example: bear, cat, dog, bird, elephant, lion, pig, etc. Make 2 sets of each, so that 2 children have a bear, 2 the cat, 2 the lion, and so on.

During class, give each child one of the cards with the name of an animal. Tell the children not to show it or tell anyone what animal they have.

Explain: The objective of this game is to find the other person in the room who has the same animal that you have on your card. You must make the sound that your animal makes, or walk or act like it, but they can't say the name. When you find your partner, come and ask me: Can we enter the ark? You'll give me your cards, and I'll compare them, and if you've really found your partner, I'll tell you, "Yes, you can enter the ark." But if not, I'll say, "No, you can't enter the ark." Play until all the children find their partner.

When finished, ask: *What bible story does this game remind you of?* (Noah's ark). *Noah lived at a time when no one else on earth loved nor obeyed God.*

Hard, Harder, Hardest

You will need: posterboard or thin cardboard, thick marker and tape.

Before class write in large letters on the posters for all the children to see: "Hard", "Harder", "Hardest". Place them on three different walls of the room.

In class say: I will read some brief stories about different times when children have to make decisions. Then you'll vote and choose if that decision is hard, harder, or hardest.

You'll vote by standing in front of the poster that you think best describes that particular decision. Read the stories. Give time for the children to decide and walk to the poster they choose. After each decision, ask volunteers why they responded as they did.

1. The teacher leaves the room. Before leaving, she told the class to be quiet and do their homework. Almost all the children start talking and laughing. How hard is this decision about keeping quiet and obeying?

2. Your mom said to clean your room before going to play. She has to go out and do a quick errand. You look at your room ... it's a mess. How hard is this decision about obeying your mom?

3. The children went to a birthday party. One of the boys had a magazine with bad jokes and bad pictures. Your parents don't let you look at that kind of magazine. All the children at the party look at it. How hard is it to say, "No, I won't look at the magazine," and start doing something else?

4. You're with your best friend in a store near your home. You both want candy and chocolates, but you don't have money to buy them. Your friend tells you, "Just take some and hide them quickly." How hard is it for you to refuse to steal?

5. One of the children in your class hit a child on the playground. The school principal is talking to the students and asking who did it. Nobody responds. How hard is it for you to tell the truth?

Say: *Deciding to do the right thing is difficult. Especially when you're the only one who wants to do it. Today's story talks about a man who decided to obey God, even when no one else wanted to.*

BIBLE STORY

Discussions! Fights! Hate! Death!

Every place on earth where God looked, he saw people doing what they wanted instead of what was right. Their selfishness was much more plentiful than the love and goodness of God. God felt terrible pain and suffering in his heart. Everyone did the wrong thing. Nobody obeyed him or did the right thing. Nobody, except one man. His name was Noah. Noah loved God and always tried to obey him. God wasn't happy and couldn't allow the world to continue the way it was. It was getting worse. Sadly, he decided, "I must destroy this world and everything in it!"

God spoke to Noah and said, "Noah, the world is full of violence and evil. I will destroy everything in it with a huge flood. But I promise you that I will save you and your family. But this is what you have to do to be saved."

"You must build an ark, a very big ship. And you will cover it inside and out with pitch. You will make it three stories tall, and place a door on the side and a window on the top. When you have finished with the boat, you will take two animals of each species and put them in the ark for them to live (see 19-20). You must also put enough food in it for you, your family and all the animals."

How surprised Noah must have been with all those instructions! It had never rained on earth before. Noah had no idea what rain was, much less a flood! And the ark that God asked him to build was huge! He had no idea what a boat was, or what it was for!

It would be much bigger than a football field, and taller than a two-story house. It would take a long time to build!

No doubt, Noah must have had many questions to ask God, but he didn't. He simply trusted him. He believed in what God had said, and he obeyed. He quickly began to build the ark. The Bible doesn't specifically say it, but Noah's three sons - Shem, Ham and Japheth - probably helped him. Noah built the ark as God had instructed him.

For many years, he built and built. All the people who passed by looked at what Noah was doing. What did they think? The Bible doesn't say it. But as they watched, Noah worked, and announced the message of God. The Lord was giving them another opportunity to be saved. He would save anyone who repented of their evil ways and asked to be forgiven. But nobody did.

Finally, the ark was finished. Noah obeyed God in everything. Finally came the time when he, his family and all animals had to enter the giant boat. What would happen next? He didn't know. He only knew that God would protect him and his entire family, as He had promised.

ACTIVITIES

Mural: Noah and the ark

This is a good lesson to make a large mural, which the children will enjoy doing. You will need: paper or cardboard, colors, crayons, brown paper for the ark, blue paper for water, tape, glue, etc. In this and the next two classes in which you'll talk about Noah, they can add more illustrations to the mural. Today they can paint the silhouettes of Noah, the members of his family, people watching Noah as he builds the ark, trees, houses, the ark, etc. Draw the ark very large, as well as other figures. Have the children color them. In the next class they can add the animals and so on. Use this activity to review the bible story. While children work coloring, you can ask appropriate questions.

Animals are coming

This game will serve to review the bible story. Ask that the children form a horizontal line at the end of the room. Then assign a different animal to each child. They will have to make the sound of that animal. There may be repeated animals. Let each one practice what they should do.

Say: I will ask questions about today's Bible story. Everyone must respond. If you answer correctly, you will advance one step forward and make the sound of the animal that corresponds to you. If you answer incorrectly, you will have to stay where you are and in silence. Let's see if everyone can get to the ark.

Play until everyone has reached the ark or until the questions are finished.

1. *Who made the earth?* (God)
2. *Why was God sad?* (Because people were violent and did wrong.)
3. *Who obeyed God?* (Noah.)
4. *What did God ask Noah to build?* (An ark.)

5. *Did Noah know how to make the ark?* (No, but God gave him the instructions.)
6. *How many animals of each species should enter the ark?* (Two.)
7. *What else did Noah put in the ark?* (Food.)
8. *Did Noah listen and obey God?* (Yes.)
9. *How many people stopped sinning and entered the ark?* (None beside Noah's family.)
10. *To whom did the Lord show mercy?* (Everyone, but only Noah and his family entered the ark.)

Teacher Attention: The purpose of this activity is to help the children remember the lesson and not take a test. If they answer wrong, you can give them the correct answer and have them repeat it, and then they can make the sound of their animal, and move forward one step, until they reach the ark, which can be a place surrounded with chairs or benches.

Decide to obey

Ask the children to cut out the puzzles from Lesson 36 of the student book. Give each one a plastic bag to store the pieces. The figures are appropriate to be able to talk about what they must do to obey.

Memorization

Memory verse race

Before class, prepare 2 pennants (flags) in the shape of a triangle. Paint them with bold colors (if you want you can make them big). Attach a wooden rod about 40 cm. long.

In class, repeat the memory verse (Daniel 9:9). After doing it several times, divide the group into 2 teams. (It's better to do this activity in an open courtyard.) When you say "GO", the first child of each team, with their team pennant in hand, must run to the other end (place something to mark the spot) and say in a loud voice the text of Daniel 9:9 and the reference. Then they will run back to their team, hand the pennant to the next child and so on. Pay attention to the repetition of the verse. Help those who have problems.

Play until one of the teams - the winner - has finished. Conclude by repeating the memory verse together. Save the pennants for the next class.

To end

Pray for your students to be obedient to God. Sing an appropriate chorus about obedience. Pray for those little ones who find it hard to obey their parents or teachers. Encourage them to pray for each other during the week.

 Notes:

God saves Noah

Biblical References: Genesis 7:1-8:19

Lesson Objective: To help the children understand that those who love and obey God experience His love and care in a special way.

Memory Verse: *The Lord our God is merciful and forgiving* (Daniel 9:9a).

PREPARE YOURSELF TO TEACH!

I will never forget the flood that I saw in a Bible story book for children when I was little. In the front part of that black and white painting, representing the waters and the fierce rain, there were figures of babies on the rocks that would soon be submerged by the water. I loved babies and I asked myself again and again why God hadn't saved them.

It's good that today's publications no longer make materials for children like those. Even so, the most sensitive students in your class will feel worried about the death of all those people and creatures that were left out of the ark.

Pray a lot for this lesson, because it teaches a difficult truth. God loves all people with a love that has no end. And those who respond to him with trust and obedience will experience his love and care in ways that others can't. But some refuse to obey and that's why the consequences come to them.

In this lesson, emphasize the ark of salvation that God provides for Noah and his family. Remind your students that Noah, like every person, had sinned. But unlike the rest of the people who hated and ignored God, he loved him and wanted to obey him. And as he did, God protected him. The Lord will do the same for the children in your class.

BIBLICAL COMMENTARY

There is Good News between last Sunday's lesson and today's: Noah survived! Between God's command to "enter the ark" (7:1) and "come out of the ark" (8:15) we see multiple evidences of God's love, mercy and care.

There are many points in this story where the result could have been different. What would have happened if God hadn't given Noah the plans to make the ark from the beginning? Or what if Noah had taken on other construction projects at that time? What if the animals had refused to go on the ark? What if the ark had leaked and sunk?

Thank God, Noah survived! After he, his wife, his children, his daughters-in-law and the animals entered the ark, God closed the door behind them (7:16). What a reassuring thought this must have been for Noah and his family during the long dark days to come! The flood had swept away all the creatures except the fish, and the animals and the people who were in the ark.

God provided the ark as a means to survive. Sheltered inside, Noah, his family and the animals escaped the terrible destruction that hit his friends and neighbors. After the flood, the ark took them gently to land, perched on Mount Ararat, and placed them in front of a new life. That new life was offered by God to those who had obeyed him.

Chapter 8 begins with the words: "Then God remembered Noah." When the Bible uses the term "remembered" in relation to God, it means one's concern for someone, which is expressed in actions of love.

God's judgment on the people was over. Now began a period of redemption.

God began again with a family and a holy creation. He extended his grace through his creation through righteous survivors. From the line of Noah emerged Abraham, Isaac, Jacob, Moses and Jesus.

Later, the word "ark" continued to appear in the Jewish religion. The ark of the covenant was the place where the symbols of God's presence were kept. While it was with the Israelites, they were safe.

In our culture, we talk about people entering the "ark of salvation" when they accept Christ as their Savior. When we enter that "ark of salvation", God delivers us from the death and destruction that accompanies his judgment on sin.

In these days of instability and sin, we want to see more than ever that our children will survive the evil that surrounds them.

God provided the "ark of salvation" through Jesus Christ. We must teach the children that God loves them and, above all, guides them to enter the ark of salvation, which is Jesus Christ, the Savior.

How can we provide an ark of salvation for our children?

✘ Through Sunday School, Vacation Bible School, etc.

✘ Through the church.

✘ Through Christian friendships and the influence of the faith community.

✘ Through good advice.

✘ Through our Christian testimony.

✘ Through varied Christian activities.

LESSON DEVELOPMENT

Receive your students with affection and ensure that the classroom is clean and tidy when they arrive. Before entering today's topic, review briefly the two previous lessons and ask your students to tell how God has protected them and helped them during the week.

Important words: "Obey" and "Sin"

Hide the cards with the important words in the classroom. Ask the children to look for the two important words of the unit: "obey" and "sin."

When they find the cards, read the meaning of obedience and sin. Ask questions about it. Help the children with clues about the previous lessons.

1. Who were the main people in the first lesson of this unit? (Cain and Abel.)

2. What did Abel offer God? (A sheep.) Did he sin or obey? (He obeyed.)

3. What did Cain do to his brother Abel? (He killed Abel.) Did he sin or obey? (He sinned.)

4. What was Noah supposed to do? (Build an ark.)

5. Did he have instructions on how to build the ark? (Yes, God had given him the instructions.)

6. How many animals of each species was he supposed to put on the ark? (Two.)

7. Who entered with Noah into the ark? (His family.)

8. What else did Noah put in the ark? (Food for all.)

9. Did Noah obey? (Yes, he obeyed.)

Count the animals

Before class, cut 2 sets of 26 cards (8 cm x 8 cm) from posterboard or cardboard. Write the letters of the alphabet on the cards - one letter on each card. Make two sets. Place all cards in a bag or basket.

During class, ask the children to sit in a circle to play the "Ark, Ark." In a rap tone you can say, "Ark, Ark, how many animals do you have?" And repeat the same thing several times, while the bag with letters goes from child to child. When you stop singing, the child who has the bag will draw a letter and say as many animals that they can whose name starts with that letter before you count to 10. Examples with the letter c: cat, crocodile, camel, etc. Meanwhile in silence, you count to 10. Write on the board the name of each animal, without repeating. Then continue singing: "Ark, ark ...". Continue if there is time until each child has the opportunity to participate. Count on the board how many animals they named.

Say: *Very well, you remembered a lot of animals. Think of how many animals Noah would have put on the ark, two of each kind. Since the ark was so big, some people think that there were about 45,000 animals. But we don't know for sure. There were a lot of animals! Today's story tells us about how God rescued Noah, his family and many animals.*

BIBLE STORY

Mural: Noah and the ark

Ask the children to continue working on the mural, drawing and coloring figures while you tell the story. (You can bring prepared waves, blue water, the silhouettes of various animals, etc. for the children to color, cut and paste on the mural at the appropriate time.) Ask some questions from the last class and give them time to match the pairs of animals).

"It's ready!" Noah said.

"It's finally finished!" exclaimed his family.

Together, Noah, his wife, sons and daughters-in-law looked at the huge ship standing on dry land in front of them. The boat was much bigger than a football field. It had taken Noah and his family more than 100 years to build it. At last it was finished!

Once again, God spoke to Noah. "In seven days I will send rain on the earth. It will rain for 40 days and 40 nights. You, your wife, your 3 children and their wives will enter the ark. Take two animals of each species and put them in the ark. And take seven pairs of clean animals. (You can stop the story here and explain what the clean animals were. They were animals that God considered fit to be sacrificed to him. Since they would be given as an offering to God, they had to have more than two of the clean animals.)

Continue with the story.

Noah did everything that God had commanded him. For a whole week, the animals arrived and Noah helped them enter. What a busy time it must have been! Can you imagine Noah, his wife, his children and their wives trying to accommodate so many animals? The huge elephants had to be in places where they didn't crush the small animals, and the birds needed space to fly. Can you imagine the noise that there would have been? And where would they have put the skunks?

At the end of the seven days, Noah and his family entered the ark. God closed the door with total security. He wanted everyone to be safe and secure, because that same day the rain would begin to fall.

It had never rained on earth! And now it didn't stop for 40 days and 40 nights. The water began to rise and rise (Give time for the children to start covering the mural with the waves of blue water, remove the figures of Noah and his family, and the ark. Put the water parts on top of the rest of the people, animals and plants), *each time higher. It began to cover the plants and trees and the houses* (make the story dramatic), *and it even began to cover the mountains. Everyone had died! The only ones who were alive were Noah, his wife, his children and his daughters-in-law, plus the animals on the ark and the sea creatures that lived in the water.*

After 40 days and 40 nights the rain stopped (place the ark floating on the water). *Now God was making the land ready once again for Noah, his family and the animals. God blew wind to make the earth dry.*

The water had been falling for several months. Noah wanted to know how things were now. At first he sent a raven (place the raven). The bird flew and returned, because there were no dry places it could make its nest.

Later, Noah sent a pigeon (place the figure of a pigeon). This is a bird that likes to walk on the ground. But it returned soon because there was still no dry land. The next morning, Noah sent the pigeon once more. It came back again, but it had an olive branch in its beak (place the olive branch on the pigeon's beak). What great news for Noah and his family! The water was already under the tops of the trees (ask some children to remove some of the water that covered the trees).

A week later, Noah sent out the pigeon once more. But this time, the pigeon didn't return. Noah thought:, "The earth must be dry so that the pigeon can walk." Would Noah open the door of the ark? No doubt he really wanted to do that. They had been on the ship for almost a year. But Noah didn't open the door of the ark, but waited for God to give him instructions.

At last the beautiful day arrived! One year and 10 days after God had closed the door behind Noah, his family and the animals, God spoke with Noah again.

"Get out of the ark! Take your wife, your children and their wives, and all the animals out with you. Live in this land and have children. I want to see the birds flying once more and the animals multiplying."

With joy, Noah, his family and all the animals obeyed God. As they left the ark, they could walk on the cool green grass. They could feel the warmth of the sun, hear the chirping of birds and smell the fresh flowers. God had lovingly protected them from the flood. Now they could start a new life on earth. Noah's heart was full of gratitude, love and praise to God.

Say: *God loves all the people of the world. How the Lord wished that people would have said, "Forgive us for how bad we've been and what we've done, please forgive us!" Had they done so, God would have saved each one and given them the opportunity to enter the ark, or maybe he wouldn't have had to send the flood. But Noah was the only one who believed, loved and obeyed God.*

Decide to obey (model in shoe box)

Give each child a shoe box, and guide them to follow the instructions on the activity sheet of the student book, lesson 37. Since Noah obeyed God in everything, ask the children: *How can you obey God in your home, while playing or at school?*

"I obey God" (headband)

Before class, cut 60 cm long x 6 cm. wide strips from posterboard or light colored construction paper. One strip for each child.

In class, write on the board: "I obey God." Hand out the strips, colored pencils and small figures or stickers so that the children can write on them: "I obey God." Then they can paste the figures and decorate their headbands. When finished, they can measure their heads and join the two ends of their headband with tape. They will definitely need your help.

While the children decorate their headbands, ask:

1. *Did Noah obeyed God?* (Yes.)

2. *What did he do to obey?* (He listened to God, he built the ark, he preached to the people, he gathered the animals.)

3. *What should you do if others disobey God?* (Continue obeying.)

4. *What should we do if we make mistakes and disobey God?* (Repent and ask God to help us to not do wrong.)

Say: *Remember, each person (even children) decides to obey or disobey God. Nobody can decide for you.*

While the children finish decorating their headbands, you can help them measure them on their heads and attach them with tape or join the ends with a stapler. They can leave the classroom with their headbands on their heads. Encourage them to tell their family and friends the Bible story about how Noah obeyed God.

Memorization

Bible Memory Verse Race

(Repeat of this game from last week.) After several repetitions of Daniel 9:9, divide the group into 2 teams and ask them to form 2 rows. (It's better to do this activity in an open courtyard). When you say "Go", the first child of each team, with their pennant in hand, must run to the other end (use something to mark the spot), and say in a loud voice the text of Daniel 9:9 and the biblical reference, run back to their team, hand over the pennant to the next child and so on. Pay attention to the repetition of the text. Help those who have problems.

Play until one of the teams - the winner - has finished. Conclude by repeating the memory verse together. Save the pennants for the next class.

To end

Ask the children: *Are there times when you find it hard to obey?* (Give them time to respond.)

If so, let's pray for God to help you remember this lesson. You decide to obey or not; the Lord is an almighty God.

Let's pray: Holy God, please help each child to be obedient to your Word and do everything that pleases you. Encourage them to pray for each other during the week. In Jesus' name, Amen.

God makes a promise

Biblical References: Genesis 8:20-9:19

Lesson Objective: To help the students have the certainty that when God makes a promise, we can be sure that He will fulfill it.

Memory Verse: *The Lord our God is merciful and forgiving* (Daniel 9:9a).

PREPARE YOURSELF TO TEACH!

I was one of those lucky kids because I knew that if my parents promised me something, they would do it unless they couldn't because of extreme circumstances. Being truthful was an emphasis in our home, and that was put into practice by both mom, dad, and us the children. I feel sad for those children who constantly hear "I promise," and then discover that they are meaningless words. It's a very weak foundation for those who wish to trust in God.

"Promise" is the subject of this lesson.

As you teach this last lesson on Noah, keep in mind that there will be children in your group who know from their own experiences what unfulfilled promises are. Even when a well-meaning father breaks his promises, his children can't understand.

Throughout this lesson, remind children that God is different from any other person who makes promises. He is God, and there isn't anything that limits him or prevents him from fulfilling what he promised. He kept the promise he made to Noah for thousands of years. And he has also kept the promises made to mankind. No matter what the children have experienced with the promises made to them, they can trust that God loves them so much that he will always keep his promises, both those he made to them and to others.

BIBLICAL COMMENTARY

At the conclusion of the story of the flood, we see that God made a promise and sealed an covenant with Noah. A covenant is a commitment between God and people. God initiated the covenant and defined both the terms of it and the blessings. In a covenant, human beings agree with the terms and promise to obey. The covenant is sometimes compared to a contract; although there are some differences. An covenant is based on interpersonal relationships and requires commitment and loyalty between the parties.

The promises God made to Noah affect us all equally. God promised that he would never again curse the earth because of the wickedness of people (8:21).

Although the plants survived the flood, there is no doubt that they would have suffered during that time. But the most important thing is that God promised never again to destroy "living creatures" (v.21). He declared his intentions with poetic beauty:

"As long as the earth endures,

seedtime and harvest,

cold and heat,

summer and winter,

day and night

will never cease"(v.22).

God promised that he would never again send another flood of such destructive magnitude upon the earth. For that reason, he placed something in the sky to remind us of it. The rainbow would be a reminder to Noah, and to every human being who lived after him, of what God had promised. It would also remind God himself. "Whenever I bring clouds over the earth and the rainbow appears in the clouds, I will remember my covenant between me and you and all living creatures of every kind." (9:14-15).

During the years between Noah and us, God has kept his promise. Never again has he sent a universal flood to destroy living beings. That doesn't mean that God ignores the evil that men continue to commit. He promised not a flood, but fire the next time. "By the same word the present heavens and earth are reserved for fire, being kept for the day of judgment and destruction of the ungodly" (2 Peter 3:7).

History testifies, and the second coming will finally prove what Christians know and believe: that God keeps his promises.

Here are some other promises of God in which we can meditate and believe:

✗ "Never will I leave you; never will I forsake you" (Hebrews 13:5).

✗ "But the Lord is faithful, and he will strengthen you and protect you from the evil one" (2 Thessalonians 3:3).

✗ "God so loved the world, that he gave his only Son, so that everyone who believes in him may not perish, but may have eternal life" (John 3:16).

✗ "Through these he has given us his very great and precious promises, so that through them you may participate in the divine nature, having escaped the corruption in the world caused by evil desires." (2 Peter 1:4) .

LESSON DEVELOPMENT

Welcome your students with affection and make sure that the classroom is clean and tidy when the children arrive. Give them a welcome hug, let them know that you love them. Tell them you pray for them.

Important words: "Obey" and "Sin"

Before class, hide in the classroom the 2 cards with the important words: "obey" and "sin".

Once again review the meaning of each one. You can write it on the board or read it if you have it written on a poster on the wall.

When the children have found the cards, ask everyone to sit or stand in a circle.

Pass a ball or sachet full of seeds from child to child. You will be out of the circle, turning your back. When you start clapping, the ball will begin to circulate from hand to hand. When you stop clapping, you will immediately turn around and the child with the ball in hand will answer a review question of the last 2 lessons about Noah. For example: *Who entered the ark? What does it mean to obey? Did Noah sin or obey?* If the child answers correctly, he will leave the circle and stand or sit next to you to help clap. You can continue with the review game while there is time.

Who does what he promises? (21 letters and a question mark)

Make 21 dotted lines on the board before class. If you want you can put a letter in the middle of each word.

For example:

_ _ O _ _ E _ _ _ A_ H_ _ _ _ M _ _ _ _? (Who does what he promises?) Place the question mark.

In class, divide the group into 2 or more teams. Start with the first child of the first team. She will have to say a letter of the alphabet. If the letter is part of the question, write in the letter and the child will earn 10 points. If it appears more than once, she will earn 50 points. Then goes to the second child and so on. Continue until a student says a letter that isn't in the question. Then go to the next team and continue child by child, etc. until one team discovers the question. Then discuss that question.

Who does what he promises? (Children will talk about their parents, teachers, or God.)

Ask: *How do you feel when someone keeps the promises he or she made?* And then: *How do you feel when someone doesn't keep the promises they made?*

Today's story is about someone who kept his promise. That person was God. Listen to what the promise was.

BIBLE STORY

One year and ten days is a long time.

During that time we have (name the holidays that are in your country). We celebrate one more year, we are bigger, we go to school, we finish the school year, Christmas arrives, then the New Year, we go on vacation. All that and much more happens in a year and ten days.

Noah and his family were in the ark during all that time. They waited and waited for the day to come when they could leave the ark and begin their new life on earth. At last that wonderful day arrived! One year and ten days after Noah, his family and many animals entered the ark and God closed it! When that special day arrived, God spoke with Noah and said, "Get out of the ark. Take your wife, your three children: Shem, Ham and Japheth with their wives and all the animals. Get out of the ark and start living on the earth."

(If you left the mural without the water last Sunday, ask the children to now place the figures of Noah, his family, the animals, etc.)

With great pleasure, Noah, his family and all the animals obeyed God.

Imagine that you were with Noah all that time. What would be the one thing you would want to do the most back on dry land? (Allow the children to respond).

Noah knew that God had kept his promise to protect him from the terrible flood. That's why his heart was full of gratitude and praise to God.

The first thing Noah did was build an altar to worship God. He looked for rocks and placed them in a large pile. (Children can draw and color large rocks, to place them as an altar, others can draw firewood and color them, some can draw and color some sheep for the offering.) *Then he killed some of the clean animals and birds that God had determined and offered them as sacrifices. Noah offered an offering to show God his love and gratitude.*

God was happy with Noah and said in his heart,

"As long as the earth endures,

seedtime and harvest,

cold and heat,

summer and winter,

day and night

will never cease"(v.22).

Then God said to Noah, "I want you and your children and their wives to have children. I want the birds and all animals to reproduce. They must fill the earth again. From now on, Noah, you can eat meat from animals and birds. You can also eat from the plants. You will never kill another person. I will punish anyone who kills another person."

128

Then God promised Noah and his family that the next promise was for them, and for their offspring that would come after them. This was also for the animals and birds that were in the ark.

(As you continue to tell the Bible story, give the children the opportunity to place a rainbow of different colors on the mural, over the ark and stone altar. They can be strips of paper, cut in a semicircle that they themselves have colored. They can add glitter if you wish.)

While God spoke, suddenly, something beautiful appeared in the sky. It was a semicircle with beautiful colors.

While Noah and his family looked at the rainbow of colors, God told them, "I will never curse the earth again with a flood, nor will I destroy every living thing again, as I have done. I have put the rainbow in the sky ... sometimes when I bring clouds over the earth, my rainbow will be seen and then I will remember my covenant with you ... and there will be no flood of waters to destroy every living being. I will keep this promise forever."

Noah believed in God's promise. He had fulfilled all His promises He had made. He had protected Noah and his family. He had made sure that the ark floated and that water didn't get inside it. He took care that people and animals weren't afraid. Can you imagine if a stampede of animals had begun inside the ark? God had taken into account every detail. He took care of the plants, allowed the wind to blow so that the earth would dry out. God had protected them until the day he told them to leave the ark. Without a doubt, Noah could continue to trust that God would fulfill all his promises.

ACTIVITIES

Review "rainbow"

Before class, write several questions on paper or cardboard strips of different colors. Use light colors representing the rainbow.

Place the strips with the questions in an envelope or box so that the children can see the colors.

Then call volunteers to take out each strip and read the question for the rest of the class to answer.

1. *What was the name of Noah's ship?* (Ark.)
2. *What did Noah build when he left the ark?* (An altar.)
3. *Why did Noah build an altar?* (To worship God and thank him for being faithful to his promises.)
4. *How did God feel about Noah's offering?* (Happy.)

5. *What did God say to Noah, his sons and daughters-in-law?* (That they should have children to fill the earth.)
6. *What could people eat?* (Meat and vegetables.)
7. *What was God's promise?* (That he wouldn't again destroy living things with a flood.)
8. *What sign did God give us to remember His promise?* (The rainbow of different colors.)
9. *What was the name of Noah's wife?* (Naamah, but the teacher didn't say it.)
10. Who remembers the name of Noah's children? (Shem, Ham, Japheth.)

Mobile: Rainbow with promise

Guide the children in making the mobile from the activity sheet from the student book, lesson 38. This craft will help them remember God's promise for all humanity.

Tell them to tell the beautiful story of Noah's obedience in their homes, stressing that God always keeps his promises when people love and obey him.

Memorization

Memory verse race

(Repeat of this game from last week.) After several repetitions of Daniel 9:9, divide the group into 2 teams and ask them to form 2 rows. (It's better to do this activity in an open courtyard). When you say "Go", the first child of each team, with their pennant in hand, must run to the other end (use something to mark the spot), and say in a loud voice the text of Daniel 9:9 and the biblical reference, run back to their team, hand over the pennant to the next child and so on. Pay attention to the repetition of the text. Help those who have problems.

Play until one of the teams - the winner - has finished. Conclude by repeating the memory verse together.

To end

Have an activity ready to thank God for his promises. It can be a time of meeting with the children's parents. Prepare the little ones to tell the whole story of Noah's life. Let the children tell their parents what they learned during this unit.

All together give thanks to God because he always keeps his promises. Then they can have a snack previously planned so that children and parents can share together. It may include: pieces of ham, cheese, sausage, cookies and fruit. Water or milk.

Year 3

Introduction – Unit X

GOD'S FAITHFUL SERVANTS

Biblical References: Ruth 1-2; Ruth 3-4; 1 Samuel 1:1–2:11,18-21; 1 Samuel 2:12-17, 22-26; 3

Unit Memory Verse: *But be sure to fear the Lord and serve him faithfully with all your heart; consider what great things he has done for you* (1 Samuel 12:24).

Unit Objectives

This unit will help the elementary students to:

- ✗ Develop a spirit of service to God.
- ✗ Learn that God want us to be his faithful servants.
- ✗ Learn that God uses faithful servants to fulfill his plans on earth.
- ✗ Discover beautiful examples of faithful servants in the Bible.

Unit Lessons

Lesson 39: Ruth

Lesson 40: Boaz

Lesson 41: Hannah

Lesson 42: Samuel

Why Elementary Students need the teaching of this unit:

This unit presents the opportunity to verify, with very illustrative biblical examples, that God values in a special way those who serve him faithfully. And not only that, but also has great esteem for those who see the needs of others and do the impossible to supply them.

These lessons also provide the opportunity for your students to compare the selfishness of the world with the attitude of service that the Lord asks of us.

Help them understand that those who strive to serve others are actually serving God, and that brings as a reward a good reputation among their friends and joy to their hearts.

Ruth

Biblical References: Ruth 1, 2

Lesson Objective: That the students learn that God wants them to be his faithful servants.

Memory Verse: *But be sure to fear the Lord and serve him faithfully with all your heart; consider what great things he has done for you* (1 Samuel 12:24).

PREPARE YOURSELF TO TEACH!

It's common for most children this age to be helpful. It's precisely at this stage of their growth that they really want to help others, and therefore, it's not strange that they volunteer to set up the classroom chairs, erase the blackboard or hand out the crayons to their classmates.

Children feel valued and appreciated when they contribute to daily activities.

Your students feel the need to work together to improve their environment. They want to show that they are trustworthy to carry out responsibilities. In a sense, they begin to develop their capacity to be faithful servants. This lesson will help them understand what it means to be a faithful servant for God.

Sadly, it's also likely that some of the members of your group have felt cheated by someone who didn't keep their promise or lied to them. However, through the study of this lesson, they will learn that God is always faithful and worthy of our trust. Remind them that the Lord always keeps his promises and wants us to be faithful people too. Use this opportunity to help your students understand that God wants to use our faithfulness to bless other people.

BIBLICAL COMMENTARY

The book of Ruth is a masterpiece in Hebrew literature, but not only that, it's also a beautiful example of the way God works through the people who are faithful to him.

Although at first sight the book seems to focus on the life of two women, it's actually a revelation of the power of God acting through the life of a faithful servant.

The first five verses tell us the background of a dramatic situation. A crisis triggers another and everything seems lost and hopeless. However, within a situation seemingly out of control for these two women, God shows his care and mercy in a majestic way.

Ruth responds to God's care with fidelity and obedience, and that's why the Lord chooses her, not only to be an example of faith and loyalty, but to be part of the genealogical tree of our Lord Jesus Christ.

LESSON DEVELOPMENT

Receive your students with joy and welcome those who attend for the first time. Begin the class by singing choruses of praise and prepare them to listen to the biblical truth using some of the following activities.

Spelling faithfulness

Before class, draw on a piece of posterboard the outline of all the letters of the alphabet and cut them out. Also write the word "faithfulness" twice and cut out the individual letters.

Mix up all the letters and place them in a basket. Then divide the class into 2 teams and give them a piece of posterboard and glue. Ask each team to find the letters that form the word "faithfulness" and paste them on the top of their poster board.

The team that finishes first will be the winner and will be able to choose a recreational activity to play at the end of the class.

What is faithfulness?

For this activity, you will need: used magazines, newspapers, scissors, colored pencils and glue.

Group your students into teams, and have them look in the magazines or newspapers for some images or words that represent "faithfulness" and paste them on their posterboard, under the word they placed in the first activity.

When both teams are finished, ask them to explain the content of their work, and use their answers as a basis to start today's bible story.

BIBLE STORY

Gather your students to hear the Bible story and tell them that each time they hear the word "Ruth" during the narration, they should clap once and when they hear the word "Naomi," clap twice.

Ruth, a faithful servant

Long ago, when the people of God were ruled by judges and not by kings, there was hunger in the land of Israel. The people didn't have enough food. For that reason, Elimelek, his wife Naomi (two claps) and their two sons went to live in a distant place called Moab.

After some time, Elimelek died and his sons grew up and married Moabite women: Ruth (clap) and Orpah. Ten years later, Naomi's sons (two claps) also died.

Naomi was very sad because she was alone in a foreign country, far from home.

"I'll return to my homeland; I have heard that God has blessed Israel and now there is food," said Naomi to Ruth and Orpah.

"We'll go with you," her daughters-in-law told her.

"My children," Naomi said, "go back to live with your families. You were very good to my sons and me. May

God have compassion on you and prepare new husbands for you."

Naomi went over to kiss them before leaving and they began to cry sadly.

"God be with you," Orpah said and kissed her goodbye and took the road back to Moab.

"Look, Ruth," said Naomi, "Orpah is returning to her village to be with her family; go with her."

"I won't go," said Ruth, "I won't leave you. Wherever you go I will go with you; your people will be my people, and your God will be my God."

When Naomi saw that Ruth wasn't going to change her mind, she stopped insisting.

The two women set out on the road to Israel and arrived in Bethlehem just as the harvest began. When the reapers cut the grain and picked it up, a little grain always fell on the ground. God had commanded the Israelites to leave the falling grain on the ground for poor people to pick it up and have food. That's what Ruth did. She went behind the reapers collecting the falling grain.

She was a hard-working woman and didn't stop to rest. She knew that if she didn't work, Naomi and she wouldn't have anything to eat.

While Ruth worked continuously, Boaz, the owner of the fields, was supervising the harvest.

"Who is that woman?" Boaz asked the manager of the reapers.

"Her name is Ruth; she came from Moab with Naomi," he answered. "She has worked all day without rest."

Boaz went to where Ruth was working and said, "Don't work in any other field; someone could hurt you. It's better to work in my fields where you will be safe."

"You are very kind!" Rut said to him. "Why are you so good to me, a foreigner?"

"I've heard that you're very good to Naomi," Boaz said.

When Ruth returned home that night, she told Naomi about all the grain she had collected and the kindness of the owner of the fields to her.

"Boaz is a relative of my husband," Naomi told her. "I'm glad he treats you well, so don't be afraid to work in his fields; he will protect you."

Ruth obeyed her mother-in-law and continued to gather the grain near Boaz's maidservants. She worked in the fields until the end of the harvest. In this way she managed to store large amounts of grain to ensure enough food for her mother-in-law and for her.

ACTIVITIES

Mobile: I can be faithful to God!

For this activity you will need: colored pencils, scissors, glue, yarn and punch.

Before class, cut a piece of yarn of 30 cm. and four pieces of 15 cm. for each child.

Distribute the Student Activities page of the student book, lesson 39, to your students and ask them to follow the instructions to assemble the mobile. Give them time to color the figures while reviewing the content of the lesson. Once the children finish coloring the figures, provide them with scissors to cut out each section of the craft. Help them make holes to assemble the mobile following the instructions.

Direct the attention of the children to the back of the figures of the mobile and tell them, Here it says, "I can be faithful to God." In what ways can we show our faithfulness to God? (Attending church, praying, obeying our parents, etc.)

If time and space allow, prepare a simple presentation for parents to observe the work their children did during class.

A faithful helper

Provide the children with pieces of paper cut out in a rectangular shape, and colored pencils.

Explain that on each piece of paper they should write a way in which they want to show their faithfulness to God and their parents during the week. For example: read the Bible daily, help my little brother with his homework, pick up the trash, pray for a sick person, etc.

It's important that your students focus on two or three activities, otherwise they will feel that they have committed to too much and will fail to keep their promises.

Pray asking God to help everyone to be faithful servants during the week.

Memorization

Before class, write the memory verse on a poster board and cut it into several puzzle pieces.

During class, have your students take turns putting the puzzle together and reading the Bible verse aloud. Record each child's time putting the verse together, challenge them to do it faster each week.

To end

Briefly review the important word of this unit (faithfulness) and sing some choruses of praise before saying goodbye. Remind your students that the next class will continue to study about being faithful servants for God, and encourage them to attend on time.

Boaz

Biblical References: Ruth 3-4

Lesson Objective: That the students learn that God uses faithful servants to fulfill his plans on earth.

Memory Verse: *But be sure to fear the Lord and serve him faithfully with all your heart; consider what great things he has done for you* (1 Samuel 12:24).

PREPARE YOURSELF TO TEACH!

Children are aware that they depend on their parents' care. They know that they provide them with food, clothing and the roof that covers them. It's likely that most of your students live in a home where they feel safe, thanks to the love and care of their parents. However, in other cases, this isn't the case, and some of your students will surely suffer from deficiencies because their parents don't fulfill their responsibilities as they should. Surely it will be harder to talk with them about God's care. Therefore, it's very important that your class, and the lessons that the children receive at church, are the means that God uses to show those children that he takes care of them.

Use the story of Boaz to teach your students that God needs faithful and obedient servants who are willing to be instruments of blessing to others.

BIBLICAL COMMENTARY

God's care and provision for this woman and her mother-in-law is evident by reading the first chapters of Ruth's story. However, Naomi's concern for the future of her young daughter-in-law emerges in chapter three. At the time of the conquest, Joshua distributed the land to the twelve tribes of Israel. However, no individual owned the land, because it was part of the family's inheritance. In Leviticus 25:23, God said, "The land must not be sold permanently, because the land is mine."

This portion of Scripture clearly details the procedures necessary to own, sell or recover a property. If the person needed to sell property (Ruth 4:3), it was the obligation and duty of the closest relative to buy it so it would remain in the family.

Naomi knew that Boaz was her closest relative and wanted him to take responsibility, not only for the land, but also for Ruth, as specified in Deuteronomy 25:5-10.

Ruth's loyalty and commitment were permanent while following the instructions of her mother-in-law. However, Boaz became the central figure in chapter 4. He did for Ruth and Naomi what they themselves couldn't have achieved: he took the initiative (4:1); rescued the property (4:8-9); restored the name of these women (4:9-10); and provided for their future (4:14-15).

Boaz followed all the legal and religious procedures necessary to help Ruth and her mother-in-law. He was obedient and fulfilled God's will by taking Ruth as his wife and being part of the genealogy of King David.

Sing with your students happy choruses to praise God before beginning the study of the Bible lesson. Pray for each other and collect the offering. Then briefly review the previous class so that the children relate the characters with today's story.

LESSON DEVELOPMENT

Loving care

You will need a small plant or a picture of a pet for this activity.

Show your students the plant or illustration and explain that they are living beings that need special care to survive. Allow them to participate by giving suggestions on how to care for plants or pets. For example: a plant needs water and sunlight, and a fish needs a special place to live, food and clean water to breathe.

Ask them: *What would happen if I forgot to take care of my plant or my pet?* (They could get sick or die).

Then make the transition to the bible story by telling them: *Just as my plant (or pet) needs special care, we also need to be cared for. Our Bible story today tells us about a man named Boaz, who was a faithful servant, used by God to take care of Ruth and Naomi.*

BIBLE STORY

Make simple puppets that represent Naomi, Ruth and Boaz to illustrate the story. Make them by using socks or paper bags, and decorate them with recycled materials. If you wish, prepare a simple scene with cardboard boxes, then you can use it for future presentations. Ask adults to help with the puppets as you tell the story.

Boaz helps Ruth

The life of Ruth and Naomi wasn't like before. Thank God they now had food and lived in a safe place. Every day, Ruth went to the fields of a man named Boaz to pick up grain. Boaz was very kind to Ruth,

133

allowing her to eat with the women who worked for him, and made sure that all his workers left enough grain for Ruth to pick up.

Ruth and Naomi were very grateful to God for having provided someone like Boaz to help them.

However, there was something that worried Naomi. Ruth was a young woman and she needed a husband who would love her and take care of her, who would also give her the possibility of having her own family.

One day Naomi spoke with Ruth and said, "I wish the best for you. I would very much like you to start your own family. Boaz is a close relative of our family. Tonight he will be separating the grains in his barn, so you must go see him. I will tell you what you should do."

Ruth dressed in her best dress and went to find Boaz. She waited until Boaz stopped to rest.

When they were alone, Ruth told him, "You are the protector of our family. Please, I would like you to take care of me by marrying me."

"Don't be afraid," Boaz said. "I'll take care of you because I'm your relative and all the people know that you're a good woman. But you have another closer relative than me. I'll go talk to him in the morning. If he wants to help you, you'll be fine. Otherwise, I will marry you and protect you."

The next morning, Boaz went to talk to the other relative. He met with him and ten other older men at the entrance of the city, and asked this man if he wanted to buy the part of the land that was Naomi's and marry Ruth.

"I don't want to buy the land or marry Naomi's daughter-in-law," said the closest relative.

In Israel, there was a custom that when two people made a deal on some property, each one had to take off one sandal and give it to the other.

Boaz addressed the older men and told them aloud, "This day you are witnesses that I bought the land that belonged to Elimelek, Kilion and Mahlon. I have also taken Ruth, the Moabitess, to make her my wife. She is the widow of Mahlon and I have decided to marry her to preserve the family."

Finally Rut and Boaz got married. Some time later they had a cute baby boy who was called Obed. Everyone was very excited about the birth of the child.

When Obed grew up, he had children and then many grandchildren. One of those grandchildren killed a giant named Goliath. He was King David, who was a descendant of Ruth and Boaz.

Many, many years later, another baby was born who was also a descendant of Ruth and Boaz. This baby was also born in Bethlehem and slept in a manger.

God rewarded the faithfulness of Ruth and Boaz by allowing them to be part of the family of King David, but above all, of the Lord Jesus.

The story of Ruth and Boaz

You need: Simple tunics or fabrics that can be used to cover, grains of corn or wheat, a doll and a blanket.

Provide the costumes and allow the children to act out some of the following scenes about the biblical story:

1. Naomi tells Ruth that she should go find Boaz;
2. Ruth talks to Boaz and he gives her grain to take home;
3. Boaz talking to the men at the gates of the city;
4. Ruth and Boaz get married;
5. Naomi takes care of baby Obed.

Animated card

Distribute the activity sheet from the student book (lesson 40). Read the prayer with them and have them sign it. Then give them enough time to follow the instructions on the sheet and make their animated card.

Ask them to take the cards home and tell their parents what they learned in today's lesson.

Memorization

Use the puzzle you made in the last class to review the memory verse.

Hide the pieces in different parts of the room before the students arrive. Let the children look for the pieces and assemble the text. Then, everyone can repeat the memory verse together. If there are volunteers who have learned the text by heart, ask them to say it. As a reward, they will receive the applause of the rest of the children.

To end

Repeat the memory verse aloud and remind them of the important word for this unit: "Faithfulness".

Form a circle, holding hands and there address them in a sentence. Conclude the class by singing a praise that speaks about God's faithfulness.

Don't forget to give them the work they have done during the class so that they can use them to tell their friends and family what they learned in this class.

Hannah

Biblical References: 1 Samuel 1:1-2:11, 18-21

Lesson Objective: That the students learn to trust in the faithfulness of God and increase their desire to pray.

Memory Verse: *But be sure to fear the Lord and serve him faithfully with all your heart; consider what great things he has done for you* (1 Samuel 12:24).

PREPARE YOURSELF TO TEACH!

Children who regularly attend church or belong to a Christian family are increasingly familiar with prayer. For them to pray is very simple; all they have to do is talk to Jesus. It's common to hear them give thanks for their pets and toys, and asking for protection for their parents while they work.

Children know that they have a direct line of communication with God, and that they can talk to him at any time of the day and in any place. This lesson will help you reinforce what they have learned over time about prayer. It will also make it easier for new believers to understand and trust that God listens to us and responds when we pray.

BIBLICAL COMMENTARY

Read 1 Samuel 1:1-2:11, 18-21. The first and second books of Samuel tell the story of Israel, from the conquest of Joshua to its captivity in Babylon. They reveal to us an astonishing and holy God who works through his servants and circumstances to fulfill his purpose. In the same way, they proclaim the presence and faithfulness of God in the history of his people.

At the beginning of today's story, Hannah lived with feelings of frustration, sadness and guilt. Being sterile in Hebrew society filled a woman with shame. Sons were important in preserving the name of the family, and for providing security for their parents in later adulthood. In addition, the husband had the legal right to divorce a sterile wife.

Hannah sought consolation and help from the only one that would listen and attend to her cry: God. She prayed humbly before him, expressing to him her frustrations and needs, and promised that if he gave her a son, she would dedicate him completely to His service.

God heard this woman's prayer and answered her request. Samuel was probably three years old when Hannah took him to the temple to fulfill the promise she had made to the Lord. Surely it was difficult for her to leave her little son for whom she had waited so long, under the care of the priest Eli. However, once again God showed his faithfulness to Hannah by granting her to be the mother of five other children.

LESSON DEVELOPMENT

Prepare in advance the teaching materials you will use for this lesson, and have your classroom ready before your students arrive.

Remember to welcome visitors and collect their info to contact them during the week.

Important words

Write the important words of this lesson (sacrifice, offerings) on the front of two cards, and write their meanings on the backs. Show them to your students.

Ask them: *Can anyone tell me what "sacrifice" means?* Allow the children to respond. Then read the definition on the back of the card and repeat the same procedure for the word "offering."

Sacrifice: A sacrifice is a priceless gift that we offer to God.

Offering: An offering is a gift that people give to God. It doesn't necessarily have to be money. It can also be time, obedience, service, etc.

Make sure your students have no doubts about these two concepts. And to make the transition to today's study topic, tell them: *In today's Bible story, we will talk about a woman who offered God a priceless gift. Her offering was a great sacrifice. Let's see what Hannah offered and why.*

Puppet

For this activity you will need: A paper bag and two strips of construction paper 5 cm. x 12 cm for each student, pieces of colored construction paper, scissors, glue, pencils or colored markers.

Tell your students: Our story today tells us about a woman named Hannah. Now we're going to make puppets with the figure of Hannah so that everyone can participate in the bible story. Give each student a paper bag and ask them to fold the construction paper strips to form the arms, then cut four circles of construction paper to form the hands and feet. They should stick their arms inside the folds of the bag, and the hands and feet where they go.

Give time for the children to draw their faces, hair and clothes.

Hannah's baby

For this activity you will need a doll. Hold the doll in your arms and say: *The bible story today is about a woman named Hannah who wanted to have a child, but couldn't. That's why she was very sad.*

Allow the children to hold the baby for a few moments and tell them that if they want to know what happened with Hannah, they should be alert during the Bible story.

BIBLE STORY

Ask the children to put the puppets they made onto their hands, and that each time they hear Hannah named during the Bible story, they should move their hands to pretend that Hannah is speaking.

Hannah keeps her promise

Long ago there lived a man named Elkanah who had two wives. In ancient times, it was permissible for a man to have two wives. One wife was called Peninnah and the other was Hannah.

Hannah loved God, but she was very sad. She felt this way because she didn't have any children, although she wanted them with all her heart. On the other hand, Peninnah did have children and always made fun of Hannah.

Each year Hannah and her husband Elkanah made a long journey to worship God in the temple and offer sacrifices. One day, while Elkanah was praying, Hannah began to cry.

"Dear God, you govern over all things. Please don't forget me, listen to my plea," Hannah prayed. "Please, allow me to have a child. If this happens, I promise you that I will give you my child to be your servant and I will love you forever."

In the temple there was a priest who took care of the house of God; his name was Eli. He was sitting near Hannah and watching her. While she was praying, her lips moved, but her words weren't heard because she was praying in her heart. Eli thought that she was drunk and that she had drunk wine, so he went over to talk to her.

"Leave the wine."

"I haven't drunk anything. I was praying to the Lord because I have a very big problem and I'm very sad," Hannah replied.

Eli told her, "Go in peace and may the God of Israel grant you what you ask."

When Hannah left the temple, she felt much better and wanted to eat. The next morning after worshiping God, Elkanah, Hannah and the rest of the family returned home. God heard Hannah's prayer and later gave her a son whom she called Samuel. Hannah was very happy because God had answered her prayer.

When it was time to return to Shiloh to worship God and offer sacrifices, Hannah stayed at home with baby Samuel. She told Elkanah, "When Samuel is older, I will return to Silo with you and leave Samuel in the temple to serve the Lord as promised."

The following years passed quickly. Although Samuel was still small, Hannah was ready to return to Silo and fulfill the promise she had made to the Lord. So she took her little son to the house of God.

After Elkanah had delivered his sacrifices to the Lord, Hannah took Samuel to Eli. And she said, "I'm the woman who came to pray to the Lord some years ago, asking for this child. Now I have returned to fulfill my promise to God and to deliver Samuel to his service. As long as Samuel lives, he will belong to God."

When Hannah and Elkanah returned home, Samuel remained in Shiloh and began helping Eli the priest in the temple work. But although Samuel didn't live in her house, Hannah still loved him, and every year she made him a new tunic and took it to him.

Eli knew that God was pleased that Hannah had fulfilled her promise, so he gave her a special blessing.

God was very kind to her and gave her three other sons and two daughters. When she saw Samuel serving in the temple, she always remembered that God had answered her prayer.

ACTIVITIES

After telling the Bible story, use this game to review what they learned. Divide the class into two teams. Use masking tape to form a large square on the floor. Divide the square into four parts and assign each section the following scores: 1, 2, 3 and 4 points. If you can't use duct tape, mark a square on a dirt floor with a stone, or on a cement floor with chalk.

Each team must form a row behind the square and move away at least half a meter from it.

You will need a bag full of grains or some other heavy object for the children to throw into the square. Depending on the score in which the bag has fallen, students will answer a review question. The team that answers correctly will have that number of points. You can continue to ask them questions and they will take turns throwing the bag and adding the points obtained. The team with the highest score will win.

Trifold

Ask a volunteer to distribute the activity sheets and cut outs from the cut out section from the student book. Then, provide glue for them to glue and fold the finished sheet to form a trifold.

Memorization

Form a circle and repeat the memory verse several times as they rotate. Then, allow volunteers to go to the center of the circle and say the memory verse alone. Help those who have difficulties with memorization.

To end

Briefly review the important words of this unit and collect the offering. Encourage your students to be faithful and obedient to God during the week, praying and obeying their parents and teachers.

Remind them that the next class is the last of this unit, so attendance is very important. Say goodbye with a prayer.

Samuel

Biblical References: 1 Samuel 2:12-17, 22-26; 3

Lesson Objective: That the students know that God wants them to listen to him and obey him in every decision that they make.

Memory Verse: *But be sure to fear the Lord and serve him faithfully with all your heart; consider what great things he has done for you* (1 Samuel 12:24).

PREPARE YOURSELF TO TEACH!

Obedience is a word that children understand well. With the passage of time, they have learned that when they disobey, there are usually negative consequences. They also understand that when they obey, there are often rewards. Teaching children to obey is a fundamental step to instill self-control and discipline. As we teach children to obey their parents and teachers, we are also directing them to do so with God.

Obedience is an essential part of faithfulness. Samuel was obedient to God, and for that reason, the Lord used him to do wonderful things. Samuel learned to listen to God.

Encourage your students to be attentive to the voice of God and to obey his will.

BIBLICAL COMMENTARY

Before the Word of God was available in written form, the Lord used different means to communicate with his people, for example through dreams, visions and supernatural events. However, 1 Samuel 3:1 says, "Young Samuel served Jehovah in the presence of Eli; in those days the word of Jehovah was scarce and visions weren't frequent."

Eli's sons were central to the problem that's reported in this chapter. Samuel 2:12 states that, "Eli's sons were ungodly men, who had no knowledge of Jehovah."

They demanded a special portion (in addition to the one they received as a donation from those who came to the temple), even before God received his share of the sacrifice. In the same way, the immoralities they committed with the women who worked in the temple violated the Ten Commandments and were probably behaviors that imitated the customs of the Canaanites.

In contrast, "the young Samuel grew and became pleasing before God and before men" (1 Samuel 2:26). God found in Samuel a diligent and obedient servant with whom he could communicate.

At first, Samuel didn't recognize God's call. However, Eli's wise counsel helped Samuel recognize the voice of the Lord and know what to do with the message he received. Although it was difficult, Samuel faithfully communicated God's message to Eli. From that moment, Samuel was recognized and approved as a prophet of God.

LESSON DEVELOPMENT

Receive your students with affection and ensure that the classroom is clean and tidy when they arrive. Before addressing today's topic, briefly review the three previous lessons and ask your students to give some examples of how they have been faithful to God during this month that's about to end.

Listen to the call!

For this activity, you'll need pieces of cloth to blindfold the eyes of your students. Move the chairs and tables to one end of the room to clear the space that will be used for the game and avoid accidents.

Divide your students in pairs; one will be the child and the other the parent. Blindfold the children's eyes and ask them to listen carefully to their parent's voice. This should be done by one pair at a time. All others must remain silent to give the child the opportunity to recognize his/her parent's voice. Once all pairs have completed this part of the game, separate the parents from the children and scatter them around the room.

When you say "Now!", the children should look for their parents guided only by their parent's voice. Those who act as parent should call until their child finds them.

Repeat the game several times, allowing students to swap roles. Make sure there are no objects that can hurt them while playing blindfolded.

Reflect on the importance of recognizing the voice of our heavenly Father.

Important words

During the week, write on a poster with large letters the three important words of the unit: faithfulness, sacrifice and offering. Cut out each letter and hide them inside the room before your students arrive.

Ask the kids to find the letters and form the words as quickly as possible. Put pieces of tape on the wall so that they can stick up the letters when they are found.

Ask three volunteers to come forward and explain to the whole group the meaning of the three important words.

BIBLE STORY

Before class, place two blankets and two pillows at opposite corners of the classroom. One bed will be for Eli and the other for Samuel.

At the beginning of the bible story, assign two students to act out the characters of Samuel and Eli. Ask them to lie on their beds until they hear the second part of the story, and when you give them the signal, they will stand up and follow the instructions in the story.

A voice in the night

The priest Eli had sons. They were also priests, but they did bad things and broke God's laws. Although they knew God's commandments, they didn't want to obey them.

When someone was going to offer a sacrifice at the temple, the priest used a certain portion of the meat as an offering to

God. Then, the priest could keep a portion for himself or share it with others.

Eli's sons didn't obey God's commandments for the offerings. Instead, they took the best pieces of meat they wanted before presenting the offering to God. When the people who offered the burnt offering asked them about it, they answered them in a bad way.

A short time later, Eli began to hear complaints about the behavior of his two sons. So he went up to them and mentioned that many complained about their bad behavior. But his sons didn't listen to their father's advice and continued to do evil in the eyes of God. However, Samuel grew and became stronger in the fear of the Lord.

One night, Eli and Samuel went to sleep as usual, but suddenly, God called Samuel. Samuel had never heard the voice of God before, so he didn't recognize it and thought it was Eli who had called him.

Samuel quickly got up from his bed and ran to where Eli was.

"I'm here. What did you call me to do?" Samuel asked.

But Eli replied, "I didn't call you; go back to bed."

Samuel returned to his bed and once more he heard a voice calling him by his name, so once again he went to where Eli was.

"My son, I haven't called you. Go back to bed," Eli repeated to the young man.

For the third time God called Samuel, but Samuel didn't recognize his voice, so he walked to where the priest was.

Finally, Eli realized what was happening; God was calling Samuel.

"Go back to bed," Eli replied to Samuel, "and if he calls you, say, 'Speak, Lord, for your servant is listening.'"

So Samuel went back to sleep and when he was in bed again, he heard the voice of God calling him and he answered as the priest had told him.

God gave Samuel a very sad message for Eli.

"Tell Eli that I'm going to punish his family. I have to do it because he knew that his sons were acting badly and didn't stop them."

When God had finished speaking, Samuel went back to sleep until the next morning.

At dawn, the young man was afraid to tell Eli what God had entrusted to him, but the priest called him to tell him the message he had received from the Lord.

"Tell me everything the Lord told you. Our God will punish you harshly if you hide a single word from me," he ordered.

So while Samuel told Eli everything, he listened intently.

"He is the Lord and will do what is best," the priest replied.

God was with Samuel as he grew up, and he continued to speak to him and give messages to the Israelites. Very soon, all the people of Israel knew that Samuel was the prophet that God had chosen.

ACTIVITIES

Review game

Write the following questions on paper strips and roll them well. Then insert each roll in a deflated balloon.

Inflate the balloons with the papers with the questions inside. Then distribute the balloons to the students so they can pop them and answer the questions. (If this isn't a practical activity for you, write the questions on small papers, place them inside a box or bag, and give each child a question to answer.) Help those who don't know the answer. You can add questions, depending on the number of students in your group.

1. What were Eli's sons doing?
2. What did the people of the town say to Eli?
3. What did Eli's sons do when he told them that they should stop their bad behavior?
4. How was Samuel different from Eli's sons?
5. What did Samuel hear?
6. What did Samuel do when he heard the voice calling him?
7. What did Eli tell Samuel to do when he heard the voice again?
8. What did God say to Samuel?
9. Who was Samuel's mother?
10. Where did Samuel live?

Handwork

Give the activity sheet from the student book to the children. Ask them: *Who is the boy in the drawing?* (Samuel) Ask some volunteers to briefly repeat what Samuel heard from God.

Play background music while your students color the illustration and cut the figure on the marked outline. Explain that they can use their finished work to hang on the door handle of their bedroom door when they are talking / praying to God and thus avoid interruptions.

Memorization

Ask two or three volunteers who have learned the memory verse by heart to come forward and say it to the rest of the group. If you can, give a small incentive (pencils, Bibles or candies) to those who have learned the full text.

If you wish, invite parents to listen to what their children studied during these four lessons.

To end

Don't let the children forget to take their things home (handicrafts, clothing, etc.). Thank each one for attending today's class and make a special mention of those who attended throughout the month. Announce the theme of the next unit: "God's amazing power", to catch the interest of the children. Finish with a prayer and remind the students that they should be faithful servants and be attentive to hear the voice of God.

Year 3

Introduction – Unit XI

GOD'S AMAZING POWER

Biblical References: Exodus 3-4; Exodus 13:17, 15:2; Exodus 16:1-17:7; Esther 1:1-4:17; Esther 5-8.

Unit Memory Verse: *God is our refuge and strength, an ever-present help in trouble* (Psalm 46:1).

Unit Objectives

This unit will help the elementary students to:

✗ Discover that God has more power than any movie or television hero.

✗ Know that God's power isn't a story, it's real.

✗ Know that God supplies the needs of his children.

✗ Trust in God in difficult times.

✗ Learn that God has the power to protect his children from the dangers they face.

Unit Lessons

Lesson 43: God gives Moses a special mission

Lesson 44: God rescues His people.

Lesson 45: God provides for His people.

Lesson 46: God protects His people.

Lesson 47: God shows His power.

Why Elementary Students need the teaching of this unit:

Children from any part of the earth love the stories of the heroes who, at the last moment, save the "good guys".

If you can communicate the biblical stories, and do so with suspense and emotion (without exaggerating the text), it's very possible that children will never forget the miracles and wonders of God.

Emphasize the following points:

1. Unlike the comic books of Batman, Superman, Tarzan and others; the prodigious stories of the Bible were real.

2. We have a God with unlimited power. That should take away all fear and fill us with trust in the God in whom we believe.

3. However hard and difficult our life may be, God can help us, since nothing is impossible for him.

God gives Moses a special mission

Biblical References: Exodus 3—4

Lesson Objective: That the students learn that when God gives them a special mission, He will help them accomplish it.

Memory Verse: *God is our refuge and strength, an ever-present help in trouble* (Psalm 46:1).

PREPARE YOURSELF TO TEACH!

The society in which we live values intelligence, beauty, popularity and talent. It's common for creative and talented people to receive greater praise and consideration than those who apparently don't show these qualities. For many of your students, it's normal to feel ignored and frustrated in face of the high standards that society imposes on them.

This is the first in a series of five lessons about the incredible power of God. Search in advance for songs that relate to this and write the letter lyrics on cards for your students to learn more easily.

Attendance Control

During the week, prepare an attendance chart for your students to complete during the course of the unit.

Look for people from your congregation to help you buy or create simple prizes to give to those who attend faithfully.

Tell the children that it's essential that they are constant in their attendance and punctuality, not only to win the prize, but to learn important biblical truths.

Important words

Before class, write the definition of the word "miracle" on the board.

Miracle: it is an amazing event that happens when God shows his power and there is no other explanation.

Tell your students that an important word of this unit is "miracle," and explain that throughout this unit they will learn about many miracles that God did to free his people.

Mysterious character

Ask the children to sit down in a circle to guess who the biblical character is that they will be studying in this unit.

You will read the following phrases, while they think in silence. Then ask that those who know who it is to raise their hand and answer in an orderly manner.

1. He was born and lived in Egypt during his childhood.
2. His family hid him when he was a baby.
3. He had a sister named Miriam.
4. He grew up in Pharaoh's palace until he was an adult.
5. For 40 years he was a shepherd of sheep in the desert of Midian.

BIBLE STORY

Gather your students to hear today's story. Open your Bible to Exodus 3 and tell the children: Our Bible story is found in the book of Exodus, chapters 3 and 4, and it tells us about Moses. Listen attentively to what happened to him while he looked after sheep in the desert.

A special mission and a promise

"Baa Baa!" The sheep bleated while Moses led them through the hot, dry desert.

He wanted to hurry up because there was still a long way to go. All the sheep were thirsty, tired and hot. Finally, they came to a mountain where they could rest a little.

Suddenly Moses saw something that caught his attention.

"What is happening to that bush?" he exclaimed, surprised.

He got closer to see it better ... The bush was on fire! He decided to get closer to see why the fire didn't burn it up.

"Moses, Moses!" called a voice from the bush.

"Here I am," he said surprised.

"Don't come any closer," God said. "Remove the sandals from your feet because you are standing in a holy place."

Quickly, Moses untied and removed his sandals. He stood very still, looking at the burning bush with huge eyes. He couldn't believe that the bush wasn't consumed by the strong fire!

"I'm the God of Abraham, Isaac and Jacob."

"Oh Lord," Moses said, hiding his face, because he was too afraid to look at God.

"I have seen what my people suffer in Egypt. Now I'm going to rescue them and take them to a beautiful land called Canaan. So now go. I command you to go to Pharaoh to free the Israelites from Egypt."

"Me? Why would Pharaoh, the king of Egypt, listen to someone like me? How could I free the Israelites?"

"I'll be with you," God promised. "And as a sign of this promise, when you have returned from freeing my people, you will worship me on this mountain."

Moses was afraid, so he began to argue with God.

"What will happen if the Israelites ask me, 'Who sent you to us?' What do I say?"

"Tell them, 'I am who I am.' Tell the Israelites that my name is "I am" and that I have sent you."

"What will happen if the leaders of Israel don't believe me and think that I'm inventing everything?" asked Moses.

"What do you have in your hand?" asked God.

"My shepherd's rod," replied Moses.

"Throw it on the ground."

The moment Moses obeyed, the rod became a serpent.

Moses ran away from the serpent in fear.

"Take it by the tail," God commanded Moses.

With fear and caution, Moses slowly took the snake, which, once it was in his hands, became a rod again.

"You will be able to do this miracle before the Israelites, then they will believe that I have sent you," the Lord said. God then ordered him, "Put your hand inside your jacket."

So Moses obeyed and when he pulled it out, it was covered in leprosy.

"I'm leprous," said Moses.

"Put it in again."

"The leprosy has disappeared," replied Moses.

"If the Israelites don't believe in the first miracle, they will believe in the second," God declared, "but if they don't, you will take water from the river and pour it into the earth, and the waters will turn to blood."

"But God, I'm too clumsy to talk well," said Moses.

"Wasn't I the one who gave you speech?" said God. "Now see, I will help you talk and I will teach you what to say."

"Oh God, please, send someone else!" Moses begged.

"Your brother Aaron speaks well, so take him with you. I will help you both in this mission. Don't forget to take your rod because through it you will do great miracles."

Finally, Moses obeyed God and went to say goodbye to his father-in-law Jethro. He took his wife and two children and set out on the long trip to Egypt. On the way he met up with Aaron.

When Moses and Aaron arrived in Egypt, they told the people everything that God had said to Moses on Mount Horeb. Moses did the miracles that God showed him in the desert, and the people understood that the Lord had heard their prayers and would free them from slavery.

ACTIVITIES

God helps us

Distribute the activity sheets from the student book, lesson 43.

Ask your students to complete the bible verse and color the figures of Moses. Then, you can ask them questions about what was happening in each scene.

When finished, ask them to turn over the page to talk about the illustration and what the girl felt. Then ask them: *Do you think that all of this girl's feelings of fear disappeared when she prayed? Why or why not?* (Sometimes God takes away all the fear we feel; at other times, He helps us know what to do even if we remain afraid.)

Give them time to do the activity, while doing a brief review of what they learned in the bible story.

Memorization

During the week, draw the outline of a burning bush on a piece of posterboard and color it with bright colors.

Then write each of the words of the memory verse on cards shaped like flames of fire.

Distribute a card to each child in a mixed up manner and then have them put the words in the right order on the shape of the bush. Repeat this activity several times with different children until it's easy for them to correctly order the verse.

Hang the poster in a visible place in the room as a reminder.

To end

Ask your students to organize and store the materials they have used during the day. Then gather them to intercede for prayer requests. Remind them that God has the power to help them do whatever he asks them to do, however difficult that may be, and encourage them to attend the next class.

141

God rescues His people

Biblical References: Exodus 13:17-15:2

Lesson Objective: That the students learn that God has power to help them in difficult situations.

Memory Verse: *God is our refuge and strength, an ever-present help in trouble* (Psalm 46:1).

PREPARE YOURSELF TO TEACH!

Children love stories about miracles. The miraculous deliverance of the Israelites in Exodus 14 will allow them to learn more about the signs and wonders that our God does.

It's likely that some of your students are suffering in a situation of domestic violence or separation from one or more parents and pray for a miracle to help them resolve this situation beyond their control.

It's important that through this lesson you strengthen their confidence and belief that God has the power to help them solve even the most difficult problems. However, it's also important to emphasize that God isn't a "wish-fulfilling machine," but a loving Father who listens to us and answers our requests according to his will. Sometimes, God's answers aren't immediate, but they are never late.

BIBLICAL COMMENTARY

Exodus 13:17. Finally, after hundreds of years, the Israelites were liberated from their bondage and God led them away from Egypt. However, he took them the long way. Surely for the people it was very difficult to understand why it would be easier to survive in a dry hot desert, than to make pyramids under the mistreatment of the Egyptians.

But God had his plans, and taking them the long way was his strategy to protect them. He knew that at that time, the Israelites were vulnerable and easily discouraged, so the long way was the best way to avoid wars with enemy people.

It's very significant to know that among all the belongings that were carried with them on this long journey were Joseph's remains. Exodus 13:19 says, "Moses also took with him the bones of Joseph, who had made the children of Israel swear by saying to them, 'God will certainly visit you, and then you will take my bones from here with you.'" Joseph wanted to be buried in the land that God had promised Abraham many years before the exodus of the people. Joseph trusted God and believed in the covenant that the Lord had made with Abraham many years ago.

On the other hand, the Israelites lost their faith very quickly while they were in the hot desert. Their first mistake was to question if God had abandoned them. God knows what He's doing when He takes us the long way. While it challenges us to remain firm in our faith and trust in him, it also enables us to get to where he wants us to go. God never leaves us alone; he goes before us to open the way. The Lord went before the Israelites as a pillar of cloud and fire as they walked through the desert.

God doesn't promise to rescue us from all difficult situations, however we can be sure that he will always be there to help us get ahead with his power.

LESSON DEVELOPMENT

Wait at the door for your students and as they enter the classroom, ask them to sit in a semicircle. Pray and give thanks to God for the week that ended and the one that begins. Welcome the visitors and make them feel comfortable with each other.

Biblical review

Draw or paste on the board the figures of: a fly, hail and frogs.

Ask the children: *What do these three figures have in common with our previous class?* (These were some of the plagues God sent on Egypt to free the Israelites.) Listen to the children's responses and briefly review what they studied last week.

Who can help me?

Use this activity for your students to learn who they should approach for help in certain situations, and also to make the transition to the biblical story.

Write the following questions on the board and let your students talk to each other to find the answers. Listen to what they say and complement their ideas with the answers that appear in parentheses.

Who would you ask for help if ...?

✘ You get lost in a store and you can't find your parents. (A store clerk, a security guard or a policeman.)

✘ Someone tries to hurt you at school. (A teacher, the principal or a school employee.)

✘ You are trying to fix something that's too complicated for you. (My parents, an adult friend or my older sibling.)

✘ You have questions about God. (My parents, my pastor or Sunday School teacher.)

✘ You feel sad or disappointed. (God, my parents.)

Caught!

Ask two of the taller students to stand face to face in a open area. Ask them to hold hands and enclose a third in their arms. Suggest they don't press too hard.

Then tell the third student: *Now you are stuck and you have to find a way out of there without hurting your peers.*

Let him try to get out, and if/when he escapes, let others try it.

Tell them: *Today we will hear about a group of people who were trapped and without a way out; they were sure that they were going to die and only God could save them.*

BIBLE STORY

Ask the children to sit in a semicircle and ask them to open their Bible to Exodus 13:17. Tell them: In the last class we learned that God punished Egypt with ten different plagues because Pharaoh didn't want to free the Israelites that he kept as slaves. In today's story, we'll learn what happened when they finally were able to leave that country.

Rescue at the Red Sea

Imagine what it would be like to live for years working as slaves under the hot sun of the desert. Imagine working every day making bricks and carrying heavy rocks from one place to the other. That was the way the Israelites lived before God sent Moses to deliver them from Egypt.

God sent ten plagues upon the Egyptians before Pharaoh finally released them and let them go. The people were happy with the news. God had promised them that He would take them to a beautiful land. Everyone praised him because they would finally be free from Egyptian slavery.

The Israelites took all of their belongings, including their animals, and left happily from the land where they had been held captive for so many years. However, God didn't take them by the short way to the land of Canaan, but chose the long way.

God laid out a special plan to guide the Hebrews to the land of Canaan. He let them know that he would be with them: a column of clouds would guide them during the day and at night a pillar of fire would light there way as they traveled.

When they reached the shores of the Red Sea, the people camped, and that's where the problems began.

"Here come the Egyptians!" someone shouted.

"Look at the dust that their chariots raise; they're getting closer!"

Pharaoh had changed his mind and wanted his slaves to return to their labors.

"We should have stayed in Egypt!" others shouted. "Why did you bring us to die in the desert?" they asked Moses. God had told him that the Egyptians would come after them, but he also knew that God was more powerful.

"Don't be afraid; watch and you will see that the power of God will free us from danger!" said Moses to the people.

The noise of horses and chariots was heard closer and closer.

When it began to get dark, God moved the column of cloud and put it between the Hebrews and the Egyptians. The people of God would be able to see to continue traveling, while the Egyptians would be in darkness.

"Raise your staff over the sea," God commanded Moses.

Moses obeyed and the wind blew so hard that it opened the sea in two, forming a dry road for the Israelites to cross.

Very early in the morning, all the people began to cross the sea by the dry road, and when they looked back they realized that the Egyptians were following them on the same road.

God caused the wheels of the Egyptian chariots to break and the soldiers shouted, "We must get away from the Hebrews; their God is fighting against us!"

When the Hebrews got to the other shore, God told Moses to raise his staff and the waters returned to their place. All the Egyptian soldiers, their horses and their chariots were covered by the sea. Through his great power, God saved his people.

Moses and all the people praised God and sang happily: "God is my strength and my song, from him comes my salvation. He is my God and I praise him."

ACTIVITIES

A wonderful rescue

Give the children the activity sheets from the student book to work on. Follow the instructions to do the activity. As they do, ask them: *In what way did God rescue the Israelites? What happened to the Egyptians? What was it that caused the waters of the sea to open in two?*

Review the story as they work and turn the page and fill in the blanks with the corresponding words.

Memorization

During the week, look in a book or magazine for a picture of a castle or fortress and take it to class with you so that the students can observe it.

Explain that in ancient times, kings built these fortresses to defend themselves against enemies. They used large stones to build high walls so no one could get in. In times of war, those inside the fortresses were safe.

In the same way, the memory verse in this unit reminds us that God is our refuge and strength, therefore, we shouldn't fear.

Hand out paper and colored pencils to draw a fortress and write the memory verse as a reminder.

To end

Thank God for what they learned and don't forget to invite them to next week's class to study more about the great power of God.

God provides for His people

Biblical References: Exodus 16:1-17:7

Lesson Objective: That the students learn that God supplies the needs of His children.

Memory Verse: *God is our refuge and strength, an ever-present help in trouble* (Psalm 46:1).

PREPARE YOURSELF TO TEACH!

It's important for your students to hear about the wonderful ways God has cared for his children over time. The children will find something magical in today's class by listening to the way God fed the Hebrew people.

Without harming their childlike faith, explain that not all prayers are answered through a miracle, but that doesn't mean that God has forgotten them.

God provides for our needs in different ways and helps us trust him more. Teach the children why it's important to present our requests and needs to God in prayer. He's careful of all aspects of our lives.

As students tell their prayer requests, encourage them to be grateful to receive the Lord's answers.

Children must not only know God as the only miracle worker, but they also need to remember that he is always with them, taking care of them and helping them through all the situations they go through. And although they often feel alone, they can trust that the Lord is always by their side.

BIBLICAL COMMENTARY

Exodus 16:1-17:7. The people of God had left behind the land of Egypt, and along the desert road, complained and longed for what they had left. They wanted the fresh water and the warm bread they enjoyed in their homes in Egypt.

When they reached Mara, they found a source of bitter water. After the people complained and argued against Moses, God directed him to hit the rock with his staff and the water became sweet.

After being in Mara, the Israelites were led to Elim (Exodus 16:1). In that place there were twelve water sources and seventy palm trees that gave good shade, so they decided to camp there.

A month had passed since the miracle of the Red Sea. God had provided their needs with fresh water and a comfortable place to rest before guiding them into the desert of Sin. However, it wasn't long before they began to complain again against Moses for having led them away from Egypt.

God wanted his people to trust and depend solely on him. He responded to their complaints with great love and provided the manna, which would be the source of food for the Israelites for forty years.

Every morning they would find manna on the ground and they would gather enough for that day. If they kept a larger supply than they needed, the next day it would be rotten and covered with worms. The only day they could gather a double portion of manna would be the morning before the Sabbath.

God once again demonstrated his power by caring for his people and sending food from heaven to them.

LESSON DEVELOPMENT

Our suggestion to start today's lesson involves investing an extra hour before class to clean the class room floor very well. You will also need a packet of cookies and napkins.

Place the cookies on napkins and place them on the floor around the room. Ask your students to be careful when entering so as not to step on the surprise there.

Tell them that today's lesson talks about a special way God took care of his people when they were in the desert.

No more than one

Get a bag of wrapped candy before class.

During class, ask the class to sit in a circle on the floor. Tell them: *Close your eyes while I count to three, then I'll drop candies around the room. Then, you can open your eyes and get one. If you take more than one, you'll lose them.*

After the children have picked up their treat, ask them: *Do any of you have more than one candy?* If anyone has two or more, ask him to give you all the candy they have.

Ask them again: *Was it difficult to take only one?*

Listen to their answers and tell them: *It's very important to follow instructions, otherwise we may have problems. Today we'll learn what happened to the Israelites when they didn't follow God's instructions.*

What happened to the bread?

You need a piece of old or spoiled bread.

Gather your students and tell them: *Sometimes when we go to the store, we buy more bread than we can eat. Do you know what happens when the bread gets old?* (Mold form on it and it smells bad.)

Show the old bread to the class and ask them: *Would you like your mother to use this bread to prepare dinner?* Let them respond and tell them: *In today's story we'll hear about some people who made a wrong decision and something bad happened to their food.*

BIBLE STORY

Gather your students to hear the bible story. Ask a young man in your congregation to wear a robe and disguise himself as Moses to tell this story.

A miracle from the sky

"The exodus from Egypt and the escape through the Red Sea were just the beginning of a long journey for all of us. God led us from one place to another through the desert. Sometimes there wasn't enough water to drink. When that happened, the Israelites complained to me and began to complain about leaving Egypt. I wish they would trust God instead of complaining all the time."

"The Lord took us to Elim, an oasis in the desert with palm trees and water fountains. After that, we traveled to the Sin desert, where we ran out of food and the hungry people started to complain to me once again."

"Why didn't God let us stay in Egypt? There we had a lot of food and here we will die soon," they told me.

"I spoke with God to find a way to solve this problem."

"I will send to the people a special bread that will descend from the sky every morning. I will also send quail in the afternoon to give them meat to eat."

"In addition, he gave us special instructions about the manna and told us, "Go out every morning and collect enough food for each person in your house, but take only what you will need for that day. Don't pick up anything extra. On the sixth day of the week, pick up a double portion so that you have food on the Sabbath."

"The next morning after the dew evaporated, there were pieces of manna throughout the desert. Its flavor was sweet like honey."

"However, the Israelites didn't follow the instructions God gave us and took more manna than they needed for that day. The next morning there was a terrible smell in their tents, and they found many worms in the bread they had collected."

"However, this didn't cause them to follow God's instructions. On the sixth day, when they were supposed to collect enough manna for two days, many didn't. And then on the Sabbath, they went to collect their portion of bread, but there wasn't any. God had said that he would only provide manna on six days."

"We received the manna from heaven six days a week for the forty years we lived in the desert. God commanded us to put a portion of manna in a container and save it so that new generations would know the miraculous way in which God fed his children."

"The day came when we had to go somewhere else. We traveled for a while and finally we camped in Rephidim, a place where there was no water. The people began to complain to me again and they asked me why I had taken them to the desert to die."

"Again I approached God to ask for his help and he told me to take the leaders of Israel and go to a rock on Mount Horeb and hit the rock with my staff."

"I obeyed and crystal clear water came out of the rock. Another miracle of our great God to show the people that he had control over everything."

ACTIVITIES

God provides

Hand out the student activity sheets from the student book and ask the children to sit down to do the activity. Read the instructions aloud so everyone can hear them clearly and then complete their project.

Explain what they must do to finish the activity, and as they work, review what they learned in today's Bible lesson.

Deliver your needs

For this activity you will need a small cardboard box for each student, pencils or colored markers, and other items to decorate.

Give a box to each student and ask them to decorate it to their liking. Each box must have a hole that they can fit a folded sheet of paper through.

Then give them pieces of paper to write their prayer requests on, and place then them inside the box.

Tell them that just as Moses asked God for their needs, they can also do so by writing their petitions and keeping them in their prayer box. If they wish, they can invite others to place their prayer requests inside his/her box. Also their parents and siblings can place their requests there.

Memorization

Ask the children to walk backwards. For each step they take, they must say a word of the memory verse. Repeat the text until they have gone around the room. Then review it with them individually and encourage those who have difficulties learning it.

To end

Pray giving thanks to God for his provision and care. Also intercede for all the people around the world who need food.

Give the children the work they did, and invite them to the next class.

God protects His people

Biblical References: Esther 1:1-4:17

Lesson Objective: That the students trust God, even in difficult times.

Memory Verse: *God is our refuge and strength, an ever-present help in trouble* (Psalm 46:1).

PREPARE YOURSELF TO TEACH!

The power of our God is incomparable and is what helps, protects and provides us with the courage to follow him. While it's true that God has not called us to be "superheroes," surely the moment will come when, because of Christ, we have to do something dangerous. However, most Christians have ordinary lives. That doesn't mean that we don't have to face the danger of sin and the temptations that the world offers.

Elementary children are beginning to discover a world hitherto unknown to them. Television, friends and the media put within their reach a great variety of temptations that want to trap them in sin. It's important that through this lesson, children learn to trust God when they feel tempted or in trouble. Queen Esther's valuable example will help them know that God is willing to help them face the dangers if they humbly ask.

BIBLICAL COMMENTARY

Read Esther 1:1-4:17. The series of strange events that led Esther to occupy the throne of the provinces of Persia may seem like a mere coincidence. But Mordecai, Esther's uncle, didn't believe that. He was sure that Esther had come to that position for a particular reason.

The Scripture doesn't give us many details about this story, such as: why Mordecai refused to let Esther talk about her origins, nor do we know why Mordecai allowed his niece to marry a Gentile, as was forbidden by Hebrew laws.

Esther was chosen as a candidate to be the king's wife and had to undergo a beauty regime for twelve months. Finally, she appeared before him and he chose her as queen, instead of Vashti. According to tradition, this process took about four years.

The coming events were a combination of evil, envy and hatred of Haman towards the Jews. However, God's faithfulness was in force and he chose to use Esther to protect his people.

LESSON DEVELOPMENT

Pray giving thanks to God for the opportunity to meet again to study His Word and sing some choruses. Explain to the class that they're going to study another book of the Bible. In the three previous lessons they studied Exodus, but this time they'll study the book of Esther.

Help them find Esther in their Bibles and save the place with a pencil to use during today's story.

Who?

Write on the board the letters that make up Esther's name in disorder, for example: TSREE. Then ask your students to try to arrange the letters to find the name of the biblical character they'll study during these two lessons.

Crowns for the king

For this activity you will need: a wide strip (15 cm or more) of construction or thick paper for each child, scissors, glue, tape, colored pencils or markers, and colored pieces of paper.

Distribute the materials and place a strip of paper around the head of each child and mark the place where the strip must match so that the crown is tailored. Help them join the ends of their crowns with the tape.

Give them time to write their name on the crown and decorate it to their liking.

As you work, ask them: *Who uses crowns?* (Kings and queens.) *What do kings and queens do?* (They govern a country, they help people and they make sure everything works well.)

Explain: *Kings and queens serve their people. Their job is to guarantee the safety of the people, provide work sources and administer the resources of the community. At present, many countries no longer have kings and queens, but presidents. However, in biblical times it was Kings and Queens who ruled. Today we will study about a queen who trusted in God to help her people.*

A brave queen

King Xerxes, who ruled Persia and its provinces, decided to hold a large banquet and invite all the important officials of the kingdom. Queen Vashti also organized a party for her friends.

The king sent a messenger to tell Queen Vashti, "Come to my party, because I want everyone to see how beautiful you are."

She replied, "I'm not coming."

When the queen refused to go, the king became very angry, so he went to his counselors and asked them, "What should I do with the queen? She didn't want to obey me and refused to come to my banquet!"

"Don't let Vashti remain the queen; it's better to look for another woman to occupy the throne," they replied.

The king smiled, thought it was an excellent idea, and began the search to find the future queen.

Mordecai was a Jew who lived in Persia. He had a beautiful niece named Esther. One day the servants of the king came to Mordecai's house and saw Esther.

"She is very beautiful!" they exclaimed. "We'll take her to the palace."

Esther had no other choice; she had to obey the king's order. But before leaving the house, Mordecai told her, "Don't tell anyone that you're Jewish, and don't worry about anything. I'll take care of it."

Esther was taken to the royal palace along with other young and beautiful women. For twelve months, the servants of the king helped them to become even more beautiful. She was well received in the palace; everyone loved her and cared for her a lot.

Mordecai didn't forget Esther, and every day he went to the palace gardens to ask about his niece.

Finally the day came when Esther would meet the king. She dressed in beautiful clothes and did everything the king's servants told her to do.

When the king saw her for the first time, he was delighted with her beauty and chose her as queen. Then, he organized a big banquet in her honor so that everyone would know that she was his new wife.

Like every day, Mordecai went to the palace to hear news of his niece. However, that day was different because he heard that two soldiers were planning to kill the king. So he immediately went to see his niece and told her what he had heard.

Esther told her husband about the plan, and the plans of the soldiers were revealed. This fact was written in the book of the chronicles of the king.

In the kingdom there was also a mean officer named Haman. However, he won the approval of the king, who gave him a very important position. All the people knelt and worshiped Haman, except one person ... Mordecai.

"Why don't you obey the king's command?" the officers asked Mordecai. But he still didn't kneel before Haman.

Soon this news reached the ears of Haman, who was very angry and said, "As punishment I will kill Mordecai and all the Jews." Quickly, Haman went before the king and said, "There is a group of people who live in your kingdom but don't respect you and don't obey your laws. Please, take this money and use it to hire men to kill those people."

"Save your money," the king said. "Here is this ring that will make official what you and I have spoken of; do what you want with those people."

Haman wrote a new law that said: "On the 13th of the 12th month, all people must kill all the Jews they find and seize their property." Then he sealed the law with the king's ring and sent it to all the provinces.

When Mordecai heard the news, he became very sad, covered his head with ashes, and dressed in old clothes in pain.

One day, Esther's servant said to her, "Your uncle Mordecai is outside and wants to see you. He's crying and he's dressed in bad clothes; it seems he's very sad."

Esther loved her uncle very much, so she asked the servant to take him clean and comfortable clothes to change.

The servant returned immediately with the clothes because Mordecai hadn't wanted to accept them. His sadness was very great and all he wanted was for the queen to know what was happening.

Mordecai asked the servant to inform his niece about the bad news.

"Our people will be exterminated," said Mordecai. "I'm dressed in these clothes because of the sadness I feel."

Esther learned what Haman had planned. Her uncle asked her to talk to the king and ask him for help.

But Esther said, "I cannot go. The king has not asked to see me for thirty days. If I go without an invitation, he will kill me."

"Don't think that you will escape in the king's house more than any other Jew. Because if you keep quiet at this time, deliverance will come from somewhere else for the Jews; But you and your father's house will perish. And who knows but that you have come to your royal position for such a time as this," answered Mordecai.

When Esther heard these words, she thought of doing something to help. He asked Mordecai and the other Jews who lived in the city to pray for her, not to eat anything for three days, but to just pray.

She decided to obey God to save her people and cried out to ask for the help of the Lord.

Mordecai, Esther and the Jewish people prayed and fasted for three days.

What would happen to them? Could someone stop Haman's terrible plan? Don't miss the end of this exciting story next week.

ACTIVITIES

I'm not afraid

For this activity you will need white paper and colored pencils.

Distribute the materials among the students and ask them to draw a picture or write a story about the things that scare them or cause them fear.

Watch them as they work and talk to them about the importance of trusting God when we feel fear or situations seem out of control.

Give them time for each one to show their work and say what it represents. Talk about their fears, and use the story of Esther to teach them that God helps us to be brave if we trust him.

Then put a basket or trash can in the center of the room so that each one passes by and tears up his drawing while saying: *I'm not afraid, because I trust in God and he helps me to be brave.*

Trust in God

Prepare in advance the materials that the student book suggests and make sure there is enough for all the children. You will need: paper plates and yarn or wire for each student, colors, markers, crayons, scissors and glue.

During the class, help the children to do the craft on the activity sheet. As they work, ask: *What characters trusted God in today's story?* (Esther and Mordecai.) *God helped Esther to be brave and do the right thing to help her people. We must also trust God to help us be brave, and we must always do the right thing, no matter how difficult the situation is.*

Encourage the children to take their completed work home and tell them: *The next time you are faced with a difficult situation, look at this figure and remember that you can trust God and ask him to help you be brave.*

Memorization

Ask your students to sit facing forward and tell them to close their eyes. Write the memory verse on the board. Then the children will be able to open their eyes and read it. Ask them to close their eyes again while you erase some of the words. Then they should open their eyes and say the whole verse. Repeat the exercise until all the words are erased and they can say the full biblical passage from memory.

To end

Form a prayer circle to thank God. Say: *He helps us to be brave and to trust in his power when we face a problem.* Give them the opportunity to tell their prayer requests.

Encourage the children to trust in God during the week. Tell them to talk to their family about what they learned in today's class.

Tell them that next week they will study the last lesson of this unit, which will deal with the rest of the story of Esther and the power of God, so it will be very important for everyone to attend.

 Notes:

148

God shows His power

Biblical References: Esther 5-8

Lesson Objective: That the children know that God has the power to protect His children from danger.

Memory Verse: *God is our refuge and strength, an ever-present help in trouble* (Psalm 46:1).

PREPARE YOURSELF TO TEACH!

The most popular television programs among children are usually those about heroes with special powers that allow them to fly, freeze their enemies, become invisible and see through the walls. Children enjoy seeing how their imaginary heroes triumph. These titans defeat their enemies by means of superpowers, and it's common that in children's games, they imitate those behaviors and pretend to be those characters.

And although all of this is a product of the imagination of the creators of cartoons, it's important that they learn that only God has the power to do anything great.

Not only that, but God wants his children to enjoy his blessings and be part of his plans. He wants to use his power through us to reach a world that lives in darkness.

As you teach this lesson, ask the Holy Spirit to help them understand that God's power is beyond our understanding, and is available to all who trust in him.

BIBLICAL COMMENTARY

Esther 5-8. Anyone who says that reading the Bible is boring has definitely not read the book of Esther. In it are all the elements that an exciting story must have to catch the reader's attention.

In today's story, Esther is about to appear before the king and is prepared for what may happen. Unless King Xerxes extends his royal scepter to her when she approaches him, the guards have orders to kill her, regardless of whether she is the queen or not.

There are two characters that play a very important role in today's story. The most visible is Esther. Surprisingly, the God of all creation, who can do what he wants, chooses to work through human hands to fulfill his divine purpose. Through this story, God allowed ordinary people to do extraordinary things, even when their lives were in danger. Esther was an ordinary woman who decided to be obedient to God, and was able to save an entire people.

It's also important to emphasize the faithfulness of Mordecai. This man remained faithful to God and decided not to bow before the wicked Haman. This story reminds us once again that God desires obedient and faithful servants to follow him and trust in his power.

God used Esther in a very special way to save the Jewish people from death. It was the fidelity and testimony of her uncle Mordecai that encouraged her to obey the will of God. She trusted that the power of the Lord could make possible what seemed impossible.

LESSON DEVELOPMENT

Since this is the unit's last lesson, we suggest that you prepare something to reward students who have faithfully attended. Create simple thank-you cards or Bible verses to give to the students.

Sing some praise songs before you start the learning activities.

What does the Queen want?

In this game, the teacher will represent the queen and the students will be the subjects. The queen must sit on one side of the room, while the students will be at the opposite end.

She will give varied commands to the subjects, for example: "Robert, you must take three small steps forward." You can also ask them to jump, walk backward, etc. Repeat the game until all your students have participated.

Say: *Kings and Queens can give orders to their subjects because they are the rulers, and they have many people at their service. In today's story, we're going to hear what happened to Queen Esther after hearing that bad news.*

BIBLE STORY

Before starting today's story, it's important that together you review what you studied last week. In this way they will remember the characters and learning will be more effective.

If desired, choose volunteers to narrate what they learned the previous week or read the corresponding Bible passage.

Before class, write on a piece of posterboard or construction paper the following sentence: **God is in control!** Then, show it to your students and tell them: *When I show you this phrase during the Bible story, you should repeat these words out loud. Listen carefully so you know what the end of this story is.*

Power that saves

Esther was very thoughtful; finally she stood up and said, "I have to see the king." (Show the sentence: "God is in control.")

She had been praying and fasting for three days. (Sentence)

After three days, she went to see the king. She was afraid because nobody could see the king without an invitation. However, she knew that God was with her. (Sentence)

King Xerxes was very pleased to see Esther and gave her permission to speak with him: he extended his royal center, which meant that he spared his life. (Sentence)

"What's the matter, Queen Esther? Why did you come to see me? Ask me what you want and I will give you what you want ... even up to half of my kingdom," King Xerxes told her. (Sentence)

Esther replied, "King Xerxes, I would like to invite you to a banquet tonight that I have prepared for you. Please come and also bring Haman."

The king and Haman accepted the queen's invitation to go to the banquet. (Sentence)

The king asked her, "What can I do for you, Queen Esther?"

"I have to ask you something very important. Please, bring Haman to dinner with you tomorrow and there I will answer your question," she replied.

Haman, who was very proud, went to the banquet. He still felt annoyed because Mordecai hadn't bowed down to him, but he was very excited that King Xerxes and Esther had invited him to the banquet.

Haman boasted to his friends and family, "Today I was eating with the king and queen. I have many riches and I'm invited to another banquet tomorrow. However, none of that makes me happy when I see Mordecai sitting at the royal gate.

"Ask King Xerxes to kill him," suggested his wife.

"Surely, the king won't deny you anything," his friends said.

So Haman had a very large gallows built to hang Mordecai the next day.

That night the king couldn't sleep, so he asked one of his servants to bring him the book of the royal chronicles and to read it in his presence. (Sentence)

When they read the part in which Mordecai helped save the king's life, King Xerxes asked, "What did we do to reward Mordecai for saving my life?"

"Nothing, sir," the servant replied.

Then the king heard a noise and asked, "Who is in the yard?"

"It's Haman."

King Xerxes ordered Haman to come in and asked him, "How should we reward someone whom the king wants to honor?"

Haman thought it was about him and replied, "You must give him beautiful clothes, a beautiful horse and put a crown on him for all to see."

Then the king said to him, "That's a great idea. Hurry and do all of that for the Jew Mordecai."

Haman did everything the king asked of him. But he was very angry! So he went home and told his wife and friends everything that had happened. At that time, the servants arrived to take him to dinner with the King and Queen. (Sentence)

While at the banquet, the king asked Esther what her request was, and she told him everything that was going to happen to her people. She told him that she was Jewish and that the law he had signed endangered her life and that of her people. (Sentence)

The king did what Esther asked of him and made a new law to keep the Jews safe. (Sentence)

Haman was punished for his evil deeds on the same gallows that he had built for Mordecai. And Mordecai, along with all the Jews of the kingdom, had a great celebration and praised God. They were very happy because he had saved them from certain death. (Sentence)

The king gave Mordecai a good position and they didn't fear again because they knew that God had delivered them from the hand of their enemies.

ACTIVITIES

The great power of God

Distribute the activity sheet from the student book and pencils. Help them put the puzzles together, putting the lost words and figures in the right place. Ask some volunteers to read the sentences out loud. Encourage them to trust in the power of God when they feel fear or face a difficult situation.

You can help too!

Ask the children to sit in a circle and wear the crowns they made during the previous class. Encourage them to imagine that they are kings or queens, and think about how they could help other people, just as Queen Esther helped her people.

Ask some volunteers to go to the center of the circle and tell how they would help other people if they were the kings or queens of a nation.

Explain that even if they don't become powerful kings or queens, they can be helpful to their neighbors, for example: picking up trash from the church, helping an older person, helping with household chores, etc.

Memorization

Talk with your pastor or director of Sunday School ministries about giving the children special involvement in the worship service. Prepare the students to recite the memory verse learned during this unit.

Help the little ones or those who have difficulties with learning.

To end

Encourage the children to trust God in the midst of problems. Remind them that through all these lessons they have learned that God's power is greater than anything else. Tell them that the power of the Lord is available to all those who trust in him and obey him.

Year 3

Introduction – Unit XII

THE STORY OF CHRISTMAS

Biblical References: Matthew 1:18-25; 2:1-12; Luke 1:26-38; 2:1-7; 2:8-20; John 3:16; 1 John 4:9.

Unit Memory Verse: *For God so loved the world that he gave his one and only Son, that whoever believes in him shall not perish but have eternal life* (John 3:16).

Unit Objectives

This unit will help the elementary students to:

- ✘ Understand the importance of obeying God.
- ✘ Understand that everyone needs the Savior, Jesus Christ.
- ✘ Awaken in themselves a spirit of evangelism.
- ✘ Understand that God appreciates the praise and worship of His children.

Unit Lessons

Lesson 48: The gift of obedience

Lesson 49: The gift of a Savior

Lesson 50: The gift of praise

Lesson 51: The gift of worship

Why Elementary Students need the teaching of this unit:

This unit will allow you to help your students understand that when they obey God, things will go much better than when they disobey. The God's guidance is always for the good of the one who follows it.

As you develop the explanation of Christmas, you can awaken in them the desire to speak about Jesus to friends or relatives who don't know the Lord. But they aren't doing it as one who recruits people for a club, but because they have understood firstly that people without God are empty, sad and hopeless.

And finally, this unit provides a wonderful opportunity to instill in them the understanding that God expects them to spend time with him each day, and to hear from their lips words of worship and gratitude for the many blessings that he pours out upon their lives.

The gift of obedience

Biblical References: Matthew 1:18-25; Luke 1:26-38

Lesson Objective: That the children desire to obey God.

Memory Verse: *For God so loved the world that he gave his one and only Son, that whoever believes in him shall not perish but have eternal life* (John 3:16).

PREPARE YOURSELF TO TEACH!

"What gift do you want for Christmas?" is probably the most frequent question we hear during the Christmas season. The lists of gifts that children make seem endless, and every day they add something new.

This lesson is the first of four in which we'll study about "the gifts" that were given at the first Christmas. With the exception of the gifts (gold, frankincense and myrrh) that the wise men of the east brought to Jesus, these gifts aren't material, but part of the worship that we must give to the King of kings.

Our world is full of spectacular gifts of all kinds and styles. Materialism absorbs much of people's lives. This special time has become an exchange of expensive gifts, but they don't fill the spiritual void in people's soul. As you prepare these lessons, ask the Lord to help you teach the students the true meaning of Christmas. May everyone understand the importance of valuing the gift of love that God gave to humanity: Jesus, the Savior of the world.

BIBLICAL COMMENTARY

You've heard the Christmas story so many times that it must seem monotonous and ordinary. But we know that isn't so. It's still a spectacular story that reminds us of the suffering and triumph of mankind.

Jesus didn't come to a perfect family that was expecting a small son, and whose parents expected him to grow up to be the Savior of the world. On the contrary, God chose two common people, two who weren't even married, to take care of his son here on earth. God chose them, but they still had to accept God's offer. And their obedience didn't come without effort, because they were human, and fear is part of the human condition. These two incidents in the Scriptures show us a pattern that will help us follow God's will.

Read Luke 1:26-38. In Mary's encounter with the angel Gabriel, she heard a great announcement from God: she would be the mother of the only Son of God.

Mary's reaction was a natural reaction of anyone. Not only did she have the opportunity of giving birth to such a "special" child (it filled her with panic), but she also didn't understand how it could happen since she was still a virgin.

Gabriel patiently explained how God would do this through the Holy Spirit. He even revealed another miracle that God had recently done: her sterile cousin Elizabeth was also pregnant. Gabriel convinced Mary that God had a good plan in mind and that he was capable of carrying it out. Mary believed in the message and accepted her role in the plan.

Read Matthew 1:18-25. Joseph had the same experience soon after. When Mary's pregnancy was confirmed; He wanted to do what was right. For Joseph, that meant breaking off his engagement to Mary because marrying her in such a condition would bring public shame to Mary. Joseph was worried about Mary's reputation, because he was a righteous man.

But in dreams an angel explained how all these things were within God's plan for him, for Mary, and for the whole world. When Joseph got up, he obeyed God by accepting Mary as his wife.

We can see this same pattern in our efforts to obey God. We hear the amazing demand of the gospel, which catches our hearts. Then our natural fears arise - fear of change, fear of the unknown - and it makes us hesitate. Then the Spirit teaches us the truth (John 14:26, 16:13). Our fears become quiet, we obey and follow Christ. Following our salvation, this process is repeated many times as God asks us to take new steps of faith.

Teacher, how can we help children accept this pattern of obedience? In several ways:

✘ We proclaim the wonderful stories of the Gospels in ways that children can understand.

✘ We advise and console the little ones when they suffer and cry.

✘ We remain alert to the Holy Spirit as he speaks to the children.

✘ We help them understand God's desire to save them and guide them for the rest of their lives.

✘ We guide children to be attentive to recognize and accept God's call and make a commitment to follow the Master.

We are collaborators with God in helping children, from an early age, decide to obey the Lord.

LESSON DEVELOPMENT

We suggest that you decorate your room with Christmas things to make it more striking for the children. Remember to use ornaments that don't distract their attention from the true meaning of this celebration.

What gift do you want for Christmas?

Distribute white paper and colored pencils so students can draw a picture of the gift they want for Christmas.

Once everyone has finished, ask them to come forward and explain the meaning of their drawing. Take into account what the students have expressed as a basis to begin the presentation of this lesson.

Important gifts

For this activity you will need four lined boxes as gifts; each box must have a card inside with one of the following words: Obedience, Savior, Praise, and Worship. In each class of this unit, you will open the box containing the gift that you will study in the lesson.

Gather your students in front of the boxes and ask them: *What do you prefer, to give or receive gifts?* Surely the majority will respond that they prefer to receive. Explain: The Bible says that it's more blessed to give than to receive. In this series of lessons, we'll study about the gifts we can offer Jesus.

Open the box that corresponds to this lesson and ask them to read aloud what the card says: Obedience.

BIBLE STORY

Gather your students to hear the Bible story and keep your Bible open to Matthew 1:18-25.

Mary and Joseph's gift

"Time passes very fast," Mary thought. "In just a few months, Joseph and I will get married."

Mary was a woman who loved and obeyed God. She lived in a town called Nazareth. She was the girlfriend of a young carpenter named Joseph.

One day, Mary was sitting in her house, when suddenly in front of her appeared a man dressed in a shining robe.

"Who could it be?" thought Mary. "Is it an angel, a messenger of God?"

It was indeed the angel Gabriel. Mary was paralyzed with fear.

"Greetings, Mary," said the angel Gabriel. "Don't be afraid. God loves you very much and is with you."

Mary felt very afraid; her eyes widened in amazement and she kept looking at the angel Gabriel who was standing in front of her. "God is pleased with you and sent me to give you Good News."

Mary listened attentively to the angel who said, "Very soon, something special will happen to you. You will have a baby! And you must call him Jesus. He will be a great King. He will be King forever and will help many people because he is the Son God."

Mary tried to understand what the angel was saying, but it seemed impossible.

"How can this be possible?" Mary asked.

"Mary, the baby that will be born will be created by the power of God. God can do things that no one else can do. You are going to give birth to the Son of God."

Mary trusted in the power of God, knew that he would fulfill his promise, and was happy to be chosen to be the mother of this special baby. When the angel left, Mary praised and glorified God with all her heart.

Then she went to look for Joseph and told him everything that had happened with the angel. But Joseph wasn't very happy, and although he loved his girlfriend very much, he decided that he wouldn't marry her.

However, that night while Joseph was sleeping, the angel of the Lord appeared to him and said, "Joseph, son of David, don't be afraid to marry your girlfriend Mary. The baby that's waiting is from the Holy Spirit. She will have a son and you must call him Jesus, because he will save the people from their sins."

When Joseph woke up, he knew what he should do. Instead of breaking his commitment to Mary, he decided to obey God, so he went to see his girlfriend.

"I have also seen the angel of God," said Joseph, "I will marry you."

Mary and Joseph didn't understand what was happening, but both loved God and wanted to obey Him by being the earthly parents of the only Son of God: Jesus. They would be part of God's plans to bring the Savior of the world.

Do you obey?

Give your students two white cards or cut a piece of paper in half. They should write on one the word "easy" and on the other "difficult."

As you read the following sentences, they should pick up the card that represents the answer they want to give.

Dad says, "Get in the car, let's go get ice cream."

Mom says, "You must clean your room today."

The teacher says, "Finish all your homework for tomorrow."

Your uncle says, "I'm going to take you to play ball at the park if you learn six bible verses."

Your grandmother says, "You shouldn't eat candy before dinner."

Your dad says, "Promise me you won't watch violent cartoons while you're at your friend Luis' house."

Your Sunday school teacher says, "Don't forget to talk about Jesus to someone this week."

When they have finished, talk about why it's sometimes difficult to obey and sometimes not. Explain that God wants us to be obedient to Him even if it's sometimes difficult for us.

The Christmas cube

During the week before class, make a model of the cube / gift box according to the instructions in the student book.

During the class hand out the activity sheet from the student book and guide the children to follow the instructions to make the gift box. Give them time to color, complete the missing words and assemble the gift box. As they work, allow them to talk and review what they learned in the Bible story. Comment on the words on the cube.

Memorization

Make the outline of several gift boxes on thick sheets of paper and color them with colored pencils. Then write the words of the memory verse of the unit. Divide the text into 7 cards, as indicated by the bars [/]: "For God so loved the world/ that he gave / his one and only Son / that whoever believes in him / shall not perish / but have eternal" / (John 3:16).

Hide the cards in the room. Ask the children to look for them and try to arrange them in order when they find them. Help them organize the verse correctly and review it several times using the cards. These cards will serve you for the four classes of the unit.

To end

Make sure your students pick up the items they used during class and organize the room before leaving. Say goodbye in prayer, thanking God for teaching us to obey Him.

Emphasize the importance of giving Jesus our daily obedience as a sign of our love for him. Remind them that next week they will study about another gift we can offer God.

 Notes:

The gift of a savior

Biblical References: Luke 2:1-7; John 3:16; 1 John 4:9

Lesson Objective: That the children understand why people need a Savior.

Memory Verse: *For God so loved the world that he gave his one and only Son, that whoever believes in him shall not perish but have eternal life (John 3:16).*

PREPARE YOURSELF TO TEACH!

Perhaps one of the most difficult tasks for elementary teachers is to help them understand why the gift of Jesus as Savior is so special. To fully appreciate Jesus as Savior, the person must have a feeling of needing to be saved. To have that feeling, you must know that you sinned and repent.

We can't force children to understand this spiritual truth before they are able to do so. However, we can present this truth to them and ask the Holy Spirit to speak to their hearts and give them understanding, even at their young age. This lesson will help students understand why they need a Savior and why the birth of Jesus is so special. Some of those children may make a personal decision for Christ if you talk to them about the plan of salvation during the lesson. It's likely that others will enjoy the bible story, but don't accept Christ. However, you will have planted the seed of truth, and the Holy Spirit will give the growth in his time.

BIBLICAL COMMENTARY

Read Luke 2:1-7; John 3:16 and 1 John 4:9. Giving presents is one of the most deeply rooted traditions at Christmas time, and in many cases, it has become the central part of the celebration. However, Scripture reminds us of the importance of this special celebration.

John 3:16 gives us the perfect example of the best Christmas gift. The whole world can receive this beautiful gift. Everyone who believes in the Son of God will receive eternal life. 1 John 4:9 tells us about this same gift, but in a more personal way: God showed us his genuine love through Jesus Christ. Then, in Luke 2:1-7, we find the special gift of God: the baby Jesus, the Savior of the world.

The great love of God manifested to the world is the best Christmas gift that people can receive. The Bible is clear in telling us that ... "he will save the people from their sins." And we, as recipients of that wonderful gift, have the mission of taking it to all those who live in darkness and without hope.

Pray that during this Christmas season, the Lord will allow you and the students to be instruments of blessing for others. Train the little ones so that they can reach others and take them to the feet of Christ. Children are also part of God's plan.

LESSON DEVELOPMENT

Welcome the students, especially those who are visiting for the first time. Take their contact information so that you can stay in touch with them. Sing praise choruses to start.

Important gifts

Briefly review what they learned about the gift of obedience last week.

Then, it's time to open the second gift box, which contains the card that says: Savior.

Choose the student who arrived earliest, or who already knows the memory verse by heart, to open the box and read the card out loud.

Explain that in this class they will study about the most wonderful gift of all time.

A special baby

For this activity you need baby items. Place them on the table and allow the children to see and touch them. You can bring a doll so that the children think of the baby Jesus.

Then ask them: *Why do we use these items?* Listen to their answers and talk about the care that parents must give to newborns. Talk to the children about the possibility that Mary didn't have clean water to wash the baby. No doubt the noise of the animals could be heard, and the typical smell of a stable would be smelled. This was the place where the Savior was born. Truly a very humble place. If the children want, someone can wear clothes to represent Mary, another Joseph, and some can represent the shepherds. Tell them that in today's class they will hear a story about a very special baby.

Contaminated! (Freeze tag)

Prepare your classroom for this game by moving all the furniture to a corner. You need a large area for your students to run (you can also do it in a yard).

Choose a volunteer to be the "contaminated" one who should infect others when he touches them. The student who is touched must remain immobile (frozen), until another child gives him a gentle pat on the back and "decontaminates" him. When everyone is immobile the game is over and they can start again by choosing another "contaminated" one.

After concluding the game, ask them: *Why couldn't you move after the "contaminated" one touched you?* (Because they were contaminated.) *What did you need to continue in the game?* (Someone who wasn't contaminated to touch them.)

155

Make the transition to the bible story by explaining that just as in the game, in real life, we are all contaminated by sin and can't save ourselves. So God made a plan for us to be forgiven of our sins and we can have him in our hearts. We will learn more about this special plan in our Bible story today.

BIBLE STORY

Help your students visualize the context of the story. It's important that they understand that the birth of Jesus occurred in the midst of special and unexpected circumstances.

To visualize the story, you can use pictures or physical objects. If you don't have any, you can make them. Maybe someone has a nativity that you can use to represent the characters in the bible story. If you wish, you can photocopy the scene from the student book, enlarge the figures, color them, stick magnets or flannel on the back, and use them on a metal sheet or the flannelgraph.

The wonderful gift of God

A messenger of the Roman Emperor Caesar Augustus arrived on his horse to a market in the city of Nazareth, took a parchment from his bag and began to read aloud for all to hear:

"Caesar Augustus, the great emperor, will take a census, because he wants to count all the people who live in his kingdom. For this, everyone must travel to the city where they were born."

The messenger closed the parchment and went to another city to give the same announcement.

It had been about 9 months since the angel had appeared to Mary and Joseph. The baby was going to be born very soon.

"We must go to Bethlehem," said Joseph, "since all my family is from there."

"My family is also from Bethlehem," Mary said.

They both packed for the long trip. They would need food, water and blankets to sleep. Mary also prepared some clothes she had made for the baby. Diapers would be very necessary. Back then, there were no disposable diapers like the ones you all wore.

It was a long way to get to Bethlehem. They finally arrived when it was already night.

Joseph hurried to find a place to rest. Mary was very tired from the long trip and soon the child would be born. However, all the inns were full. Many people were there because they had to register because of the census.

Finally, they arrived at the last place in town and although it was full, the innkeeper allowed them to stay in the barn.

That wasn't the place where Mary imagined for her son to be born. Her family was very far away and they didn't have any friends or relatives nearby to help them, nor did they have a bed to sleep in.

However, that night, in a stable in Bethlehem, the baby Jesus, the Savior of the world, was born.

Mary took the baby in her arms and cleaned it, then wrapped it in the blankets she had brought, and put him in a manger filled with clean straw so he could sleep.

That night, God gave humanity the best Christmas gift ever: Jesus, his only Son.

After the story, ask the children to bow their heads and lead them to repeat this prayer after you. Pause each time you find this sign (/). If you wish, you can make a more personal invitation to each student to give their life to Christ. If the children accept Jesus, we suggest that you spend a little time after the class to pray with them individually.

Dear God, / thank you for loving us. / Thank you for making / a perfect plan for us / and for sending Jesus to earth. / We praise you / and adore you God / for the wonderful gift / that you gave us / through your Son Jesus, / our Savior. / Amen.

ACTIVITIES

Give each child the activity page from the student book, scissors and tape.

Before class, read the instructions carefully and follow them step by step to prepare the stable where Jesus was born.

Help the children do their craft and ask questions about the lesson to review the story as they work. Encourage them to use the scene of Jesus' birth to tell their friends and family about what they learned in this class.

Memorization

Use the cards you made last week with the Bible verse.

Stick them on the board so that the children read the verse a couple of times, then remove them one by one, until the board is empty and they can say the entire passage by memory.

If you wish and time allows, ask some volunteers to come forward and say the verse by heart.

To end

Pay special attention to those who prayed to accept Jesus, and explain the importance of this step of faith. Make a plan to start discipling them. (A good resource to use is "Friends of Jesus," found at: SdmiResources. MesoamericaRegion.org)

Encourage them to continue attending the class to learn more about the gifts we offer God.

Give them time to share their prayer requests and intercede for each other before saying goodbye.

The gift of praise

Biblical References: Luke 2:8-20

Lesson Objective: To teach the children about the importance of sharing the Good News with others.

Memory Verse: *For God so loved the world that he gave his one and only Son, that whoever believes in him shall not perish but have eternal life. (John 3:16).*

PREPARE YOURSELF TO TEACH!

It's common that for some of the students, the concept of being "witnesses for Christ" is a bit difficult to understand. Many children are shy and find it hard to tell others about their faith, especially if they live in a society where beliefs are completely opposed to what they learn in class or in their Christian homes.

This lesson will help them learn about the joy the shepherds felt when they met Jesus, and the way they told this Good News to other people.

The shepherds didn't have much to offer Jesus, and perhaps the students feel the same way. Help them understand that they can give Jesus what the shepherds offered him in the manger: their praise, enthusiasm and desire to tell others the Good News of the Son of God.

BIBLICAL COMMENTARY

Read Luke 2:8-20. There are stories that we could hear again and again without getting tired, and this is the case of this biblical passage.

This part of the Christmas story reveals the greatest event that happened in the history of humanity: the birth of the Savior of the world. However, it's not a simple narration about that event, but it explains the meaning of what was happening. It wasn't just the birth of another Jewish baby; it was the arrival of the Messiah, the anointed of God, who had been sent to bring the Good News to the poor (Luke 4:18).

The Messiah would also bring freedom to the captives and give sight to the blind. Definitely, the birth of Jesus completely changed the history of humanity, and the world would no longer be the same.

However, God chose humble shepherds to give the Good News to. The Gospel of Luke is the only one that tells us about the visit that the angels made to the shepherds. These humble men were the first to know that God had fulfilled his promise, and that the chosen Messiah was now on earth to fulfill his mission.

Luke clearly explains to us that God set his eyes on those humble and despised shepherds to announce the birth of his Son. With this, he established that the Good News was for everyone, from the richest and most powerful to the poorest and smallest creature.

The shepherds didn't wait. Full of joy, they rushed to Bethlehem to meet the new King. Not only that, they told everyone the Good News. The shepherds' spontaneous way of believing and responding is an example for us today. We must give all our praise to God because Jesus, his Son, came to live with us, came to die for us, and went to prepare a place for us. That's the best gift we can give to those who don't know the Good News of Jesus Christ!

LESSON DEVELOPMENT

Pray giving thanks to God for the opportunity to meet once again to study His Word. Greet each other. Sing a chorus of praise and begin the study of the lesson.

Important gifts

Open the third gift box. Like the last class, you can choose a volunteer who has shown good behavior or learning. Talk about the other two gifts you studied and tell them that in today's class they will learn about another very special gift that a group gave to Jesus.

What does a shepherd do?

In advance, invite a young man from your congregation to dress up like a shepherd from biblical times. Ask him to talk to the children about the tasks a shepherd performs, for example, caring for the sheep, defending them from wild animals, finding food and water for their flock, counting them at night, etc.

Let your students ask him questions before moving on to the next activity.

BIBLE STORY

Find two young people to help you by acting out the next scene. Make photocopies of this page so that your guests have time to study the part that is assigned to them. They can put on robes as in the times of Jesus. You can also use puppets.

The gift of the shepherds

Zetro: Miriam, Miriam come fast!

Miriam: What's the matter, Zetro? What happened? I didn't expect you to get home until three days from now.

Zetro: Miriam, I have something to tell you; something wonderful has happened!

Miriam: Tell me everything!

Zetro: Last night while we were taking care of the sheep in the field, something wonderful happened.

Miriam: Hurry, tell me, what happened!

Zetro: Angels!

Miriam: Angels? Zetro, do you have a fever? (touches his forehead) Are you sick?

Zetro: No, no, no, Miriam! I'm telling you the truth. In the middle of the night, angels appeared wearing beautiful robes and we were all very scared.

Miriam: I would have been very scared too.

Zetro: Then an angel appeared before us and told us, "Do not be afraid. I bring you good news that will cause great joy for all the people. Today in the town of David, a Savior has been born to you; he is the Messiah, the Lord. This will be a sign to you: You will find a baby wrapped in cloths and lying in a manger."

Miriam: And then? Tell me faster ... what excitement ... and what fright!

Zetro: Then the sky was filled with hundreds of angels who praised God and said, "Glory to God in the highest heaven, and on earth peace to those on whom his favor rests."

Miriam: And what does that mean?

Zetro: I was going to explain that to you. When the angels left, we hurried and went to Bethlehem to see what had happened that the Lord had told us. And just as the angel told us, we found the baby in a stable! A stable! Can you believe it? Poor thing, he was lying in a manger! There were animals in the barn, as well as his parents, Mary and Joseph! The smell wasn't very good ... it was a stable! But the baby had very clean clothes. His face was beautiful and his cheeks were pink.

Miriam: Really? It seems impossible to believe. Are you telling me the truth?

Zetro: It was amazing for us too, but everything happened just as the angel told us. Although I still don't understand why the Messiah was born in a stable instead of in a palace with a beautiful cradle of gold and embroidered blankets.

Miriam: I don't understand that either.

Zetro: However, we feel in our hearts that this baby is the Son of God. We knelt down in front of him to worship him. Then we left in a hurry because we had to tell this Good News to everyone. What a privilege to tell others that the Savior, the promised one of God, had arrived! What a privilege it was that the angels gave that beautiful news ... to us ... humble shepherds! We went throughout the town of Bethlehem worshiping God and telling what we saw and heard.

Miriam: Zetro, I still can't believe you. You are just a humble shepherd. Why would God give you such a great honor?

Zetro: I don't know Miriam. But I do know that I saw the promised one of God, the Messiah, my Savior, and I have to tell everyone. My voice isn't as beautiful as that of the angels, but I want to use it to always worship God. I want to give the Good News to all people. That's my gift to God!

ACTIVITIES

Let's share the Good News

Give your students strips of paper to write some ways to tell the Good News to others. When they are finished, stick the strips on a poster board to form a mural and place it in a visible place in the room. In this way they will remember that it's important to tell others about the birth of Jesus.

Here are some suggested ideas:

✗ Invite our friends to the Christmas service.

✗ Send a Christmas card with a message about Jesus.

✗ Visit hospitals to tell the story of Jesus' birth to children who are sick.

✗ As a class project, each person can make a Christmas card and send it to a relative or friend who doesn't know Christ.

The shepherds

Distribute the activity sheets, scissors, glue, and the figures from the cut-out section and give them time to cut out the figures and paste them in the corresponding spaces. As they work, talk about what they imagine the shepherds felt when the angels visited them.

Christmas songs

Lead a time of Christmas songs, accompanied with instruments. Here's a simple way to make them.

You need: cans or empty canisters (empty plastic soda bottles) of different sizes, seeds, buttons, and small stones. Ask the children to place the seeds or stones in the cans. Hand out sheets of paper or aluminum to make a kind of lid. Teach them how to tape the lids. The shakers are ready.

If you have rhythm instruments in your church, don't hesitate to use them, and dedicate a time of praise to celebrate the birth of Jesus. Explain to your students that a way to praise God is through our songs, just as the angels did the night Jesus was born.

Memorization

Hide the cards you used the previous lesson before class. Tell the children to look for them. Then ask them to arrange the verse in order and say it aloud. If you want you can make two or more sets of cards with the figure of gift boxes. This will help you divide the class into two or more groups.

To end

Form a prayer circle and intercede for the needs of each one. Then encourage them to take advantage of this Christmas season to follow the example of the shepherds. Ask the children to tell others the story of Jesus' birth. Encourage them to tell of God's perfect plan to save mankind from their sins.

Say goodbye by singing a chorus of praise. Invite them to next week's class to discover the last gift.

The gift of worship

Biblical References: Matthew 2:1-12

Lesson Objective: That the children want and search for ways to worship Jesus.

Memory Verse: *For God so loved the world that he gave his one and only Son, that whoever believes in him shall not perish but have eternal life* (John 3:16).

PREPARE YOURSELF TO TEACH!

Can children worship God? Yes, of course they can! Many times we think that they are unable to concentrate in an attitude of worship. However, even with their dynamism and excess of energy, children have the ability to learn to worship God.

To worship doesn't only mean to sing with our eyes closed and our hands raised. To worship is an attitude of the heart, which is born of the love we feel for God.

Use this lesson to teach the little ones the example of the wise men from the East who traveled many miles to offer not only material gifts, but also their worship and devotion to the King of kings.

Help them understand that true worship comes from the heart. Tell them that God is pleased when we humble ourselves before Him. Contrary to what happens during Christmas, when everyone expects to receive something, children will learn that God wants us to give Jesus our sincere gift of worship.

BIBLICAL COMMENTARY

Read Matthew 2:1-12. A bright star in the sky was what caught the attention of wise men from the east. It wasn't an ordinary star; they had never seen it appear before, and it seemed to indicate something important. But what was it? It was the fulfillment of God's plan for humanity! God had fulfilled his Word and the Messiah was about to be born.

The Bible doesn't tell us how many men came to visit Jesus or what their names were. Tradition tells us that there were three, because of the number of gifts they offered to the Lord.

We also know that they came to Jerusalem from the east and went to look for King Herod to ask him, "Where is the one who has been born king of the Jews? We saw his star when it rose and have come to worship him" (Matthew 2:2).

Herod immediately summoned the priests and scribes of the people to investigate where the Christ was to be born. After some deliberations and calculations, they informed him that it would be in Bethlehem of Judea, as the prophet Micah wrote.

Herod secretly called the sages to inquire about the time of the appearance of the star, and sent them to Bethlehem to look for the baby. He told them that when they found him, they must let him know so that he too could go to worship him.

When the wise men met Jesus, they bowed down to worship him and offered him symbolic presents: gold, frankincense and myrrh.

Then, they had a revelation in a dream. God told them in the revelation not to return to see Herod again. The three magi went to their land by another path. God knew that Herod's plans were sinister.

These men give us an example, not only of obedience to leave their land and undertake a journey to seek Jesus, but of surrender and worship before the Savior of the world.

But not all people respond as the wise men did. Some react to the announcement of Jesus as Herod did, with hatred and hostility. Herod thought of Jesus as a king who would compete with him for power. That's why he said that he wanted to go worship him; but the truth was different - he wanted to kill him.

Others respond to Jesus with indifference. This was the typical response of many scribes and Pharisees who ignored Jesus during his years of ministry. But the wise men responded to Jesus with true worship. That's how we all want to be. Let's ask the Lord to help us to be "true worshipers" of Christ Jesus.

LESSON DEVELOPMENT

Since this is the last lesson of the unit and of the year, we suggest you prepare a simple Christmas party. The main reason will be to celebrate the baby of Bethlehem, Jesus. It will also be to thank the students for their attendance and participation throughout the year.

It will be necessary to prepare the crafts and materials that the children will take home. Today they can take home there candy jars with the Sweet Verses. Ask them to stick the last candy verse on the jar. Tell them to keep remembering and memorizing the bible verses. Suggest that they repeat the passages to their parents, grandparents and friends.

Important gifts

Today is the day to open the last of the four gifts. Review briefly what they learned from the previous three lessons and open the fourth box to discover the card that says "worship."

Mention to the children that in this class they will study about another gift they can give to Jesus.

Three gifts for a King

Get three small boxes, the size of your hand, wrapped as a gift, and put inside each box a card that says either gold, frankincense or myrrh.

Hide the three boxes in the room and ask the students to help you find the three gifts that the wise men brought to Jesus when he was a baby.

Give them a few minutes to look for the boxes and bring them to the front. Then choose three volunteers to read the cards out loud. Use this activity as an introduction to today's Bible story. When they open the small boxes and read what the cards say, explain the meaning of each gift the magicians brought:

Gold: it was the perfect gift for a King. Jesus was the King of kings and Lord of lords.

Frankincense: it was the perfect gift for a Priest. Jesus was the High Priest.

Myrrh: the perfect gift for someone who would die as the perfect offering. Jesus would die on the cross for us.

BIBLE STORY

Prepare some visual material to illustrate the content of the lesson. Use figures for flannelboard or other illustrations to capture the students' attention.

The Wise Men's gifts

A long time ago, in a very distant place, lived wise men. They were scholars of the stars. One night, they observed something different in the sky, a very big and bright star had appeared.

"This star means that a special baby has been born," said one wise man. "This baby is a very important King; let's worship him!"

The wise men climbed onto their camels and set out on the long journey.

"We must get to Jerusalem," said one of them. "The people there will tell us where to find the new King."

When they reached the city, they went to the royal palace to speak with King Herod, who ruled Jerusalem.

"Where is the new-born King of the Jews? We have seen his star and we have come to worship him," said the wise men.

King Herod became very nervous when he heard this, and gathered the chief priests and other educated men and asked them, "Where is the new King to be born?"

"In Bethlehem of Judea, the city of David," they replied. The prophet Micah had written about it. Long before the birth of Jesus, God had chosen faithful men to announce to the people that he would send his Son into the world as a special King.

The wise men took their camels and began the journey to Bethlehem. The bright star they had seen guided them as they advanced. After a while, the star stopped over the stable where the baby Jesus was. The wise men were very happy! When they entered the house, they saw Jesus with his mother Mary and they knelt down to worship him. "This is the new King," they excitedly proclaimed. The wise men gave Jesus three special gifts: gold, frankincense and myrrh.

Soon, they had to return to their land; the trip would be very long, but that wasn't so important. They were very happy because they had met Jesus, the Son of God, the expected Savior. And they were happy that they were able to bring their gifts of worship to the baby of Bethlehem, to the King of kings.

ACTIVITIES

Let's decorate the tree

You'll need green construction paper or thick green paper, strips of brown paper for the trunk, scissors, glue, colors. Ask a volunteer to distribute the activity sheets. Help the children understand and follow the instructions to make the Christmas tree.

Take this time to review with them what they learned throughout these four lessons about the Christmas story.

A hidden star

Cut an apple in half and show your students the star that forms in the center when you split it in half. Tell them that some people think this star is a reminder of the one that led the wise men to where Jesus was.

We are glad that God sent that special star. It's a sign that Jesus isn't only the King of the Jews, but also our King. The magi who traveled from the east to Bethlehem were the first non-Jewish people to worship Jesus.

Share apples with your students if you have enough.

Memorization

1. Organize a special participation of students who have learned all the memory verse, and give them simple prizes to encourage them to continue studying and learning the Word of God.

2. If there are children who remember all the Bible verses of the year, it would be exciting if they could have a special time to recite the verses in front of the congregation. For this, ask the pastor to give you the opportunity to introduce your class and the children who learned all the verses. You can give certificates of recognition to the children who participate.

To end

Thank God for this year of study, and also for the beautiful gift of Salvation that He has given us through Jesus. Encourage the children to move forward in their Christian life by trusting Jesus as their personal Savior.

Ask them what gifts they will give to Jesus this Christmas. Begin by telling the children what your special gift or gifts will be for Jesus:

✗ Time: teaching the class, preparation time, attendance at the services, etc.

✗ Personal and public prayer

✗ Consecration: all of your life

✗ Offerings: money, talents

✗ Worship: songs of praise, telling the Good News, testifying to others about Jesus.

Pray for each of them and remind them of the importance of always seeking God.

Either that Sunday or the next, have a ceremony of advancement in which the older children move on to the next class. (See The Importance of Students Advancing in Sunday School, p. 11.)

Printed in the USA
CPSIA information can be obtained
at www.ICGtesting.com
LVHW080557090823
754668LV00019B/1797